The African Caliphate
The Life, Work and Teachings of Shaykh Usman dan Fodio

The African Caliphate

The Life, Work and Teachings of Shaykh Usman dan Fodio

Ibraheem Sulaiman

The African Caliphate: The life, work and teachings of Shaykh Usman dan Fodio

Published by: The Diwan Press Ltd.
311 Allerton Road
Bradford
BD15 7HA
UK
Website: www.diwanpress.com
E-mail: info@diwanpress.com

By: Ibraheem Sulaiman
Edited by: Abdalhaqq Bewley
Typeset in Gentium by: Abdassamad Clarke
Cover by: Muhammad Amin Franklin
Cover image courtesy of NASA through the Visible Earth website (http://visibleearth.nasa.gov/)
A catalogue record of this book is available from the British Library.

ISBN-13: 978-1-84200-111-0 (paperback)
978-1-84200-112-7 (casebound)
978-1-908892-13-3 (ePub)
978-1-908892-14-0 (Kindle)

Contents

Allah has promised those of you who believe and do right actions that He will make them successors in the land as He made those before them successors and will firmly establish for them their deen, with which He is pleased, and give them, in place of their fear, security. They worship Me, not associating anything with Me. Any who disbelieve after that, such people are deviators.

(Surah an-Nur Ayat 55)

Foreword

OF ALL BELIEFS, ideologies and civilizations, Islam stands out distinct and unique in its resilience. No matter what damage it suffers, no matter what opposition and obstacles it faces, no matter how long the time that passes, it always reasserts itself. Islam has consistently and persistently stood on the side of the weak and oppressed, checked the excesses of the corrupt and strong, and insisted on the establishment of justice, equity and fairness in human society. It has thus offered the weak and the oppressed their only real and lasting hope and presented the corrupt and the unjust with the only real and unflinching curb on their power.

The rise and fall of nations and civilizations – indeed the entire history of mankind – is nothing but a reflection of this reality, which the future of human society will inevitably continue to reflect. The Most High says:

"If it were not for Allah's driving some people back by means of others, the earth would have been corrupted. But Allah shows favor to all the worlds." Qur'an 2:249

In *Bilād as-Sudan*, as in other parts of the world, this reality has manifested itself in the rise and fall of states and the series of *jihads* the region was destined to see. In the nineteenth century in particular the region saw a series of *jihads*, prominent among which were those led by Usman dan Fodio in Hausaland, Aḥmadu Labbo in Macina, 'Umar al-Fūti in Senegambia, Muhammad 'Abdallah Hassan in

Somalia and Aḥmad al-Mahdi in Nilotic Sudan.

Of these *jihads*, that of Usman dan Fodio was perhaps the most spectacular and far-reaching and the one with the most lasting effect. It brought the various peoples that made up Hausaland into a single polity, unprecedented in scope and complexity, and gave them the security, stability and justice they had lacked under the warring Hausa states. The wave of Islamic revival it triggered reached as far as the shores of the Atlantic to the west and those of the Red Sea to the east, disturbing the geopolitical situation everywhere it went, causing radical socio-economic changes, and building Islamic states of varying sizes and complexity throughout the region of *Bilād as-Sudan*.

Bilād as-Sudan (lit. the countries of the blacks) is the name early Muslim historians gave to the vast region of savanna grassland lying between the Sahara Desert and the dense forest to the south, from the shores of the Atlantic in the west to the Nile Valley in the east. This region has from time immemorial been in constant contact with North Africa, with which it traded its gold and ivory for metal goods, salt, horses, and other such things. Over time a network of routes developed, linking various locations in North Africa to trading centers in *Bilād as-Sudan*. Because of this, trans-Saharan caravans, constantly moving backwards and forwards, became common between the two regions.

When North Africa became Islamized in the seventh century, the trans-Saharan caravans began to bring into *Bilād as-Sudan* not only Mediterranean goods but also, and far more consequentially, the good tidings of Islam. Once the message had reached the caravan destinations, it became largely the job of the indigenous populations to spread it throughout the whole of this vast region. With its universal appeal and superior culture, Islam easily found its way to all parts of the region. Wherever it went, it generated a cultural, societal and political transformation, which saw the rise of such great states as Ghana, Mali, Songhay, Kanem Borno and Darfur Funj. It also developed centers of learning and a body of students and scholars whose activities furthered Islam in the region.

The obligation on Muslims to go in search of knowledge, the need for them to travel to Makkah (Mecca) for Ḥajj, and their responsibility to teach and spread the message, generated currents of intra-regional traffic and waves of migration that saw a massive integration of this vast region. Within only a few centuries *Bilād as-Sudan* integrated into a single entity with a common intellectual tradition, culture, economy and ideology, and it was this that facilitated, in the early nineteenth century, the spread of the wave of Islamic revival triggered by the *jihad* of Usman dan Fodio in Hausaland.

Hausaland is located in the central *Bilād as-Sudan*, bordering on Kanem Borno to the east and Songhay to the west. At certain periods prior to the *jihad*, it came under the political control of both Songhay and Borno. As the name implies, it is the land of the Hausas. The Hausas were neither an ethnic group nor the only inhabitants of the land. The bulk of inhabitants were believed to have migrated into the region some time before the tenth century from the central Sahara, perhaps due to desiccation or some such natural phenomenon. They settled in the central savanna and mixed with the indigenous people. The result was a multi-ethnic society sharing a common language – Hausa. This heterogeneity further facilitated the absorption of other ethnic groups that arrived subsequently. When the Fulani, for example, reached Hausaland early in the fifteenth century, those who settled in the towns lost not only their nomadic lifestyle but also their native language.

Prior to the spread of Islam into Hausaland, the inhabitants toiled under a variety of pagan beliefs. Though varying in detail from one community to another, these pagan beliefs usually revolved around a high distant god (*ubangiji*), who was not actively connected to everyday life, and was supplemented by a chain of supernatural forces (*iskoki*) directly in touch with men and controlling their everyday lives. Natural resources such as agricultural land, forests, rivers, iron ore and salt deposits were believed to be in the custody of certain of these *iskoki*. Harmony with the *iskoki* was understood to be essential for a good harvest and for the success of such pursuits as hunting and fishing. Therefore, farmers, hunters and fishermen performed sacrifices and rituals, usually around stones, trees or places believed to be the habitat of the *iskoki*, to maintain harmony and secure their livelihood. Such conditions naturally supported a class of priests (*bokaye*) who acted as intermediaries between them and the people.

Islam spread into Hausaland as a result of the trans-regional movement of scholars and traders. This is popularly thought to have occurred at some time in the fourteenth century. Available historical evidence, however, suggests that Islam reached Hausaland much earlier than this and that it was not limited to one direction or to one group. The ancestors of Usman dan Fodio, for example, moved into Hausaland in the fifteenth century under the leadership of Musa Jokollo and settled in the Hausa State of Gobir.

Working day and night, collectively and individually, formally and informally, these assorted indigenous groups carried the message of Islam throughout the length and breadth of Hausaland. As it had in other parts of *Bilād as-Sudan*, in Hausaland too Islam transformed the socio-economic and political structures, boosting the economy and paving the way for the emergence of numerous independent Hausa states such as Kano, Zaria, Katsina, Gobir, Kebbi, Zamfara and Daura. With the spread of literacy and the accompanying flow of Islamic literature, Hausaland became increasingly incorporated into the wider Islamic fraternity, with its people becoming well informed about Islamic thought and ideas and about the history, geography, politics and economy of the known world. Eventually, Islam emerged as a political force in the latter part of the fifteenth century, bringing changes in the political leadership of some major Hausa states.

These developments were particularly notable in Zaria, Kano and Katsina, which at that time formed the core axis of Hausaland. The leadership of these states in that period is still remembered for the bold changes they effected in their administrations to make them conform to Islamic standards. In Kano, for example, Muhammad Rumfa invited Shaykh Muhammad al-Maghili, a North African Muslim jurist of international repute, to advise him on administering an Islamic government. Al-Maghili's visit to Kano was of great significance to the process of Islamization in Hausaland, for his books and religious rulings (*fatwās*) gained wide circulation. One of his books, *Taj ad-Dīn Fī Mā 'Ala-l-Mulūk*, described as a comprehensive treatise on government, seemed to have been highly influential throughout Hausaland.

As Islam gained strength in Hausaland, its significance as a pilgrimage route and center of learning increased. By the sixteenth century, the reputations of some Hausa state capitals as centers of Islamic learning – Kano and Katsina in particular – were already high enough to attract many Muslim scholars and students. The Ḥajj, serving as a permanent link with the rest of the Muslim world and a source of continuous flow of Islamic thought and ideas, further reinforced the intellectual development of Hausaland. In due course, an educational system with a clearly defined curriculum and methodology was fashioned along the lines of Sankore University of Timbuktu, from which it seemed to have received its greatest impetus.

However, the Moroccan invasion of Songhay at the end of the sixteenth century, with its attendant seizure of Timbuktu, weakened that intellectual impetus and upset the political stability of Hausaland, because the power of Songhay had kept some of the leaders of the Hausa states in check. With the rise of another axis of power in Hausaland, the seventeenth and eighteenth centuries saw the almost equally powerful Hausa states engaged in continuous and devastating interstate warfare without a clear winner emerging. Quite naturally, the security, economy and learning of Hausaland were affected by this situation.

Though learning continued, even in these difficult circumstances when movement was restricted, there were many obstacles to the spread of knowledge. Entrenched in warfare and desperate for victory, rulers in Hausaland were willing to go to any lengths to win battles, even if it meant violating the limits set by Islam. Political leadership gradually degenerated into tyranny and corruption resulting in injustice, oppression and misery for most of the people. The consequent materialism and permissiveness gave the receding paganism a chance to resurface and some Muslims started once more to mix Islamic practices with traditional pagan rituals.

Muslim scholars, who form the backbone of any Muslim society, were also affected by the pervading decadence. Some gave support to the tyrannical order by joining the rulers, whereas others withdrew into silence, leaving only a few courageous scholars to raise objections and to point accusing fingers at the tyranny and corruption around them. One of the few, who dared to raise his voice and who in fact organized a *jihad*, was Shaykh Jibril ibn 'Umar, with whom Usman dan Fodio studied and from whom he may have acquired his fervor to revive Islam and to restore the Sunnah. It was out of this rising tide of discontent on the one hand and expectation on the other that Usman dan Fodio emerged. How Usman responded to this challenging situation is precisely what this book is about.

Because this work has been produced outside of a conventional scholastic environment, it is blessedly free from those pointless academic technicalities for which universities today are so well known. The imaginative capacity, analytic insight and unique style of the author give the reader a rich and profound account of the great phenomenon that is the Sokoto *jihad*. By drawing on the rich intellectual inheritance of the Sokoto *khilāfah*, and relying on the original Arabic works of the Sokoto *jihad* leaders and their contemporaries, the author has rescued the reader from the distortions, misconceptions and fabrications, which permeate the works of European scholars and their heirs.

For almost a century, the Muslim mind has been under the sway of imperialism, especially as manifested in its educational institutions. Muslim history has been distorted and all access to the true message of Islam has been denied. The Muslim personality has been under persistent attack and the Muslim mind fed entirely on euro-centric thoughts and ideas. Muslims, therefore, have lost self-confidence and have developed an inferiority complex. This has led to meekness and docility and a tendency to readily imitate European thought. However, history, it is said, has a habit of repeating itself and Islam, with its characteristic resilience, is reviving itself from within the very fortresses of imperialism. More and more Muslims are seeking out their true history and the true message of Islam, and abandoning the false goals they have been pursuing.

Coming at a time when an increasing number of Muslims are working to develop Islamic solutions to their problems, this book will provide them with an important part of their history and will help them define their own future. For, indeed, a people without a past are a people without a future. At this critical point, one hopes and prays that Muslims will not betray their history because if they do so, history will certainly betray them. The Most High has informed us:

"You who have iman! If any of you renounce your deen, Allah will bring forward a people whom He loves and who love Him, humble to the believers, fierce to the unbelievers, who do jihad in the way of Allah and do not fear the blame of any censurer. That is the unbounded favor of Allah which He gives to whoever He wills. Allah is Boundless, All-Knowing." Qur'an 5:54

Usman M. Bugaje

Introduction

HISTORY moves at so slow a pace as to be almost imperceptible to the observer. Ideas that shape nations take years to take root and grow and it requires decades to mold a generation capable of undertaking and sustaining change. So the rise of a nation may take place very gradually. On the other hand, the reasons for a nation's decline may be so ingrained that they are invisible and its downward progress towards its own demise goes almost unnoticed.

What shapes history are people's moral attitudes and changes in their inner state of being. So alterations in human society occur basically because people change their beliefs and, consequently, their conception of life, basic attitudes and behavior, and in an ultimate sense, their destiny. In this way human beings are responsible for their own destiny and are the shapers of their own history.

At any given moment in his life, a man may face the moral responsibility of making a choice between striving after an exalted life or pursuing a base one. This takes as read that man is a moral being with an inherent sense of right and wrong; that he is a free agent under an obligation to choose his own path; that he has a faculty of inner sight, enabling him to visualize the ultimate result of his actions, and an inner voice, warning against evil and urging good; and that potentially he is endowed with the ability to achieve whatever end he chooses for himself.

The slow pace of history offers considerable opportunity

for people to make the right choices and to make amends for any wrong ones. The unvarying characteristics of natural processes provide ample lessons for man. He is constantly reminded that day follows night, seasons come and go, one bursting with life and luxuriance, the other dry and barren. Every day this illuminating drama is re-enacted before his eyes. Every day is a sentence in a book of lessons, every season a paragraph, and generations and epochs are simply pages and chapters in that book.

True understanding of a single day is also understanding of millions of days past and millions to come. The exactness, the order, and the perfect patterning that characterize the workings of the universe also embrace the life of man. History is, therefore, a single chain of connected events, just as mankind is a chain of connected individuals and the world itself a chain of connected eras. As Allah Himself reminds us: *"Your creation and rising is only like that of a single self."* (31:27)

Decline is also integral to all natural processes and is a stage through which all nations must pass. A critical moment arrives in the life of every nation when a decisive choice must be made: whether to take the path that leads upwards to renewal or to continue on the downward slope of inevitable decline. The upward move demands tremendous courage and willpower. It entails much social sacrifice but is nevertheless the only honorable and redeeming course to follow. To continue the moral drift means the nation has despaired of progress and given up on its future – a course of action, which runs counter to the very notion of life and to the purpose of human existence.

A nation, which has given itself up to a condition of moral decline, is said to be *fasiq* – succumbing to the iniquitous, the immoral and the offensive. The inclination towards evil stems from a perversion of faith, from a blunting of ethical sensibility, and from a violent disruption in the inner state of individuals and in the soul of society as a whole. People in this condition are spiritually blind and materialistic in their approach to existence. They ignore history and the ultimate purpose of human life. They fail to perceive the destructive turn that the economic and social polarization of society have taken and the consequences resulting from it.

There are several reasons why a nation begins this process of decline. It has to have abandoned its belief in, and commitment to, the Supreme Being. It may have taken up another god or gods and transferred allegiance to them. This inevitably causes a serious rift in its crucial relationship with its True Sustainer and brings about a profound disturbance in its own soul. This social apostasy is the principal cause of decline. It inexorably changes the values and norms of the society involved and, by implication, its whole world-view and way of life. The world is now perceived as a permanent reality and this means that the restraints that should characterize the moral life of society are done away with. The immutable principles, which should uphold society and on which legal, moral and social rules should be based, are now regarded as a cumbersome nuisance. People are free to flout them. The general attitude which allows this permissiveness will lead to the downfall of the society concerned.

In such critical moments nations always produce rare people who perceive the direction in which the nation is moving. They operate on a higher level of ethical and intellectual consciousness and are therefore able to understand what is happening and redirect the national course. Foremost among them are the prophets or messengers of Allah. Next come the truly learned – those who combine knowledge with moral excellence. Such people are able to implement the guidance brought by the prophets.

A prophet's duty is to transmit to his nation the Divine guidance he receives, sharpen its intellect, and raise its level of consciousness. He presents a challenge to society to awaken its conscience. This is a continuous process which is called 'warning'. The society in question must respond to this challenge and awaken from its deep sleep in order to reach a level where it can assume full responsibility for the choices it makes. The prophet extends this challenge repeatedly. The society, now morally disturbed, makes its response each time it is challenged until its fate is decided.

The challenge issued by the prophet hinges on three things: ideological commitment, way of life, and leadership. In concrete terms, the final objective of the prophet, and by extension of a truly learned man, is to return his people to faith, to Islam. It inevitably entails the dissolution of all the illusions that have crept into the intellectual and moral fabric of society and become the basis of its ideology. It means the overthrow of the institutions that sustain the apostate life of that society. It also involves the demolition of the unyielding and unrepentant social, economic and political forces that have enslaved it.

So while the prophetic challenge is essentially ethical, it nevertheless manifests itself in all spheres of life, since its basic objective is to create a totally new socio-political grouping – an *ummah* – which may be the formation of a new society, the building of a new nation or the ushering in of a new epoch.

The process of raising people's consciousness operates on three levels. On an individual level a person is trained to see himself in relation to his Lord, in relation to the complex structure of the universe, and in relation to himself. It is also necessary for individuals to comprehend the position they hold within the social strata. Peasants who toil hard, only to have the fruits of their labor usurped and squandered by the idle, should be aware of that; laborers should be conscious of any exploitation by powerful masters; the poor should know the reasons for their poverty; women should understand any oppression and humiliation they suffer arising from gender bias. In short, all persons should know their positions in society, why they are there, and what should be done individually and collectively to correct any imbalances that exist.

Finally it is necessary to have an intellectual perception of an ideal society, a concept of the future based on a correct understanding of life and history, and ways of dealing with the prevailing untenable state of affairs. The elevated consciousness thus generated inevitably crystallizes into a social force, so that the men and women who have been imbued with a prophet's elevated vision become a distinct, active and vigorous social entity.

To act as a historical force, a prophet firstly needs the moral authority to enable him to influence the minds of people and to sway events. Moral authority is the most potent and enduring force in history. The symbolic embodiment of it in prophethood has commanded loyalty from the larger part of humanity since the beginning of human history. A prophet also needs knowledge to enable him to understand and interpret events accurately, to tell him the absolute values upon which a society should be established, and to provide him with insight into the operation of universal forces. Finally, a prophet must have political power to enable him to administer society properly, to uproot evil and to expand the frontiers of justice. Moral force and knowledge come to the prophet without a struggle, but political power is invariably gained only through struggle.

In any reflection on the need for social change, the essential question to be answered is what makes a society so bad that it requires changing? The answer is *fasād* – corruption. *Fasād* brings about distinct social and political divisions, engendering a small but extremely powerful element in society called the *mutrafūn* – those who live in decadent and undeserved ease and luxury and who thrive off of unbridled corruption – and the rest of the people called the *mustad'afūn* – the oppressed masses of the population.

The *mutrafūn* enjoy a monopoly over the wealth and economy of the state. The impact on their characters of the luxury they enjoy invariably results in undisciplined behavior. Their control of the economic forces leads to arrogance, a characteristic manifested not only towards other people but also even towards Allah. They grow oppressive and constitute a tyrannical minority. The *mustad'afūn*, who comprise the poor, the needy, the beggars, the debtors and the slaves, constitute the workers who generate the resources and produce the wealth of the state.

In such a society injustice becomes legitimized state policy and justice a remote and strange possibility. Society, though divided, is unified in its acceptance of injustice as an absolute value. The transformation of this society is only possible when the distinct and separate social entities are identified, the oppressors are unambiguously known as such, and the oppressed are seen to be oppressed.

A third social grouping then comes into existence who may be called the *muṣliḥūn* – people of right action. They stand between the *mutrafūn* and the *mustad'afūn* and take on the responsibility of bringing society back to a correct human balance, of acting as a force to liberate the oppressed. In doing this they will certainly incur the wrath of the tyrannical power elite. Paradoxically, however, the cord that binds together the *mutrafūn* and the *mustad'afūn* has, in many cases, proved unbreakable. This may be because oppression has the effect of destroying the spiritual qualities of human beings to such an extent that they lose the moral stamina to resist evil and resign themselves to it. Or perhaps it is just that human beings can reach a stage of moral degeneration when they simply lose interest in striving after justice or excellence.

This paradox is responsible for many of the tragic political realities of world history and the terrible contradictions which still exist in so many societies. It creates the conditions and justification for slavery and has been responsible for the sorry plight of the peasantry in all but a few periods of history. We find a handful of families controlling the great bulk of the wealth and resources of a nation, while the majority of its citizens can barely meet their basic needs. Dignified patience is required from those who take on the task of transforming such societies. The work is thankless and tedious, a Divinely imposed responsibility which has to be discharged without anticipation of any earthly reward.

It is within the framework of this philosophical

understanding of social history that Hausaland – the large area of *Bilād as-Sudān* which lies between Lake Chad in the east and the Middle Niger in the west – of the twelfth century A.H./seventeenth century A.D, and the later emergence of Shehu Usman dan Fodio, must be seen. This framework is necessary if we are to appreciate the circumstances, both negative and positive, which created the generation of the spiritual and social momentum that, in turn, culminated in the establishment of the Sokoto *khilāfah* and the eventual social and political transformation of the *Bilād as-Sudan* as a whole.

The Shehu divided the people of Hausaland into three groups. The first were those who believed sincerely in Islam, the second were straightforward idolaters who worshipped stones, trees or the like, and the third, whom he named the *mukhalliṭūn* (syncretists), were those who practiced an outward show of Islam but combined that with a simultaneous observance of various pagan rites. To the Shehu, the last group constituted the main problem because it included the bulk of the leadership of Hausaland.

The result was that unbelief, iniquity and open defiance of Allah's laws had become the order of the day. The social system was immoral. Women were oppressed and, in Shehu's words, "neglected like animals". There was unrestrained mixing of men and women. Cheating and fraud were rife. In the legal sphere the *Sharī'ah* had been subjected to significant alteration and property laws were geared towards benefiting the rulers. Hausaland was at a critical stage in its history, needing a profound challenge to stir its conscience. Shehu Usman dan Fodio was the man who emerged to lay down this challenge, to awaken the vast land to its religious and social responsibilities and to provide an alternative political, moral and intellectual leadership.

1. Hausaland before Usman dan Fodio

HISTORY does not allow a vacuum. There is a ceaseless interplay between the forces of decay and those of regeneration. Conditions of seemingly unremitting darkness – such those existing in Hausaland towards the end of the twelfth Islamic century – do in fact create the conditions necessary for the initiation of a process of rebirth. However, there have to be positive forces at work to provide the nourishment and atmosphere for a sustained process of regeneration within the dark environment.

Hausaland was not lacking in these positive forces. They constituted the self-perpetuating, indestructible factors that kept the fire of Islam burning even in the overwhelming atmosphere of corruption and degeneration. They included the philosophy of *tajdīd* (Islamic regeneration), which had been kept alive in *Bilād as-Sudan* for centuries and was never affected seriously by the triumph of *takhlīṭ* (the practice of mixing Islam and paganism). These positive forces also included the philosophy of law, which had always acted as a dynamic agent for change, and the resilient and thriving tradition of learning that had been maintained throughout the centuries.

It is also the case that people do not emerge from a void but are necessarily the products of their history and environment. So to gain a rounded picture of the great Shehu Usman dan Fodio it is necessary to see what forces for change existed in Hausaland before his time, to trace the traditions which may have influenced him, and to identify any predecessors who might have been sources of inspiration for him. In order to do this we must go back to Hausaland in the ninth Islamic century.

The Philosophy of *Tajdīd*

The idea of *tajdīd* is ingrained in Islamic thought and is perpetuated as a living tradition in all Muslim societies. The ceaseless conflict between good and evil, right and wrong, justice and injustice makes regeneration of Islam a continuous necessity. Indeed, the concept of prophethood is synonymous with the philosophy of *tajdīd*. It implies that human society should not be left in darkness and corruption but be guided back to righteousness on a regular basis.

Injustice should not be allowed to frustrate the Divine purpose for mankind, which is essentially the establishment of justice on earth. Man has an obligation to overthrow systems of injustice. Indeed, deviant, godless and misleading ideologies should not be allowed to predominate. Human beings have a perpetual duty to strive until the Word of Allah becomes supreme. In short, the world should not be left in peace until corruption, injustice and false ideologies have been uprooted and the religion of Allah is being implemented everywhere.

The philosophy of *tajdīd* was given a new impetus in *Bilād as-Sudan* in the ninth Islamic century/fifteenth century A.D. by an unusually revolutionary and highly respected North African scholar, Muhammad bin Abd al-Karim al-Maghili at-Tlimsāni. The treatises he wrote while staying in some of the key cities and states of *Bilād as-Sudan*, such as Kano, Katsina and Gao, and the advice he gave to certain rulers, notably Muhammad Rumfa of Kano and Askia Muhammad of Songhay, were largely instrumental in the enhancement of the *Sharī'ah* as the legal modality of those states and in the Islamic transformation of those societies in general. The fire of revival he kindled kept burning until the thirteenth century when it was translated again into a political and social force by men such as Shehu Usman dan Fodio.

Our sources for al-Maghili's philosophy of *tajdīd* are firstly *Ajwibat al-Maghili*, which comprises his replies to the questions of Askia al-Hajj Muhammad, for which we have drawn on Dr. Hunwick's impressive translation. Secondary sources of reference are provided by the treatises written by al-Maghili for the Amir of Kano, Muhammad Rumfa: *Taj ad-Dīn Fī Mā Yajibu 'Ala-l-Mulūk* on government; and *Wasiya* on the establishment of the rule of law.

In *Ajwibat*, al-Maghili states that *tajdīd* is a historical imperative and is essentially the responsibility of scholars imbued with knowledge and piety. Its ultimate purpose is to ascertain the truth, banish falsehood, overthrow a tyrannical order and establish justice. He maintains in it:

> "Thus, it is related that at the beginning of every century Allah sends a scholar who regenerates their religion for them. There is no doubt that the conduct of this scholar in every century in enjoining the right and forbidding what is disapproved, setting aright people's affairs, establishing justice among them and supporting the truth against falsehood and the oppressed against the oppressor, will be in contrast to the conduct of other scholars of his age. For this reason, he will be an odd man out among them on account of his being the only man of such pure conduct and on account of the small number of men like him."

This struggle to support truth against falsehood and the oppressed against their oppressors has two distinct dimensions. It inevitably involves a confrontation between scholars who distort the truth in order to gain favor with the oppressors and those who strive for the spiritual and economic wellbeing of the people. In al-Maghili's view, the first kind are not Muslims and are worse than the oppressors themselves.

In the second place, and indeed more importantly, support for the oppressed must inevitably involve a struggle against tyrannical rulers until they are overthrown. Concerning an oppressive ruler, al-Maghili told Askia Muhammad in *Ajwibat*:

> "If you can bring to an end his oppression of the Muslims without harm to them, so that you set up among them a just amir, then do so, even if that leads to the killing of many of the oppressors and their supporters and the killing of many of your supporters, for whoever is killed from among them is the worst of slain men and whoever is killed from among your people is the best of martyrs. . . . If you cannot bring to an end his oppression of the Muslims except by causing harm to them, then here two evils are conflicting; so beware lest you change one reprehensible practice for another like it or worse than it. So make sure here and commit the lesser of the two evils, for committing the lesser of the two evils is a widely accepted rule and a firmly transmitted Sunnah. It is not reprehensible to kill unjust miscreants and their helpers – even if they pray and pay *zakāt* and perform pilgrimage. So fight them, even if they kill many of your number and you kill many of their number, so long as your fighting them is for the victory of truth over falsehood and the victory of the oppressed over the oppressor."

Thus as far as al-Maghili was concerned, one of the objectives of *tajdīd* is to set aright the affairs of the people and establish justice among them. This implies, essentially, the transformation of the polity and the restoration, enhancement and consolidation of the Islamic order. Hence, it involves the establishment of wide-ranging measures, policies and institutions designed to give the state a thoroughly Islamic character.

In the administration of the state, recourse should be had to right-acting scholars for the formulation of policies, decision-making and the running of affairs in general, for such scholars are like the prophets in former communities. In general, the Islamic leadership should be guided in its decision-making and policy formulation by a number of principles.

It should commit itself to the establishment of whatever

Allah has commanded to be done and eradicate what He has forbidden. Muslim leadership should, as a matter of policy, keep away from matters of dubious legal status. In concrete terms, if there is doubt as to whether a particular matter is an obligation or not, the safer course of action is to undertake it, but if there is doubt as to whether a particular matter is obligatory or forbidden, then it should be avoided altogether. Where there is a conflict between two courses of action which appear to be equally sound, then the more exacting should be preferred.

In social matters, the fundamental duty of the state is to ensure comprehensive social justice in society, and this is the theme of al-Maghili's *Taj ad-Dīn*. The state must be generous to its citizens. On the one hand, this implies that people should be allowed to retain possession of their own wealth, thus contributing to the permanence of the state. On the other hand, it implies that the authorities should handle public wealth with restraint, for greed on their part will lead to instability and the collapse of the state.

Social justice also entails the distribution of state wealth and resources in such a way that the general welfare of Muslims is advanced. To achieve that, the Imam should start with the areas of society with the greatest need – possibly the rural areas. Workers, including scholars, judges, *muadhdhins* and civil servants, need to be paid. The poor have to have their share as well: "The Imam should give to the poor, first to the neediest and then to the needy, until it is spread to all of them both male and female, young and old, according to the degree and variety of their need." Social justice also implies refraining from and prevention of injustice. Hence, authorities should not take undue advantage of their position, indulge in bribery, confiscate people's property, or impose unjust and illegal taxes.

Basic economic life is dealt with under the heading of "Markets" in *Ajwibat*. Al-Maghili wrote that the leader of the Muslims has a duty to prevent fraud in every aspect of economic activity and to organize the market system in a way that will "safeguard people's means of subsistence". To that end, he should standardize all weights and measures to ensure that "the scales and the weights are just and that the weights are equal". Similarly, the leader of the Muslims must restrain people from encroaching on the rights of others in economic dealings and should be hard on those who defraud and cheat. All wealth obtained from such means, said al-Maghili, should be confiscated and restored to the state treasury.

The preservation of public morality and social integrity entails a number of measures. The most important is to safeguard the sanctity of the office of the judge. This office, al-Maghili wrote to the Amir of Kano, pertains to the Prophet of Allah ﷺ and, therefore, only men of learning and piety should be appointed as judges. The rule of law should be strictly maintained and all people should be treated equally before the law. The institution of public complaints should also be strengthened, especially to defend the rights of the weak – women, children and the poor. Criminals should be dealt with appropriately but, al-Maghili warned, severity should be tempered with mercy lest the course of justice be perverted.

In the specific area of public morality, especially as it related to the free mixing of men and women and immodest dress, al-Maghili exhorted the ruler in *Ajwibat* to "appoint trustworthy men to watch over this, day and night, in secret and in the open. This is not to be considered as spying on the Muslims, it is only a way of caring for them properly and curbing evildoers."

Such, briefly, was al-Maghili's philosophy of *tajdīd*. Indeed, it was a great credit to *Bilād as-Sudan* that, whereas much of the Muslim world at that time was unprogressive, *tajdīd* was being carried out there in several places at that time. Askia Muhammad, for example, was so keen on establishing Islam and fighting wars in its cause that many leading scholars in *Bilād as-Sudan* regarded him as a *mujaddid* (reviver of Islam) himself. The efforts of the Amirs of Kano and Katsina were no less impressive. Even though al-Maghili left North Africa in utter despondence, because of hostility against his zeal for restoring the authority of the *Sharīʿah*, his influence was extensive, profound and enduring.

Shehu Usman paid a glowing tribute to this remarkable man. Al-Maghili, Shehu wrote in *Taʿlīm al-Ikhwān*, was "the seal of inquirers, the learned and erudite Imam... the exemplary, the pious Sunni, one of the truly intelligent, which lent him an abundance of energy and insight. He was a man of prestige in arms, a hater of the enemies of Allah, intrepid in affairs demanding courage, constant, eloquent of tongue, a lover of the Sunnah."

The Philosophy of Law

We shall now consider another important area which played a significant role in creating the necessary atmosphere for the eventual transformation that took place – the philosophy of law. Jurisprudence was seen as a vehicle of protest and a means of dissemination of the principles necessary for the revival of Islam in a time of decline. If al-Maghili personified the philosophy of *tajdīd*, Imam Muhammad ibn Abdur Rahman al-Barnawi, who hailed from Borno in the present northeast of Nigeria, personified the ideal of social morality and a dynamic, revolutionary approach to law. His *Shurb az-Zulāl*, a short composition in verse written in 1119/1707, summarized that approach.

Shurb az-Zulāl was a work of protest in a social and political atmosphere that had become corrupt and oppressive. It was written with the specific purpose of eroding the influence of the rulers over the people and destroying their credibility. It may also have been directed at venal scholars who colluded with the kings and supported their oppression.

It appears that the political and social climate under which al-Barnawi wrote *Shurb az-Zulāl* was not different from the one Shehu Usman described in *Kitāb al-Farq*. In both we are given a list of oppressive policies instituted by rulers – illegal taxation levied on common people, arbitrary confiscation of property, corruption by judges, perversion of the legal process, alteration of the sacred law to suit the interests of rulers and rich men, and large-scale corruption in government quarters.

Al-Barnawi added another dimension to this picture by considering what seemed to be an operative, perhaps prevalent, economy based on usury in a society that was supposed to be Muslim. He also assailed what he termed usurpation, oppression, marauding, illegal imports and unjust enrichment carried out by those in power. Associated with the oppressive social atmosphere was the general social disorder and the growth of crime. Thus, al-Barnawi declared the proceeds of gambling, singing, theft, wheedling, deception and secret perfidy to be illegal.

Al-Barnawi did not spare the scholars either, though his attack on them was rather veiled. He censured those engaged in the thriving but pernicious trade of fortune telling. Writing in the sand, astrology, the spells of jinn and incantations were declared to be illegal means of livelihood. With regard to the more respectable scholars, al-Barnawi appeared to be saying that, even if association with the rulers was unavoidable, it was important to limit it to the barest necessity. Piety demanded that they do all that they could to avoid the oppressors altogether.

Al-Barnawi was also uneasy about those who created artificial scarcity, especially of essential food items. Similarly he objected strongly to an economic system which favored only the rich and abandoned the poor, saying: "He who does not help (the needy) in a year of dearth has sinned. He has neglected the command of Allah." Any food item in excess of a person's requirement must, in a time of scarcity, be sold and at a price which reflected the plight of the poor.

Al-Barnawi was concerned about the way people acquired their wealth through illegal means. His theme, expressed in the phrase, "the sources have become corrupt", impelled him to warn those rich men, who felt that they could remain good Muslims despite their unlawful sources of income, that their assumptions were clearly wrong. Their worship, as long as they persisted in unjust enrichment, was null and void. They were destined for a hard time on the Day of Judgment.

To save themselves from Allah's wrath, those engaged in illegal acquisition and false trade must repent, repay their ill-gotten wealth, and seek Allah's forgiveness. More fundamentally, al-Barnawi reminded his audience that Islam has clearly defined the lawful sources of income, which include agriculture, trade, industry – all of these to be conducted with, "piety and honesty in dealing".

The state, he added, had the same obligations as the ordinary citizen to seek its resources through lawful means. These, too, had been spelled out clearly by the *Sharī'ah.* They are *al-khums* (one-fifth of the booty of war), the tithe, the poll tax, land tax, booty and what is surplus, and then property whose owner is unknown and inheritable property lacking (rightful) heirs. The idea of spelling out the sources of state income was perhaps to show that other taxes which the state levied on individuals were unauthorized by law and therefore illegal.

Finally, al-Barnawi reiterated several principles both for individuals and the state over the issue of what constitutes legality and illegality. One of the principles involved, in his view, was that, "religion is ease". The immediate beneficiaries of this principle were the poor people. As long as they remained in a state of deprivation, hunger or poverty, then much of what Islam declared to be unlawful would become lawful to them. The poor man could take for himself and family money that would otherwise be illegal. He incurred no sin thereby, as long as he neither squandered it nor took what was in excess of his needs.

Similarly, a person who was overwhelmed by hunger could take food from anywhere. "This is not illegal food," al-Barnawi stated categorically, "no, indeed, nor even dubious food." It was unfair to add to the misery of the common man by confining him to the rigorous letter of the law. He needed a degree of relief from the confines of the law in order to take the necessary social steps to overcome his deprivation.

He postulated the principle that anything with an unclear origin is legal. Therefore, in a situation pervaded by corruption and immoral earnings, it would be futile for any person to insist on absolute purity. "It does not befit us today," he said, "to ask questions, for the sources have become corrupt." Was that an answer to some civil servants who might be uneasy about the source of their salary or about those who sought the ideal in a situation of general corruption?

Further, where it was impossible to distinguish between what was legal and what was not, where things such as commodities in markets were concerned, then one must presume the legality of what was being sold unless it was obviously illegal in origin. This was so, even if one suspected a vestige of illegality. "So long as the illegal portion is not the major part... then to eat what is legal together with what is of dubious legality is the customary usage." It was advisable, however, for anyone who could afford it, to abstain totally from things that were of a dubious nature.

The Timbuktu Tradition

Perhaps the most important factor in the resurgence of Islam, after several decades of decline in *Bilād as-Sudan,* was that the Islamic tradition of learning and scholarship continued throughout the period of decline to operate as a living and thriving tradition, producing scholars, jurists and saints all over the region. The tradition preserved the best of Islam and kept alive its intellectual legacy strongly enough for any determined reformer to apply it as an instrument of societal transformation. That Islamic tradition was best symbolized by an enigmatic and highly venerated West African city that flourished for at least five centuries from the twelfth century A.D. – Timbuktu.

Timbuktu was a city bolstered by piety and, as Dr. Hunwick tells us, "it was the proud boast of its people that worship has never been offered to pagan gods within its walls." He quotes Muhammad Kati who described the city in *Tārīkh al-Fattāsh*:

> "Religion flourished and the Sunnah enlivened both religious and worldly affairs... In those days it had no equal in the Sudan, from Mali to the edges of the Maghrib, for soundness of its institutions, political liberties, purity of customs, security of life and goods and respect for, and assistance to, the students and men of learning."

The city owed its prestige and its immense influence on the subsequent history of West Africa to its being a center of learning. It was a university complex, drawing students and scholars from different parts of the Muslim world, nourishing governments with administrators, clerks and judges, feeding cities with imams, teachers and jurists, and providing, for the wider society, a long chain of muftis, saints and above all, *mujaddids*. The unusually high number of *mujaddids* which the *Bilād as-Sudan* has produced – perhaps higher than any other part of the Muslim world – can be attributed in part to the tradition of learning fostered by Timbuktu.

"The tradition of learning in Timbuktu," Elias Sād writes in his *Social History of Timbuktu*, "assured the city a status and prestige." He continues:

> "The Muslim sciences, which the various settlers brought and fostered in the city, went hand-in-hand with the widespread commercial contacts of these groups to secure for the growing town a measure of non-interference from outside. For one thing, the settlers themselves commanded considerable wealth along with widespread networks of trade and alliances in the area. Additionally, however, the security of the city was in its Islamic image. Its mosques, schools and shrines began, at an early stage, to be seen as its guardians. In the psychological mood which prevailed after pilgrimage of Mansa Musa of Mali (and again on the return from the Hajj of Askia Muhammad over a century

> and a half later), Timbuktu gradually gained an aura of 'sanctity' and assumed for itself a sort of inviolability."

In this tradition of learning, after the elementary stage of Qur'anic recitation and literacy, a student was introduced into the world of scholarship via the Arabic language. Versatility in Arabic, Sād suggests, was highly valued, and so fields of learning associated with language, such as grammar, rhetoric, logic and prosody, became an essential part of the learning process.

The fundamental goal of learning in this tradition was to acquire comprehensive understanding of Qur'an, *ḥadīth* and *fiqh*, and, to some extent, *taṣawwuf*. As a result of this, the science of *tafsīr* – Qur'anic exegesis – was perhaps the most important of all the sciences studied. Then followed study of the *ḥadīth*, in which, Sād states, "the abilities of a jurist came to be measured by his familiarity with the precedents set by the Prophet ﷺ."

In the study of *fiqh*, the Timbuktu tradition insisted on achieving as high a level of competence as could be found in any other part of the Muslim world. The *fiqh* studies revolved almost wholly around the Māliki School, to which the entire region has subscribed until the present day. Other fields of knowledge, such as *taṣawwuf*, *uṣūl* (the philosophy of law), *tawḥīd* (the science of the unity of Allah), history, medicine, astronomy and mathematics were also given due attention. A relatively wide range of textbooks was available to the students.

Knowledge was sought in this tradition precisely in order to enable the students to organize their lives as Allah had ordered, and subsequently to organize society and state on those lines as well. Scholarship was, therefore, an institution in its own right, distinct from and almost totally independent of the state. It remained self-reliant, maintaining and generating its own funds through a high level of commercial activities, and in this way preserved its own prestige and sanctity.

Scholars were never subservient to the rulers. Indeed, in some respects, the tradition was so strong that it forced the rulers to concede to the supremacy of the scholar over the ruler. For example, it was the monarch who visited the Qāḍī of Timbuktu, and not the other way around. The idea was that a *qāḍī*, as the custodian of Allah's sacred law, was pre-eminent over the temporal ruler. This tradition gave the scholars of Timbuktu an aura of sanctity and respectability that made them the symbol of the people and the conscience of society.

The Timbuktu tradition persisted in Hausaland, and in the whole of *Bilād as-Sudan*, producing scholars who upheld the spirit of Islam and nourished Islam itself both in the periods of light and of darkness. The Moroccan invasion of 999/1591, in which almost all the leading scholars were arrested, precipitated its decline. This deterioration, however, was merely quantitative. The quality of the tradition was maintained. So, while Hausaland was sunk in moral degradation, this intellectual and moral tradition carefully nurtured a cadre of scholars who were able to bring about a revival of Islam and create a society dedicated to Islam – a state entirely committed to the defense and enhancement of Islam.

2. The Education of Usman dan Fodio

SHEHU USMAN was born into a highly cultured family in 1168/1754. His father was Muhammad ibn Salih, known generally as Fodio. His mother was Hawwa bint Muhammad ibn Usman. Shortly after his birth the family moved to Degel, where the young Usman grew up. In the Timbuktu tradition, the parents were invariably the first teachers and Shehu Usman received most of his early education from his parents and relatives.

Our main sources concerning his education are *Idā' an-Nusūkh* and *Tazyīn al-Waraqāt* of 'Abdullahi dan Fodio and *Asānīd al-Faqīr* of Shehu Usman himself. In *Idā' an-Nusūkh*, 'Abdullahi described the Shehu's early education:

> "The Shaykh read the Qur'an with his father, learned *al-Ishriniyyah* and similar works with his shaykh, 'Uthman, known as Biddu al-Kabawi. He learned syntax and the science of grammar from *al-Khulāsah* and other works at the hand of our Shaykh 'Abd ar-Rahman ibn Hammada. He read *al-Mukhtasar* with our paternal and maternal uncle, Uthmān, known as Bidduri.... This shaykh of his was learned and pious, well known for righteousness and the ordering of the right and the forbidding of the wrong, and for being occupied with what concerned him. He it is whom our Shaykh Uthmān (dan Fodio) imitated in states and in deeds. He accompanied him for nearly two years, molding himself according to his pattern in piety (*taqwā*) and in ordering the right, and forbidding the wrong."

We can see from this that the Shehu's character was initially molded by Usman Bidduri. His inclination towards the career which eventually turned out to be the sole purpose in his life, and his keenness to call people to the way of Allah, were instilled in him by this shaykh, whose influence on Shehu Usman was fundamental, enduring and far-reaching. Associated with this influence was that of Muhammad Sambo, who supervised part of the Shehu's early education. According to 'Abdullahi, this scholar, "used to attend (the Shehu's) reading of *al-Mukhtasar.* If he made a mistake or let anything slip, this maternal uncle of ours would correct it for him." Though he was away in the Hijāz during most of the period of the Shehu's early activities his influence on the whole community was beyond question.

Continuing his account of the Shehu's education, 'Abdullahi wrote:

> "Now Shaykh Uthmān informed me that he had learned Qur'anic exegesis (*tafsīr*) from the son of our maternal and paternal uncle Aḥmad ibn Muhammad ibn al-Amin, and that he was present at the assembly of Hāshim az-Zamfari and heard from him Qur'anic exegesis from the beginning of the Qur'an to the end of it... He learned the science of tradition (*ḥadīth*) from our maternal and paternal uncle, al-Hajj Muhammad ibn Raj... reading with him all of *Ṣaḥīḥ Bukhāri.* Then he gave us license to pass on all that he had recited of that which he had learned from his Madinan Shaykh, the Sindi of origin, Abū Al-Hassan 'Alī."

Muhammad ibn Raj's knowledge of *ḥadīth* was indeed profound. He had studied all of the most important works of *ḥadīth,* such as those of the Imams al-Bukhāri, Muslim and Mālik, through an uninterrupted chain of authorities. His other teacher of note was Salih Muhammad al-Kanawi, through whom Shehu Usman also traced his *isnāds* in *Bukhāri, Muwaṭṭa* and *ash-Shifā'.*

'Abdullahi told us further in *Idā' an-Nusūkh* that the Shehu sought knowledge from Shaykh Jibril and accompanied him for almost a year until they came to the town of Agades. Jibril ibn 'Umar's influence was both intellectual and moral. In *ḥadīth*, for example, the Shehu traced his *isnād* in all the essential *ḥadīth* works, notably *Bukhāri*, *Muslim*, *Abū Dawud*, *Muwaṭṭa* and *Ibn Majah*, through him. Shaykh Jibril was his most important authority in *fiqh* (jurisprudence) and also, most significantly, in all the various aspects of *taṣawwuf* (spiritual training). His *silsilah* (spiritual genealogy) in this sphere of life and especially in the Qādiriyyah order, and his *silsilah* in *Dalā'il al-khairāt*, are all traced, in *Asānīd al-Faqīr*, through Jibril. There seemed to be no aspect of learning that the Shehu undertook in which Jibril ibn 'Umar did not leave his indelible imprint.

The real significance of Jibril ibn 'Umar, however, is that he gave the Shehu the idea of *tajdīd*, the foundations of which he himself laid. He gave his student the intellectual, moral, spiritual and ideological training he needed for the gigantic task of *tajdīd*. Later, Jibril was the first to pledge allegiance to the Shehu, even before the *jihad*. Despite certain differences of opinion the Shehu acknowledged his profound indebtedness to Jibril, which 'Abdullahi quoted in *Idā' an-Nusūkh*: "If there be said of me that which is said of good report, then I am but a wave of the waves of Jibril."

Influence, though of an indirect nature, was also exerted on the Shehu by Sidi Mukhtar al-Kunti, who was born in 1142/1729 and died in 1226/1811, and was thus a direct contemporary of the Shehu. Sidi Mukhtar belonged to a highly venerated Kunta family which, over many years, had produced an uninterrupted chain of scholars and saints, the most influential being Sidi Mukhtar al-Kunti. Knowledgeable and charismatic, he soon became a veritable institution in himself.

According to Abdalaziz Batran, Sidi Mukhtar attracted multitudes of students, people who came just for his *barakah* and guidance, and scholars seeking enlightenment. He assumed the leadership not only of the Kunta family but, more significantly, also of the Qādiriyyah order, giving unity to branches that had been estranged from one another for nearly two hundred years. Thereafter, he initiated an ambitious and, indeed, successful though peaceful, moral transformation of a large part of Africa.

Sidi Mukhtar taught that the study of *taṣawwuf* was essential, as it was imperative for self-fortification and for achieving nearness to Allah. This nearness itself involves a progressive moral transformation of the individual under the guidance of a shaykh. He also taught that it was necessary to give as much attention to the mundane aspects of life as to the spiritual. Wealth, therefore, was essential, as it is the cornerstone for *jāh* – social standing and dignity – as well as for *haibah* – authority and respect. He wished for a return to the basic sources of Islamic jurisprudence and for the teachings of the Companions of Muhammad ﷺ to be reinstated. Moreover, he rejected exclusive adherence to one *madh-hab* (school of jurisprudence) and opened the door of *ijtihād* (independent judgment) to all who were juristically qualified.

Sidi Mukhtar believed that he was the *mujaddid* of the thirteenth century of the *Hijrah* whom Allah had called upon to renovate Islam and to restore the *ummah* to its glorious past, not only in West Africa but also throughout the whole Muslim world. Like Aḥmad Baba before him, he expressed the opinion that several *mujaddids* appeared periodically in different territories, including West Africa.

We shall now look at some of the principal ideas of Sidi Mukhtar, namely his ideas on *tajdīd*, the *'ulamā'* and *taṣawwuf*. *Tajdīd* for him was, "the resuscitation of what has withered away of knowledge of the Qur'an and the Sunnah and the commandment of their observance." Because the *ummah* was bound to sink from time to time into degeneration or turmoil, *tajdīd* would always remain imperative.

In western Sudan, this degeneration was first precipitated by the despot, Sonni 'Alī, who appeared in the ninth Islamic century, and therefore necessitated, by implication, the contemporary *tajdīd* of Askia Muhammad. Further degeneration was brought about by the invasion of the Moroccan hordes who killed many of the inhabitants of western Sudan, slew the *'ulamā'*, captured as many as thirty thousand people and sacked the towns. This destruction of the life and knowledge of a large part of the western Sudan also precipitated a moral and intellectual decline, which in turn necessitated the initiation of a new process of *tajdīd* throughout the region.

Tajdīd, Sidi Mukhtar said, could take various forms and thus could be led by individuals who emphasized different aspects of Islam, depending on the prevailing situation. The *mujaddid* could be a statesman who would preserve the principles of the law, make justice triumph among the people and protect the lives and property of the people, so that they could carry on their temporal affairs and their religious duties without any hindrance. The *mujaddid* could also be a *zāhid* (ascetic) who would remind the people of the world to come, call them to righteousness and renunciation of the world. Or he could be a pure scholar who would regenerate the knowledge of the Sunnah and establish the authenticity of the Prophetic tradition. Few individuals could undertake *tajdīd*, for the standard of learning needed, coupled with exemplary moral probity, is extremely high. Sidi Mukhtar said of such a person:

> "Assuming that all religious knowledge was forgotten, all literature burned, and he were resorted to, he would have the capacity to resuscitate that knowledge and write similar books."

It was Sidi Mukhtar's view that the center of gravity in the Muslim world had shifted to western Sudan by the eleventh Islamic century. In the century before, those who had undertaken the *tajdīd* were firstly the *mujaddid* of all branches of knowledge, al-Maghili, secondly Jalāl ad-Dīn as-Suyūti, thirdly the *zāhid*, Sayyid Muhammad as-Sanūsi, and fourthly the statesman, al-Hajj Askia Muhammad. But in the eleventh century, the three *mujaddids* that appeared in the Muslim world were, according to Sidi Mukhtar, all from the western Sudan. These were the *faqīh* Aḥmad Baba at-Timbukti, the famous *ḥadīth* scholar Muhammad Baghyu at-Takruri, and the ascetic Baba al-Mukhtar at-Timbukti. In the twelfth century, two of the three *mujaddids* that appeared were from western Sudan, Sidi Mukhtar al-Kunti himself and Shehu Usman dan Fodio.

Sidi Mukhtar attributed the decline of knowledge and the triumph of *bid'ah* (innovation) in the western Sudan in the twelfth and the thirteenth Islamic centuries partly to the activities of corrupt scholars (*'ulamā' as-sū'*), whom he grouped into as many as sixteen categories. They included those who had knowledge, but failed to put it into practice; those who presented an appearance of compliance with the outward religious duties, but had not eliminated characteristics such as vanity, hypocrisy, ambition, and desire for political office and high rank; those who presumed that they had the exclusive right to guide the common people and yet entered into unholy alliance with the *sulṭāns*, thus encouraging the *sulṭāns*' oppression of the people; those who engaged in *jihad*, but only to obtain fame and wealth; and those scholars who used false methods, such as music, to lure people into spiritual practices. The danger of those scholars, Sidi Mukhtar said, could be seen from the *ḥadīth* of the Prophet ﷺ:

> "I fear for my *ummah* after me more from *'ulamā' as-sū'* than from the Dajjal", and when asked who these were, he replied that they were *'ulamā' al-alsinah*, 'the *'ulamā'* of the tongue.

Sidi Mukhtar insisted that *taṣawwuf* (sufism) is an indispensable aspect of Islam but that true sufism is none other than honest and sincere adherence to the Sunnah:

> "If the *murīd* observes the commands of the *Sharī'ah* and refrains from doing what is prohibited by it, truly and

> sincerely, Allah will open in his heart a portal through which he can perceive *'ulūmu-l-ḥaqīqah* (knowledge of spiritual realities). And if he adheres to the rules of *'ulūmu-l-ḥaqīqah,* Allah will cause to open a further portal within his inner self through which he shall see the Kingdom of Heaven and realities of Allah's might."

The combination of law and moral purification seemed to him the best way to practice religion.

Sidi Mukhtar's views on the use of music in sufism and on *zuhd* (abstention from this world) are worth noting. "Allah, the Almighty, is not worshipped by dancing and chanting... We the Qādirīyyah do not approve of dancing, frivolous playing and merry-making because they are degrading to man's dignity and damaging to his honor." *Zuhd* does not mean squandering one's wealth or declaring illegal things that Allah has decreed to be legal, such as taking up a profession or other economic pursuits. According to him *zuhd* is to dispense with the world willingly when one possesses it and to be at rest in one's heart when one loses it. "The Companions ؓ of the Prophet ﷺ," he said, "possessed the world and held it like the trustworthy treasurer, kept it in the lawful manner and distributed it in the legal way. They neither clung to it nor had any inclination towards it."

Sidi Mukhtar's influence on the Shehu and his movement was first and foremost spiritual, for, as the undisputed head of the Qādiriyyah order, to which the Shehu belonged, and as a dynamic intellectual personality, he was bound to exert a deep influence over the Shehu. Some of the three hundred or so books and treatises he wrote were certainly brought to the attention of the Shehu, and his students and companions also made their own particular impact. Significantly, Sidi Mukhtar used his vast and profound influence in support of the Shehu and his movement, a support that advanced the course of the *jīhad* in considerable measure.

We have mentioned some of the men who influenced the Shehu to indicate the kind of training he had, although it is impossible for us to know all of them. There are certainly other personalities who contributed to the making of the Shehu in much the same way as those we have mentioned but who are not known to us and may never be known. What cannot be denied is that the Shehu drank deeply from the great lake of knowledge, which the western Sudan had to offer.

It is to his credit that he sought knowledge wherever he could find it and that, even when he had grown important and more famous than most other scholars, he still sat humbly before them, learning from them. He also learned the primary sources – the Qur'an and *ḥadīth* – from as many authorities as possible. At the end of the day he had acquired not only a deep and indelible knowledge of these sources but also of the different interpretations of them that had been developed over the centuries.

The Shaping of a Character

The Shehu, from what we can understand, must have seen in al-Maghili, the early scholar from North Africa mentioned above, a vigorous intellectual who had a deep knowledge of those sciences necessary for changing people's intellectual precepts, and also a noble character imbued with the requisite moral persuasion to sway even the most powerful of men. In al-Maghili, the Shehu saw how an individual, despite having refugee status, could effect a lasting change in the life of nations and set their history, almost single-handedly, on a totally different course by the sheer force of his intellect, his moral authority and his absolute reliance on Allah. He took time to study al-Maghili properly, taking from him, as faithfully as possible, the concept of the Islamic renewal of both society and government and also the nature of the ideological divide between Muslims and those who serve the cause of evil.

From al-Barnawi, as well as a number of scholars of his time, especially those of the intellectual centers of Borno, Katsina and Kano, the Shehu must have understood the importance of an active, purifying and transformative jurisprudence which, even though it had been relegated to the background and lost its supremacy, could still serve as a potent forum for protest and mobilization for the revival of Islam. Indeed, the point that came out clearly in al-Barnawi was that what was wrong in respect of law was not so much the stagnation it had suffered through the loss of genuine *'ulamā'* but rather the neglect it had suffered through its abandonment by society as a whole. Law grows and develops through application.

In Sidi Aḥmad Baba, who epitomized the spirit of the Timbuktu tradition, the Shehu must have perceived the role and place of the scholar in society. The scholar's first responsibility is to acquaint himself with the basic knowledge of the sources, then of the law, then of different sciences that support the life of society, and then of history and so on. This will place him in a position to guide society in all essential areas and to put himself at the disposal of every segment of society.

His second responsibility is to stand up boldly as the guardian of the conscience of society, preventing any assault or outrage on the values of society or on the sanctity of its beliefs and institutions. In this way, he serves as the force behind the preservation of the moral and social purity of society and respect for the integrity of the nation.

The scholar's third responsibility is to stand up for the poor and the oppressed, to defend their rights and strive for the accomplishment of their aspirations. The scholar's fourth responsibility is to stand up for the defense of the nation and enhance its integrity as a nation faithful to Allah and submissive to His laws.

As an institution in himself and an active observer of events and history, the scholar is morally bound to warn his nation with all the power and means at his disposal against possible deviations from Islam and to state as clearly as possible the moral, political and historical consequences of such deviations. Finally, it is his responsibility to raise a generation of men and women capable of taking on their true societal responsibilities and steering the course of society in a positive direction when the signs of degeneration are apparent.

When considering his teachers and contemporaries, the influence of Usman Bidduri should not be underrated. He was a scholar, who combined learning and piety, who was dissatisfied with the prevailing corruption and who felt the acute need for change but who, at the same time, had the wisdom and patience to first sow the seeds of change. He quietly transferred his desire for change to a future generation and died silently, leaving a legacy for the future. The Shehu, we are told, imitated him in almost all situations relating to his work, recognizing that restraint and patience, as well as a depth of understanding of the issues at stake, are essential ingredients for social transformation.

It was the learned and pious Jibril ibn 'Umar, however, who gave him the weapons with which to strive against the currents of the time. In the Shehu's studies of *ḥadīth*, in his efforts to acquire a deep knowledge of law and jurisprudence, in his studies and practice of *taṣawwuf*, in his endeavors to get a more intimate spiritual relationship with the Prophet ﷺ, and in his endeavors to understand his society and work for its improvement, he found in Jibril a worthy and eager mentor. He learned from him the importance of restraint, of open mindedness and sympathy for the inadequacies of the common people, and he also learned from the reverses, which his teacher had suffered in his attempt to change society too quickly.

Other scholars also left their mark. The supervision of his teachings by the saintly Muhammad Sambo, the vast knowledge of *ḥadīth* acquired from Al-Hajj Muhammad Raj and the important studies of the Qur'an and its exegesis from Muhammad al-Amin all influenced the Shehu deeply.

In Sidi Mukhtar al-Kunti, he found the true embodiment of sainthood and a versatile and richly endowed scholar who had the view that concern for this world and the more lofty concern for the Hereafter had to be combined in a single individual to create a saint. Sidi Mukhtar also maintained that both temporal and spiritual matters had to be brought under the single authority of Islam if the world was to be a better place in which to live. In him Shehu Usman must also have seen a dynamic sufism concerned with securing for man both a just society on earth and Allah's pleasure in the Hereafter.

He must have seen in Mukhtar al-Kunti the extent to which an individual possessing sanctity and prestige could penetrate people's hearts and secure their allegiance for the task of creating a better society. It was to the credit of both the Shehu and al-Kunti that they did not view each other as rivals but rather as two *mujaddids*, each engaged in the same endeavors in the cause of Allah but each employing slightly different methods.

There were many other aspects to the shaping of the Shehu's personality. All that he had learned of the Arabic language, Qur'anic exegesis, and the science of *ḥadīth* was just an introduction to the wider world of learning and scholarship. From the *Mukhtasar* of Khalil the Shehu moved further to drink from the great pool of jurisprudence of not only the Māliki but also the other three schools because, although the Māliki school was sufficient for his needs, he felt he should know the principles of other schools as well. As he himself said: "There is no rule in Islam, other than that of mere convenience, that restricts a community to following one particular school of law."

Then, the Shehu ventured boldly into the world of sufism and learned and practiced the rites of several branches of the Qādiriyyah, including that of Sidi Mukhtar al-Kunti. In addition, he read almost everything that reached him of the works of al-Ghazali, most especially the *Iḥyā'* from which he derived much profit. His book, entitled boldly *Ṭarīq al-Jannah* (The Way to the Garden), was simply a summary of what al-Ghazali had written on piety and moral purification. He also examined the works of other great *ṣufi* personalities –

the sage Ibn al-'Arabi, the saint az-Zarrūq, his teacher Ibn 'Ata Allah, amongst others. He also studied other *ṣufi* orders because, as far as he was concerned, sufism, like Islamic jurisprudence, is a tree with many branches.

The Shehu also studied history, especially that of the Rightly-Guided *khilāfah* and of Islam in general. He took a special interest in the history of the western Sudan in which he noticed the inevitable confrontation between the forces of light and darkness that had periodically occurred in the region.

But there is no doubt that the most important of the Shehu's personal efforts were devoted to the study of the Qur'an and *ḥadīth*. By investigating these two sources over and over again and by teaching some of them from beginning to end many times over, he acquired a deep knowledge of them. In his *Asānīd al-Faqīr*, the Shehu leaves no one in doubt as to his tremendous knowledge of the *ḥadīth* – it seems that he had read and taught almost all the *ḥadīth*s contained in the authentic collections.

As a result of all this Shehu Usman was a forest of knowledge, a jurist, a saint. "He grew up penitent and devout," Muhammad Bello tells us in the *Infāq al-Maysūr*, "possessed of pleasing qualities, and none was his equal. People trusted him, and flocked to him from the east and west." Bello continues:

> "He instructed the *'ulamā'* and raised the banner of religion high. He revived the Sunnah and put an end to heresy. He spread knowledge and dispelled confusion. His learning dazzled men's minds. He showed how spiritual reality (*ḥaqīqah*) was to be reconciled with the *Sharī'ah*. For years he explained the Qur'an in the presence of learned and righteous men of importance, vying with them, through his reading and the different branches of his learning, in rhetoric and in the knowledge of the authorities, and of what is written and what is abrogated. At the same time, he was pre-eminent in knowledge of the *ḥadīth* and learned

in its unfamiliar parts and different branches. Revered by both great and small, he was a *mujaddid* at the head of this generation."

3. Raising the Students

ONE OF the most important tasks in the process of *tajdīd* is the cultivation of a crop of people through whom the message, calling for the revival of Islam, can be transmitted to the generality of society and who will eventually shoulder the responsibility of running the new social order when it is established. The greater the number of people so trained, the greater the prospects of transformation taking place. This cultivation is nothing but a process through which the *mujaddid* is able to multiply himself on a continuous basis. He creates people in his own image who in turn create others in the same fashion and so on. This ensures continuity in the process of change, because the movement is being continuously nourished morally and intellectually. Moreover, it ensures for the movement the loyalty and dedication it requires if it is to move successfully through the lengthy process of change to the desired state of the established transformation of society.

The Shehu was well aware that, if he was to transform society, he had to mold men and women who would subscribe to his ideas and share his aspirations to bring about an *ummah* dedicated to Islam. As he knew that he could not rely on other scholars to achieve his purpose, he established his own "school", trained his own students and created his own community of scholars, teachers and saints. It was through these students – the *ṭalaba* – that he spread his message; it was from these students that he formed the inner core of the movement; and it was these students who spearheaded the prosecution of the *jihad* and carried it to a successful end.

The Shehu's methods of raising the generation that brought about the transformation of central Sudan encompassed three areas: intellectual, spiritual and profound training in *taṣawwuf.* In all this, the Shehu was at the center, drawing students to him from far and wide and nurturing them until they had attained full moral and intellectual maturity. Some became centers of learning themselves, as great as anyone could find in *Bilād as-Sudan*, while others became statesmen, carving out for themselves worthy places in Muslim history. Yet others took their place in the company of saints, having acquired both knowledge and piety.

Intellectual Training

The nature of the education offered was in the best Timbuktian tradition, little changed from what the Shehu himself had received. The content of what was taught had remained almost unchanged for several centuries, so in terms of the quantity of books studied, the learning remained the same. However the quality of the students raised by the Shehu differed fundamentally – a difference due to the new orientation and general intellectual outlook introduced by the Shehu. He widened his students' intellectual horizons and introduced pertinent social issues into the scheme of their education.

It was his view, as expressed in *Iḥyā' as-Sunnah*, that it was the knowledge of the exact nature and implications of the aberrations existing in society – such as nepotism, moral indiscipline and political tyranny – rather than the knowledge of Islam that was missing in Hausa scholarship. Scholars, he thought, knew the law in minute detail but had not grasped its social and political implications. The Shehu's inclusion of these fundamental issues of the day made all the difference. In addition, he developed a new approach to jurisprudence. Law should not be studied out of mere curiosity but should be practiced as well. Hence, making the sacred *Sharī'ah* a living and dominant reality in society was part of the process of education. A student was obliged to aspire to the actual realization of Islam as a faith, as a body of law and as a political system.

Students had roughly ten subjects to learn, judging from information available in the *Iḍā' an-Nusūkh* of 'Abdullahi and the *Shifā' al-Asqām* of Muhammad Bello. Students were not required to excel in all subjects but they had to have a fair knowledge of them before deciding where to specialize. Arabic language was essential, for it was the language of scholarship. Therefore, Arabic grammar was a priority, as well as other subjects associated with Arabic – logic, rhetoric, and so on. Poetry had a special place in language study for two reasons: because so much knowledge, especially of law and the fundamentals of religion, is compressed in verse and also because poetry is a means of reaching people's hearts.

Naturally, students would not wait until they had mastered Arabic before beginning the study of other subjects which were studied simultaneously. *Fiqh*, the science of law, was the most popular subject. It followed a progressive pattern, starting with the elementary knowledge contained in *al-Akhḍarī* and ending with the towering *Mukhtasar* of Khalil. The *Mukhtasar* seemed to represent the ultimate in *fiqh* in the Timbuktu tradition, though there were quite a few other basic textbooks available to the students as well. The science of *uṣūl* – philosophy of law – was also available for students who wanted to specialize in that field but it was not as popular as *fiqh*, because *fiqh* is concerned with the regulation of both individual and social life. In his *Iḥyā' as-Sunnah*, the Shehu introduced another dimension to the study of *fiqh*, showing that it could also act as a forum for the criticism of contemporary society and a subtle call for change.

The most important field of knowledge was that of the Qur'an and Sunnah. The Qur'an is the ultimate knowledge, the source of knowledge and the yardstick for measuring all other aspects of knowledge. The most popular textbook for the study of *tafsīr* (Qur'anic exegesis), at least before 'Abdullahi wrote his *Ḍiyā' at-Ta'wīl*, was *Tafsīr al-Jalalayn.*

For further studies, Baydawi, Razi and several others were available. Qur'anic legislation and rules of recitation were among other subjects studied. The Shehu himself taught *tafsīr*. 'Abdullahi stated that he studied *tafsīr* under the Shehu, "from the beginning of al-Fātiḥah to the end of the Qur'an, more times than I can tell." There were some students whose education was fundamentally confined to the memorization, study and recitation of the Qur'an.

In *ḥadīth*, attention was centered mainly on Bukhāri and Muslim and, to some extent, *al-Muwaṭṭa* of Imam Mālik. But for those who wanted to go further, other *ḥadīth* works were available – notably Tirmidhī, Abū Dawud, Ibn Majah and Nasai. Others were *Mishkāt al-Maṣābīḥ* and other similar collections. However, as-Suyūti's two collections, *Jāmiʿ al-Kabīr* and *Jāmiʿ aṣ-Ṣaghīr* were of immense value in *ḥadīth* studies, especially for students who wanted reference books. Commentaries on the major *ḥadīth* books were also studied, especially al-Qastalāni's *Fatḥu-l-Bāri*, a commentary on *Ṣaḥīh al-Bukhāri*.

The study of *tawḥīd* (the science of the Divine Unity) centered mainly on the books of as-Sanusi. It was a highly prized knowledge. "The greatest favor done to me," was how 'Abdullahi saw the imparting of the knowledge of *tawḥīd* to him. *Taṣawwuf* was also studied and practised, though it was confined to the Qādiriyyah order. History was an important subject in the Timbuktu educational tradition since it was regarded as a guide to the future. Muhammad Bello articulated this concept in *Infāq al-Maysūr* when he declared that many a great man had failed because he had neglected to learn from history. Medicine was also a highly rated subject. Emphasis was laid on Prophetic medicine without limiting the scope of 'practical medicine'. Astronomy, mathematics and related subjects were also part of the curriculum. Education revolved generally, however, around the Qur'an and Sunnah; every other subject was derived from, or at least related to, these two sources.

This approach to education was imperative for a movement

dedicated to creating a society on the pattern established by the Prophet Muhammad ﷺ. Imperative also was the ideological stance given to education by the Shehu himself. If students were to spearhead the struggle for an Islamic society, then a belief in Islam as the way of life, in *Sharī'ah* as the law, in *khilāfah* as the ultimate political system, in *jihad* as the ultimate form of struggle, in Muhammad ﷺ as the leader par excellence, in the Hereafter as the true domain of life, in Allah as the ultimate goal, all these had to be carefully nurtured and imparted to them through the process of education. At the end of the day, no student would be left with any doubt in his mind regarding the way of life, the law, the kind of society and the ultimate goal he should strive for; nor any doubt that the existing order, characterized by oppression and corruption and heedlessness of Allah, was illegitimate and had to go.

The imparting of the idea of *tajdīd* – the revival of Islam – in his students and involving them in the process of *tajdīd* as a necessary part of their education was, perhaps, Shehu Usman's greatest contribution to education in Hausaland. Yet he introduced another aspect that was also of prime importance – a new approach to law and society, the gist of which is contained in his *Hidāyat aṭ-Ṭullāb*.

The *Hidāyat* dealt with several issues relating to Islamic law and Muslim society, the first of which was the very definition of law itself. In Hausaland, as elsewhere in the Muslim world, the notion of *madh-hab* (school of jurisprudence) dominated the entire concept of law and the term was taken as being synonymous with *Sharī'ah* itself. The practical implication was that both the Divine aspects of Islamic law and their human derivations became inseparable and were given equal treatment and weight by Muslims. This was obviously a dangerous attitude to law for, while Divinely prescribed law is perfect and immutable, humanly derived law is far from perfect and should not be immutable.

Shehu Usman felt it necessary, therefore, to distinguish between the law proper – *Sharī'ah* – and the human understanding and application of the law embodied in the idea of *madh-hab*. *Sharī'ah*, he stated, is the body of laws revealed to Muhammad ﷺ by Allah and is therefore the universal, unalterable law and cannot be regarded as the *madh-hab* of any particular person. The *Sharī'ah* is absolutely binding on every Muslim wherever he may be, but a *madh-hab*, being essentially human in formulation, is not absolutely binding on all Muslims. Laws formulated by a *madh-hab* are subject to change and modification in response to human needs and differing circumstances.

This notion of *madh-hab* put forward by Shehu Usman raised the whole issue of the relevance of the concept of *madh-hab* as a whole. The Shehu answered that basically Islam places no obligation on any Muslim to follow a particular *madh-hab*, nor did the Imams themselves insist on being followed. A Muslim is free to choose any *madh-hab* of his liking, or in fact, to refuse to subscribe to any, provided that he is of the status of a *mujtahid* himself.

The Shehu went even further in trying to limit the scope of any particular *madh-hab* by distinguishing between the rulings and opinions of the Imam of a *madh-hab* and the ideas of his immediate students and later scholars. The former is what constitutes the *madh-hab*, the latter is of secondary importance only. Thus, even if Muslims feel bound by a *madh-hab*, they should nevertheless allow themselves freedom to hear the opinions and rulings of scholars other than the Imam.

Granted this, all the schools of law are in the right. Therefore, no Muslim should feel constrained to follow the rulings of any one of them. Equally, a Muslim does not commit a sin by following rulings of a *madh-hab* other than his own. Indeed, he sins by nursing aversion to following such rulings. In other words, all the schools are the common property of Muslims and should be seen as a source of strength for the *ummah* rather than as a source of disunity and conflict. No one school is superior or inferior to another; each one is on a right path and within the bounds of Islam.

But the situation confronting Shehu Usman was one in which *fiqh* was almost totally divorced from the Qur'an and Sunnah, so much so that it seemed as though these fundamental sources were relegated to the background in the scheme of things. The re-establishment of the supremacy of the Qur'an and Sunnah – or the *Sharīʿah* – became imperative in those circumstances. Hence, the Shehu issued the statement that any rulings of a *madh-hab* which contradicted the Qur'an, Sunnah or *ijmāʿ* (consensus) should be ignored. *Fiqh* had to be subordinated to the primary sources. Shehu Usman's *Iḥyā' as-Sunnah* should be seen as an effort to return to the true spirit of *Sharīʿah*, where primacy is given to what the Prophet ﷺ said and practised.

Finally, the Shehu dealt in the *Hidāyat* with the issue of right and wrong in society. He sought to limit both the authority and scope of the concept of *madh-hab* by emphasizing that it is *Sharīʿah* alone that is absolutely binding on Muslims and that a *madh-hab* is essentially the opinions and rulings of its Imam. Secondly, he attempted to establish the supremacy of the Qur'an and Sunnah over the entire Islamic legal order. Thus, what is right and what is wrong for society can only be determined by the Qur'an and Sunnah. Human legislation cannot be prescriptive in matters about which the Qur'an and Sunnah have not been categorical. Nor can anyone be repudiated for not performing a duty, or for doing a deed, which neither source has declared as unlawful.

Shehu Usman's *Hidāyat aṭ-Ṭullāb* can be seen as an attempt to instill in his students a universal approach to law and to expand their attitudes to society. When incorporated into the scheme of education, this approach was bound to create broadminded scholars with an incentive for wider reading and research. They were to regard all schools of law as correct and equally valid for all Muslims. They were to look at the weaknesses and failures of their society with sympathy and flexibility.

The common people might do many things that offend the spirit, if not the letter, of the law but, as long as the

Qur'an and Sunnah have not been dogmatic about the prohibition of those deeds, such lapses should be overlooked. The students should concentrate on the fundamentals and view the common people with sympathy, with the idea of drawing them into the *Jama'a* (the Shehu's Community) and correcting them by a gradual process. This approach to people's moral failings was a significant factor in the expansion of the *Jama'a* and its impressive social and ethnic spread.

On the whole, the quality of the students produced by the Shehu rested more on the personal initiative and effort they exerted in private research than on what they were taught formally. Knowledge was the most fundamental criterion in the new scheme of things. The acquisition of knowledge was part of the effort of the individual to ensure for himself a place in the new order but, more importantly, the atmosphere of ideological and social struggle under which the *ṭalaba* were being nurtured, was most conducive to study. The need to find solutions to new problems that confronted the *Jama'a*, the intellectual challenge posed by *'ulamā' as-sū'*, the desire to reach the high standard of learning achieved by earlier scholars and the intellectual climate fostered by the Shehu himself all contributed to the general upsurge in scholarship. The Shehu devoted the larger part of his time to teaching and raising his students.

In addition, the growing intellectual character of his *Jama'a* attracted revivalist scholars from all corners of Hausaland and beyond, and this influx swelled the pool from which the *ṭalaba* drew their knowledge. "I cannot now number all the shaykhs," 'Abdullahi wrote in *Tazyīn*, "from whom I acquired knowledge. Many a scholar and many a seeker after knowledge came to us from the East from whom I profited, so many that I cannot count them. Many a scholar and many a seeker after knowledge came to us from the West, so many that I cannot count them."

The Shehu's advice to his students and companions in his *Wathīqat al-Ikhwān* to go out to seek knowledge from pious, learned scholars wherever they might be, coupled with the pressure exerted by the process of reviving Islam, which required a body of scholars to articulate and disseminate its message, created that fertile intellectual climate that was to feed Hausaland with knowledge.

The scale of research and scholarship was astounding. There seemed to be the realization in the *Jamaʿa* that the process of reviving Islam depended almost entirely on the soundness and amplitude of the learning which its members were able to acquire. Scholars among them gave their time to developing other scholars and learning more themselves. Students strove for intellectual excellence. Muhammad Bello told us in his *Shifāʾ al-Asqām* that in all he had read as many as twenty thousand books. Books were bought, others were borrowed from different parts of Hausaland, and many were written in response to the demands of the *Jamaʿa*. What came out of this extraordinary devotion to learning was an intellectual revolution on a scale unprecedented in Hausaland.

Spiritual Training

Intellectual training went hand-in-hand with the spiritual development of Shehu Usman's students and companions. A summary of this development process is contained in a concise but precious treatise, *ʿUmdat al-ʿUbbād*, which the Shehu wrote to provide guidelines for the minimum voluntary acts of devotion: prayer, fasting, Qur'anic recitation, remembrance of Allah and acts of charity. Muhammad Bello wrote an addendum to the *ʿUmdat* entitled *Tamḥīd al-ʿUmdat al-ʿUbbād*, which might perhaps have been his first book. It should be stressed that supererogatory devotion presupposes the fulfillment by a Muslim of his obligatory duties, otherwise it is meaningless. It is on this premise that *ʿUmdat* was written.

Ṣalāt

In the area of *ṣalāt* (prayer five times a day), three categories of *nawāfil* (supererogatory devotion) were recommended in the *'Umdat*, chosen because they constitute the median way, where the Prophetic practice is concerned, and because they are easy to perform. The first is *Ṣalāt aḍ-Ḍuḥā* which is performed between daybreak and noon and is of great significance because it is performed at the very start of the day's work or in the busiest part of it. It gives people the chance of turning to their Lord and being intimate with Him at even the most mundane of times. Thus, the Prophet ﷺ extolled this *ṣalāt* by calling it the "prayer of the penitent" and indicated that it contained within it the qualities and ingredients of almost every deed which a Muslim is recommended to do for the day:

> "An act of charity is due from each part of the body of each one of you every day. Thus, the glorification of Allah is charity; the declaration of His Unity is charity; the declaration of His absolute greatness is charity; to praise Him is charity; to command what is good is charity; to prohibit evil is charity; but the two *rak'ats* performed during the morning suffice."

A further category of *nawāfil* are the prayers following each obligatory prayer, such as the *nāfilah* (sing. of *nawāfil*) of *Ṣalātu-dh-Dhuhr.* The time of *Dhuhr*, according to the Prophet ﷺ, "is the hour at which the gates of heaven are opened and I would like any good deed of mine to ascend there at that time." The implication is that the possibility of Allah looking sympathetically at one's actions is higher if these are presented to Him at a time when one is actually engaged in another act of devotion and more so when, according to the Prophet, "the gates of heaven are opened purposely to receive such devotional acts."

The *nāfilah* of *Ṣalātu-l-'Aṣr* was also important to the Prophet ﷺ, who said, "May Allah bestow His mercy on a person who performs four *raka'ats* before 'Aṣr." The *nāfilah* of *Ṣalātu-l-Maghrib* follows, and then the *nāfilah* of *Ṣalātu-ṣ-Ṣubḥ*, by far the most important of this category of *nawāfil.*

According to 'Aishah ﵂, the Prophet ﷺ was most constant in performing this prayer, referring to it as better than the world and everything in it.

The third category of *nawāfil* recommended in the *'Umdat* is the night prayers, called *tahajjud*. These are the most important prayers apart from the obligatory ones. The Prophet ﷺ said they were, "the customary practice of the best of men who have gone before us and therefore, by implication, one of the means through which they were exalted." Allah said to Muhammad ﷺ in this regard: "*And stay awake for prayer during part of the night as a supererogatory action for yourself. It may well be that your Lord will raise you to a Praiseworthy Station.*" (17:79) So persistent and diligent was the Prophet ﷺ in obeying this command that often his feet swelled up as a result of his long standing in prayer.

Tahajjud, the Prophet ﷺ said, "is a means by which one achieves nearness to Allah." The timing itself, when the night is in its full serenity and everything is still, creates an impression in the mind of the person who stands up in prayer, that he is directly in the presence of Allah. It is a time about which Allah Himself says that it, "*has a stronger effect and is more conducive to concentration*" (73:5), a time when it is easier to empty the mind and heart of everything that distracts the worshipper from Allah and to beseech Him earnestly. It is the best time for people to come closer to Allah, for there are no barriers between Him and them at that time. And if some people do rise to great heights spiritually, it is precisely because they have made the best use of this opportunity.

Tahajjud is also, according to the Prophet ﷺ, a means of obtaining Allah's forgiveness and other favors. He said that Allah descends, as it were, to the lowest heaven in the latter part of the night purposely to listen to the complaints of people, to respond to their needs and to forgive the sins of those who seek His forgiveness. *Tahajjud* is also a means by which a person is protected against persisting in serious wrong-action. When the Prophet ﷺ was told of a man who was constant in *tahajjud* and yet was in the habit of stealing people's property he said that he would stop his stealing on account of the effects of *tahajjud*.

Fasting

In the area of fasting, *'Umdat* gave three recommendations, to be followed by people according to their own choice and capacity. One was fasting three days a month, the minimum required of anyone who wanted to undertake the *nawāfil* of fasting. The Prophet ﷺ likened it to fasting continually on the basis that, since every act of piety is rewarded tenfold or more, fasting three days in a month is equivalent in reward to fasting a whole month. The second fasting *nāfilah* was called the "golden means" by the Shehu and entailed fasting every Monday and Thursday. "Those are the days," the Prophet ﷺ said, "on which people's deeds are presented to Allah, and it is better to be fasting at that time." The last type of fasting recommended was the fast of Dawud, which entails fasting on alternate days and which the Prophet ﷺ called the most excellent type of fasting.

Fasting is particularly important for a group undergoing a process of moral growth. It offers a moral and physical discipline which differs completely from the gluttony and permissiveness of the society in decay. It is the antidote to degeneration. The austere habits, social restraint, modesty and physical endurance which it cultivates in the individual are the ingredients of moral transformation. Fasting is also important because of the regard accorded to it by Allah. "Fasting is for Me", He said, "and I personally give the reward for it." And the Prophet ﷺ said that the supplication of a person who is fasting is never rejected by his Lord.

Qur'anic Recitation

In the area of Qur'anic recitation the Shehu recommended that its reading should be completed within a maximum period of two months and a minimum of three days. The optimum time, however, is between ten days and one month. The reasons for it are twofold, one moral and one educational. The personal reading of the Qur'an is a duty owed by each individual to Allah and He gives ample reward for it, as a number of *ḥadīths* have indicated. It has the effect of familiarizing the mind with the Message of Allah, to which eventually – if it becomes a constant practice – the mind will respond with awe and reverence, so that as the response grows in intensity the Qur'an becomes part and parcel of a person's being.

The second purpose is to enable each individual to have a personal acquaintance with and understanding of the Qur'an. During a year, a person will have gone through the whole of the Qur'an in a contemplative and devotional way, without outside aid or interference, a minimum of six times and in some cases twelve times or more. In the course of time, that individual will have been morally and intellectually transformed, be filled with reverence for the Book and be more ready to put its precepts into practice.

Remembrance of Allah

The next area of spiritual training dealt with in *'Umdat* was that of *dhikr* or remembrance of Allah. *Dhikr* is a continuous effort on the part of man to seek access to Allah, to remain as close to Him as possible, to bear Him in mind at all times and in all conditions, and to seek His assistance in every situation. It is thus rightly regarded as the best form of worship. It comprises a number of elements: giving Allah His due rights, such as constant contemplation and affirmation of His unity, glory, majesty and greatness and appreciation of His uncountable favors; seeking the means of approach to Him; turning to Him in repentance moment by moment and day by day, with the hope of obtaining His forgiveness and the expiation of sins; seeking assistance from him in respect of the numerous, intractable problems of the world; contemplating His message, His creation and His authority; and evoking His blessing upon the best of His creatures ﷺ.

The forms of *dhikr* recommended in *'Umdat* are intended to cover as many aspects of ordinary life as possible. For this reason, guidance is given as to what should be said during *ṣalāt* and when going to bed and waking up in the morning, as well as how to seek Allah's forgiveness and how to glorify Him. Some chapters and verses of the Qur'an are recommended, including the chapters *al-Baqarah* and *Āli Imrān*, which, in addition to their obvious spiritual value, are the summary and quintessence of all the themes of the Qur'an. Anyone who is familiar with them will have a fair idea of Islam and how it differs from other ways of life.

Charity

Finally, in the area of *ṣadaqah* or charity, the Shehu did not make any specific recommendations, except that he referred to the statements of the Prophet ﷺ which explain the true nature of this kind of devotion. The compulsory equivalent of *ṣadaqah* is *zakāt*, which is given, as the Qur'an commands, for the amelioration of the weak elements in society and, ideally, to eliminate poverty and social misery altogether. *Ṣadaqah*, for its part, means more than simply acts of almsgiving. Essentially, it embraces any kind of honest effort, moral, material or intellectual, expended to improve the lot of society, especially in the areas of social indignity, poverty, ignorance or disease.

We may stress that *ṣadaqah*, in the context in which it is conceived here, is a means of integrating and unifying a nascent community. Not only does it indicate the personal goals which its members should individually pursue – acquisition of knowledge, securing of a livelihood, honest acquisition of wealth for family support – it also places such goals in the broader context of communal responsibility. In this way the community is unified in mutual assistance and protection from the social, economic and political hardships foisted on it by the powers that be or simply by the vicissitudes of life.

Taṣawwuf

In addition to the general education that the Shehu

imparted to his students and companions, there was also a more intensive and systematized spiritual training in *taṣawwuf.* The Shehu had a group of people – men and women – whom he brought up in the ways of sufism. His main aim, no doubt, was to create a core of saints whose inward temperament was harmonized with their outward disposition in such a way that their utterances, behavior and characteristics mirrored their inner beings. This nucleus of people eventually formed the inner core of the *Jama'a*. It was to them that mightier affairs were entrusted.

If the Shehu were asked if *taṣawwuf* was necessary, he would reply in the affirmative. In his *Uṣūl al-Wilāyah* he said that in the early days of Islam there was no need for *taṣawwuf* as such, because the Companions ﷺ of the Prophet ﷺ had among them those from whom the rest could draw inspiration and who could serve as models for them. The proper Islamic attitudes to life were preserved and transferred from one generation to another until the time came when the moral tone of society changed and people sank into moral decadence. Then a systematized form of spiritual training (*tarbiyah*) was needed, to give individuals guidance toward intellectual and moral elevation in order to overcome the diseases of the soul that prevented spiritual development.

This kind of concentrated spiritual cultivation of individuals, the Shehu maintained, is traceable to the Prophet ﷺ himself, who trained his Companions ﷺ in accordance with the disposition of each. He would say to one, "Avoid anger," and to another, "Let not your tongue ever rest from mentioning Allah's names."

The Shehu elaborated that *taṣawwuf* entails securing from people a pledge, which has to be continually reaffirmed, that they devote themselves to moral rectitude and the search for knowledge following the example of the Prophet ﷺ. In this desire to inculcate in people knowledge (*'ilm*) and spiritual experience (*ḥaqīqah*), the *ṣufis* have added nothing to the general practice of Islam. They simply reinforce its demand for the performance of obligatory duties and avoidance of prohibited things.

The essence of *taṣawwuf*, as expounded in *Uṣūl al-Wilāyah*, is five-fold. It is to seek to attain that superior moral consciousness (*taqwā*) as a result of which a person behaves as if he is in the presence of Allah, so that, whether alone or with others, obligatory duties are always upheld and forbidden things avoided. The Sunnah should be followed in all its ramifications, manifested by good character and being a source of happiness and comfort to others. You should not harm people or cause them unnecessary discomfort, while at the same time exercising patience and trust in Allah if they cause you harm. You should cheerfully accept Allah's overriding will in all matters concerning your life, whether that entails prosperity or poverty. You should perfect the attitude of submission whereby, even in the most trying circumstances, you offer thanks to Allah, appreciate the perfect nature of His will and, in the hope of His mercy and succor, flee from the imperfect state of this world to seek refuge in Him.

Those goals are to be reached by taking the following steps: exercising zeal in seeking the highest of aims of worship; revering the sanctity of Allah by following His injunctions and avoiding His prohibitions; striving to perform your professional work correctly and skillfully in accordance with the Sunnah; carrying out your resolutions about religion regardless of opposition; and finally acknowledging Allah's favors by being thankful to Him so as to be graced with an increase in such favors.

The Shehu listed, in this order, a number of qualities that ultimately should be inculcated: basic knowledge in the fundamentals of religion, jurisprudence and *taṣawwuf*; repentance (*tawbah*) from all sins, both spiritual and social; keeping aloof from people except for spiritual, educational or other positive purposes; waging war against Shaytān; striving against lower desires and restraining the self through *taqwā*; reliance on Allah in matters of provision and livelihood, that is, self-reliance; committing affairs in their entirety to Allah; cheerful acceptance of Allah's judgment; patience (*ṣabr*), especially in times of trial; fear of Allah's retribution at all times; love of Allah in all conditions and at all times; avoidance of eye contact at work; avoidance of conceit by calling to mind Allah's unbounded favors; and constant praise and thanks to Allah.

The Shehu described the nature of the training as the gradual cultivation of a person's character through a systematic process supervised by a Shaykh until the whole being is positively changed by the good qualities being totally inculcated into the personality. This process is called *riyāḍah*. The Shehu offered an insight into this method by saying, for instance, that if the student (*murīd*) were ignorant of the *Sharī'ah*, the starting point in his training would in that case be his instruction in law and jurisprudence; if he were preoccupied with unlawful enrichment or was in a sinful political or social position, he should first be made to rectify that situation; even if he were sound in outward appearance, the diseases of the inward would have to be cured; if he were obsessed with personal appearance, he should be assigned such lowly chores as cooking until that obsession had been removed; if he were obsessed with food, he should be introduced to constant fasting until that obsession had been overcome; if he were in a hurry for marriage, in spite of being unable to shoulder its responsibilities, that desire should be curbed with fasting and other exercises. Thus, the training would be in accordance with the intellectual and moral level of the individual concerned.

What differentiates this system of training from informal, personal education is that it is under the guidance of a realised shaykh. This raises the fundamental question of how one can distinguish a true shaykh from a false one. The Shehu offered the following guidelines in identifying a fraud: if he engages under any pretext in disobedience to Allah; if he is hypocritical and pretentious in exhibiting obedience to Allah; if he is greedy for wealth and worldly status and cultivates rich people; if he sows discord among Muslims and is disrespectful to Muslims in general. All these are signs that he is not genuine. A true shaykh is known by the soundness of his knowledge derived fundamentally from the Qur'an and Sunnah, by the nobility of his character, by his spiritual soundness, by a pleasing and easy disposition, and finally by his display of pure insight through interpreting the issues confronting him clearly.

Finally, there is the question of whether a shaykh is essential for the attainment of spiritual wellbeing. Not necessarily, the Shehu stated in *Uṣūl al-Wilāyah.* The collective spirit of an Islamic group – *Ikhwān,* as he called them – could take the place of a shaykh and, in any case, the ultimate purpose of *taṣawwuf* is that an individual should reach a stage in his "direct experience" of Allah in which he dispenses with the guidance of anyone else. *Taṣawwuf* is the process of training by which an individual is brought to spiritual maturity and then freed to seek his way to his Lord.

For Shehu Usman, *taṣawwuf,* as an integral part of Islam, is derived from two verses of the Qur'an: "*But as for him who feared the Station of his Lord and forbade the lower self its appetites, the Garden will be his refuge.*" (79:39-40)

4. Building the Community

HAVING seen the sort of intellectual and spiritual training given to those men and women who clustered around the Shehu, we shall now look at the shaping of the nucleus of the Shehu's followers in the emerging new order – the *Jamaʿa*. Here we shall be concentrating on three areas as the basis of their identity and solidarity: the molding of the character, the building of the communal spirit and the development of a "new culture".

For any movement with the goal of bringing about a society superior to the one it abhors and is challenging, the test of its sincerity lies in its ability to develop individuals who are the very embodiment of its message and vision. No movement can be taken seriously if the character and behavior of the core members do not set them clearly above others. That was precisely the challenge before the Shehu. His responsibility was not only to preach the truth and attack evil but also, and more fundamentally, to produce men and women who believed in that truth and whose general disposition was a clear testimony to their faith in it.

Moral Ideals

Our concern now is to look at those qualities which the movement regarded as being vital for its members – especially those involved in the dissemination of its message – to acquire and practise in everyday life. There is nothing new in these qualities, for they were derived from the teachings and practice of the Prophet ﷺ, his Companions ‌﷽ and the early generations of Islam. They were, however, new to Hausaland where they had been all but abandoned and where, if they were still regarded as ideals at all, they were certainly not translated into action or expressed socially.

The most important work for the understanding of the moral training of the Shehu's lieutenants and students is his *Ṭarīq al-Jannah* but the moral ideals imparted in those men and women were best articulated by Muhammad Bello in *Ṭā'āt al-Khallāq bi-Makārīm al-Akhlāq*. Other sources are 'Abdullahi's *Sabīl an-Najāt* and *Minan al-Minan* and Bello's *Jalā' aṣ-Ṣuḍūr.*

Knowledge

The first and perhaps the most important of the qualities the movement considered vital for every person in the forefront of the struggle was knowledge (*'ilm*). This involved the learning of those aspects necessary for the realization of the objectives of *tajdīd,* including the understanding of the Qur'an, Sunnah, *uṣūl*, *fiqh* and *taṣawwuf,* the acquisition of the necessary skills in such sciences as medicine, and a full understanding of the means and method of government and administration.

Since knowledge was conceived as an instrument of *tajdīd*, a considerable stress was laid on its application in everyday life. Knowledge which was not put to use was not considered relevant. Thus, while 'Abdullahi in *Minan* stressed that knowledge was the "root of our work, to the extent that the work we do in ignorance is of no merit," he added that acquired knowledge must produce its results in practical life, otherwise it is meaningless. And Bello, in *Jalā'*, after quoting the *ḥadīths* of the Prophet ﷺ: "Woe to the one who does not learn!" and "Woe to the learned who does not put his knowledge to use," likened such a learned man to a lamp which, while providing light to others, burns itself out.

Cognition

Associated with knowledge was the quality which Bello

in *Ṭā'āt* called *'aql* (cognition). Essentially it means the full cognition of the aims, purposes and significance of the commands and prohibitions of Islam. "*'Aql* is what leads you to the consciousness of Allah, and saves you from passion," because the cognition of evil and its ultimate consequences is the thing most likely to help someone avoid it. Bello said that the truly cognizant is he whose words are few but whose actions are many.

The importance of cognition is twofold. First of all it gives every action not only a social or spiritual meaning but an intellectual significance as well. The man of cognition does or avoids things in the full appreciation of what they mean to him personally, what they contribute to his relationship with Allah, and what their consequences might be on the Day of Judgment. There is a qualitative difference between deeds performed with intellectual awareness and those performed merely in compliance with the letter of the law.

There is, for instance, a world of difference between a ruler who is just out of mere obedience to the law and another who is just because he is aware that it is justice that sustains a nation or because, as a leader, he will appear before Allah on the Day of Judgment in chains and it is only his justice that can release him from them. And there is a similar difference between someone who performs the four *raka'āt* before *Dhuhr* because the Sunnah requires him to do so and someone who does the same with the understanding that that is the very hour in which his deeds are being presented to Allah. This quality imposes on an individual the duty to probe deeply into the meaning of the injunctions and prohibitions of Islam and to devote time to pondering them.

Secondly, the importance of this quality is that it furnishes individuals with the necessary instruments for calling people towards religion. Questions as to why Islam has enjoined certain things and prohibited others are bound to be raised by people, some with a sincere aim to learn and obey and others with a mischievous intention. If cogent answers are given, Islam will thus be exalted; otherwise serious damage may result.

Repentance

In *Sabīl*, 'Abdullahi said of the importance of repentance (*tawbah*): "Know that Allah has made *tawbah* a covering for the nakedness of work, a cleansing of the impurities arising from error, and a means by which the sins of the past are wiped out and the deeds of the future are perfected."

We may look at *tawbah* from two angles: firstly that of a person's individual recognition of their own innate imperfection as a human being, which impels them constantly to seek to make up their deficiencies by recourse to the act of repentance; and secondly, that of repentance as a vital social imperative for a nation in a period of decline.

In its latter, wider context *tawbah* means the progressive abandonment of the path that is leading to social and political disintegration and the ultimate collapse of the society concerned, and turning to the path which leads to regeneration and rectitude. *Tawbah* thus embraces both the spiritual and socio-moral behavior of people and societies. In a yet more profound sense, on an individual level, *tawbah* means a return to the path that leads to Allah, the objective being to escape from perdition on the Day of Judgment and gain admittance into the Garden.

So for a people striving to regenerate their society, *tawbah* implies a sustained disengagement from the norms and attitudes of the prevailing order, because it is they that are the symptoms of the diseases that have plagued the society causing its decay, and the adoption of the kind of behavior and attitudes that will lead to its regeneration. *Tawbah* involves, therefore, a total change in an individual's conception of, and attitude to, life, as well as the absolute change of course necessitated by the initiation of a process of social transformation.

Zuhd

Ẓuhd is what stood at the core of that new attitude to life which was a fundamental quality of the movement. *Ẓuhd*, as explained by the Prophet ﷺ, has two elements: abstention from the world and keeping away from the possessions of other people. To abstain from the world means, among other things, that a person should live in it on the understanding that it is only a temporary abode, indeed, that it is in fact a place of trial and a place of preparation for the realm of reward and permanence which is the Next World.

Whatever one takes from the world, whether it be in the form of sustenance, power, knowledge or skill, and whatever other pursuits one undertakes in it, should all be seen as a means by which one is being tested by Allah, who will take the final account on the Day of Judgment. Nothing in this world, therefore, is an end in itself. Everything is given or taken by way of trial. The world itself will at some point cease to exist and give way ultimately to the everlasting life of the Hereafter.

Zuhd also involves, however, exerting the effort necessary to secure your own livelihood so as to be self-reliant and free from having to look towards what belongs to other people. Bello stressed in *Jalā'* the need for people to preserve their integrity through self- reliance, saying: "The Prophet ﷺ said, 'Take to trading, for it secures nine-tenths of wealth'... It is related that [Prophet] Isa ﷺ met a certain person and asked him, 'What do you do for a living'? He replied, 'I engage in worship'. Isa ﷺ then asked him, 'In that case, who takes care of your needs?' 'My brother,' he answered. 'Then,' said Isa ﷺ, 'your brother is more of a worshipper than you are.'"

In essence, *zuhd* means that one should ardently seek the realm of the Hereafter by mobilizing and channeling the materials of this world towards the accomplishment of the higher purposes of life and by living one's life, as far as possible, in accordance with the injunctions of Allah. Equally, it means exerting the efforts necessary to make one self-reliant and self-sufficient, to obviate any need to sell one's honor, or even as a last resort one's religion, in order to live.

In its ideological context, *zuhd* means the mobilization of a movement's moral and material resources with the purpose of delivering the people from the grip of this world. Moral resources provide the strength to strive against a degenerate social order, while material resources, secured through the members' extensive and serious engagement in various professions and trades, are advantageous in the struggle for economic and technical supremacy.

Ṣabr

To achieve that moral and economic supremacy another quality is, however, essential: *ṣabr.* In a narrow sense, *ṣabr* just means patience, but in a wider sense, it embraces a number of attitudes, including endeavoring to live honestly and honorably in a situation where those qualities are not tolerated by the prevailing system and putting up with the hardships and disadvantages suffered as a result. The purpose of embodying this attitude is that it serves as a shining light in the midst of pervasive darkness. *Ṣabr* also means overlooking much of the ill-treatment, harm and wrongs which come from others and which are an integral part of human life. Allah has said in this regard that He has made some people a means to test others, in order to see which of them will exercise patience.

The most important form of *ṣabr* is the endurance of hardships suffered while striving on behalf of one's religion. In their struggle against a decadent system, some people might lose social or economic privileges, some might lose their freedom, some their means of subsistence and some their very lives. In all these trials the most valuable weapon is *ṣabr,* because the path of religion is long, the steps hard and the efforts exhausting. *Ṣabr* means not personalizing any harm or injury suffered in the cause of Allah and not holding personal enmity towards those who inflict such harm, so that hostility will cease as soon as such an adversary opens his heart to the faith. It also entails overlooking temporary inconveniences and viewing such trials as moral training, not as a punishment from Allah.

The fruits of *ṣabr* are ready forgiveness, the lack of any other than ideological adversaries, the ability to overlook and overcome any obstacles placed in your path, and ultimately the attainment of your goal. Apart from knowledge and piety, there is no greater weapon for an individual striving in the cause of Allah than *ṣabr.*

Diplomacy, Forgiveness and *Ḥilm*

For a movement, the relationship of its vanguard with the generality of the people is vital, not only for its image but also, more significantly, for its very survival. In this regard three other qualities, in addition to *ṣabr*, were given prominence in the Shehu's movement. One of them was what Bello called *mudārah*, or diplomacy. It entails showing kindness, generosity and respect to others, even to those who nurse enmity towards religion, in the hope of either winning their hearts to the faith or at least neutralizing their enmity. In short, *mudārah* is another word for restraint and caution.

Bello was quick, however, to distinguish between this honest effort to safeguard religion and acts of opportunism or ambivalence, whereby a person heaps praises and gifts on a powerful enemy in order to gain the latter's acceptance or favor. "That," he said, "is squandering religion to safeguard wealth." In a wider sense, *mudārah* embraces those steps a movement takes to disarm its potential enemies by winning their hearts through persuasion, such as showing regard for their feelings and sensitivities and offering them help in a time of need.

The second quality is *'afw* or the spirit of forgiveness. In this respect Bello quoted the verse of the Qur'an: "*Repel the bad with what is better and, if there is enmity between you and someone else, he will be like a bosom friend.*" (41:33) He also quoted the words of the Prophet ﷺ: "A person does not forgive a wrong done to him without Allah exalting him on account of it; therefore, take to forgiveness so that Allah may exalt you."

The third quality is what Bello called *ḥilm*, which means to develop and perfect a gentle disposition so that people find comfort and have confidence in you. Even in anger, you should never stray from truth.

Discipline

A further extremely important quality highly prized by the movement is what Bello in *Ṭā'āt* called *adab*, which, for want of an appropriate word, we may term discipline. "The Prophet ﷺ," Bello said, "has inculcated discipline in his *ummah* by instructing them to mention the name of Allah before a meal and to give praise to Him after it; by forbidding them to drink while standing, or directly from buckets; and by forbidding them from eating with the left hand or removing impurities with the right." That is just one of the several aspects of *adab*.

In a more comprehensive sense, *adab* embraces the discipline and control of what the Shehu in *Ṭarīq* and 'Abdullahi in *Sabīl* called the five organs – the eye, the ear, the tongue, the heart and the belly. The eye must be controlled, the Shehu said, for three main reasons: firstly, because Allah himself has commanded that Muslims should lower their gaze and guard their modesty; secondly, because the Prophet ﷺ warned us that immodest gazing at women is "one of the poisoned arrows of Shaytān" and that anyone who avoids it will be graced with the sweetness of worship; and thirdly, because the eye was created, not to seek out the beauty of women, but to gain the vision of Allah – glorious and great is He! 'Abdullahi added that controlling and restraining the eyes help towards the perfection of faith and obedience to Allah.

Similarly, it is part of *adab* to keep the hearing under control. This is achieved by not listening to irrelevant or offensive things, such as vulgar music or the denigration of others. The tongue, for its part, should be prevented from making any utterances which are likely to involve the body in physical or moral danger or that will be a cause of regret when you stand for judgment before Allah on the Last Day. Such utterances include, for instance, slandering other people, which Allah likens to eating the flesh of your dead brother.

The control of the heart is, as far as both the Shehu and 'Abdullahi were concerned, the most important challenge people face. The Shehu called attention to five factors which account for this crucial importance. The first is that in all matters Allah looks into the heart, into people's intentions, as is stressed so often in the Qur'an. The second is the reinforcement of this point by the Prophet ﷺ. The third is the point that the heart is, as it were, the king of the body and all the other organs its subjects, so that if it is corrupted the whole body is likewise corrupted. The fourth is that the heart is the repository of innate human qualities such as intelligence and knowledge. "It is most fitting," said the Shehu, "that such a repository should be preserved against being contaminated or despoiled." The fifth is that the heart is, as it were, the battleground between good and evil, between angelic and satanic forces.

Controlling the heart means preserving it from inordinate ambition, haste, envy and pride and, conversely, refining it through such attitudes as modesty, where hope or ambition is concerned, deliberation in affairs, maintaining good will towards people, and humility.

The control of the belly means preserving it from taking in what is either expressly unlawful or of a dubious nature, or taking in even lawful things in excess of one's needs. Excessive consumption, even of lawful things, has the effect of hardening the heart, causing injury to the other organs of the body, weakening the intellect and the ability to pursue knowledge, reducing one's desire for worship, increasing the possibility of falling into dubious and prohibited ways and, above all, it may warrant one's being subjected to serious scrutiny on the Day of Judgment.

Besides this comprehensive discipline, *adab* also involves, according to Bello, acquainting oneself with the knowledge of good works and endeavoring to perform them; and acquainting oneself with the knowledge of evil deeds and distancing oneself from them. It encompasses the control of the senses, the positive orientation of one's total disposition, keeping within the legal limits set by Allah, the abandonment of passions and dubious conduct, striving towards good deeds and keeping the mind engaged in thought and remembrance of Allah.

Another quality related to *adab* is what Bello called *inā* or deliberation. This is important for an individual, because it enables him to ponder issues before he undertakes them, thus saving him from rushing into things which he may later regret. Deliberation is essential for a movement that regards its cause as a lifetime undertaking. In this case, *inā* involves the realization that, in the task of raising people to moral excellence, there is no need for excessive urgency, since there is no shortcut in such matters. "Haste," said the Prophet ﷺ in a *ḥadīth* quoted by Bello, "is from Shaytān," whereas caution and deliberation are from Allah. Bello made, however, six important exceptions where haste is not only allowed but praiseworthy: the payment of debt, offering food to a guest, burying the dead, prayer at the right time, the marriage of a girl who has reached maturity and *tawbah* (repentance) after doing wrong.

Other qualities pertaining to *adab* were listed by Bello as being a humble disposition, generosity, contentment, truthfulness in speech, strengthening the ties of relationship, honoring trusts, good neighborliness, fulfilling promises and obligations, modesty, keeping appointments, and being merciful to creatures. And he quoted this noble statement of the Prophet ﷺ:

> "My Lord has commanded me to do these nine things, and I recommend the same for you. He has commanded me to be sincere in all matters, secret or open; to do justice in all circumstances, in pleasure or anger; to be moderate in all conditions, prosperity or poverty; to forgive those who wrong me; to give to those who deprive me; to seek ties with those who break from me; that my silence should

> be for reflection; that my utterance should be a reminder; and that my seeing should be to gain instruction."

This emphasis on the qualities we have enumerated implies that the Shehu was determined to create individuals imbued with the qualities of the Prophet ﷺ himself and to evolve, through them, a community that embodied the qualities and characteristics of the community of the Prophet ﷺ. Every *mujaddid* knows that the course of his movement is determined ultimately by the quality of the people who champion it and, that it is only when such people are nurtured to moral and intellectual maturity through a long and painstaking process of training and education, that Allah in His wisdom will entrust them with the great task of shouldering the responsibility of forming a new *ummah*.

The Communal Spirit

We can now look into the nature of the social relationships that were being nurtured in the nascent community and see this as one of the principal means through which the new order was developed. It is natural that a special kind of relationship should exist among members of an ideological group, dictating their interpersonal conduct, establishing the rights and obligations of each member and holding the community together. This relationship is an expression of a profound mutual commitment to a cause, something absent in society as a whole, and a sense of unity, belief, purpose and destiny.

In the case of the Shehu's community, the question of the rights and obligations of its members was not determined by the development of a new code. These had already been spelled out by Islam itself. If society at large did not implement them, it was not because they were not there, but rather because a sense of unity, a sense of commitment to Islam and a feeling of brotherhood were missing. But a group committed to the regeneration of Muslim society should not only establish these mutual rights and obligations but also give them a new significance within the context of their particular situation. They are not mere rules but constitute the means of maintaining the community spiritually, morally and socially, as well as being the means of self-development and self-expression.

The rules did not only deal with the duties of one member to another but also with the duties of each member to his or her parents, children, and spouse. It was, in effect, the training of an individual in social responsibility. Our main source of information about this is 'Abdullahi's *Tibyān li-Ḥuqūq al-Ikhwān*. This short treatise, we venture to suggest, was only a written testimony of what the movement had in fact put into practice right from its inception.

Brotherhood

The first category of duties and responsibilities comprises the mutual rights of Muslims that flow from the bond of brotherhood which ties each to the other in this world and the next. The fulfillment of these mutual responsibilities has the effect of cementing that brotherhood and brings together all members into a single *ummah*, separate and distinct from the communities of other faiths or systems.

The rights cover the whole spectrum of life. A Muslim should greet a fellow Muslim whenever they meet, an action which, according to the Prophet ﷺ, increases love among Muslims, mutual love being something which assures admittance to paradise. He should accept the invitation of his Muslim brother. He should visit and care for a fellow Muslim when he falls sick. He should honor his brother's words and oaths. He should give him good counsel or advice whenever it is sought or whenever he deems it necessary. He should protect his brother's honor when he is absent. He should attend his funeral. And, above all, he should love for his fellow Muslim what he loves for himself and hate for him what he hates for himself.

These mutual duties are increased when the Muslim brother is also a neighbor. He should be helped whenever necessary. A loan should be extended to him if he is in financial difficulty and if an outright gift is not possible. He should be congratulated when good comes to him and consoled when misfortune afflicts him. He should share a meal with him from time to time. Neither his neighbor nor his neighbor's children should be made to feel any difference that might exist on an economic level. His neighbor's privacy must be respected and guarded.

Mutual rights are also increased, both in quality and intimacy, when a Muslim is a fellow traveler in a common cause. As a friend and confidant his rights are that he should be accorded almost the same status as yourself with regard to your property. At the very least, he should be considered as having absolute right to what is in excess of your needs, and at best, you should follow the example of earlier Muslims by preferring him to yourself. You should go to his aid even before he asks for it and support his family if he dies. You should refrain from exposing his weaknesses and secrets and discourage others from doing so.

You should also be silent about his dislikes, except, of course, when it is your duty to prevent evil. You should make him happy through whatever honorable means are available, such as commending his good qualities and those of his children, "without," added 'Abdullahi, "having to tell lies." You should overlook any bad behavior on his part and accept his excuses, whether they are true or not. You should also pray for him from time to time. And, finally, you should avoid putting unnecessary burdens on him, so that the bond of love is preserved and not strained.

Parent-Child Obligations

Rights and obligations flowing from child/parent relationships constitute a further relevant category. A child has a duty to obey his parents. 'Abdullahi quoted a number of traditions without, however, making any specific recommendations; but Bello might have been expressing 'Abdullahi's thoughts in *Fawā'id Mujmilah fi-Mā Jā' fi-l-Birr wa-l Sillah* when he commented briefly on Allah's injunction to be dutiful to one's parents:

> "It is narrated in the *Saḥīḥ* on the authority of Abū Hurayrah 🌼 that a person came to the Messenger of Allah 🌼 and asked, 'Who is most entitled to my best treatment?' to which the Messenger of Allah replied, 'Your mother.' The man asked, 'Who next?' He replied, 'Your mother.' The man asked, 'Who next?' He replied, 'Your mother.' He asked further, 'Who next?' And the Messenger of Allah replied, 'Your father.'"

The implication of this – that someone's affection for a mother should be three times that given to their father – is supported by what we see in life, since a mother bears the burden of conception, the burden of childbirth and the burden of nursing.

"Five duties," Bello wrote further, "devolve on a responsible person in respect of his parents. Firstly, that he should not be arrogant towards them; secondly, that he should avoid rebuking them even when they confront him with something he dislikes; thirdly, that he should address them in a pleasing, respectful manner... as a humble servant addresses his noble master; fourthly, that he should show great affection to them, not raising his voice in their presence or walking in front of them, and should do what they want, without of course disobeying the law, showing them love, compassion, reverence, and serving them in an excellent way; and fifthly, that he should always pray for Allah's mercy on them provided they are Muslims, and offer *sadaqah* on their behalf after they are dead."

Regarding the children's rights, 'Abdullahi emphasized that a child is a trust (*amānah*) in the hands of his parents, endowed with a pure, innocent heart, free from guilt. At the same time, a child's heart is impressionable so that it can be steered towards either good or evil. If a child is introduced from the beginning to goodness he will grow in that direction and will be a success in this world and in the Hereafter, and everyone who has contributed to that moral success will share in the reward. If, however, he is introduced to evil, he will grow in that direction and the burden of misguidance will be on those who are responsible for it.

A child should be suckled, 'Abdullahi insisted, by a woman who lives on lawful food and is herself upright because "unlawful milk corrupts the child, as there is no blessing in it at all." A child's correct upbringing in the home is a duty owed to it by its father. 'Abdullahi suggested that children should be inculcated with Islamic discipline in matters such as eating, dressing and sleeping.

Concerning his education, he should first be introduced to the Qur'an and entrusted to an upright teacher. Throughout his early education, the child should be guided towards developing strength of character. He should be taught not to cry loudly if beaten at school, nor to seek the intervention of anyone against his punishment by his teacher, but rather to endure the punishment patiently. He should be allowed sports and playtime after school to prevent depression, blunting of the intelligence and loss of interest in schooling altogether.

Regarding general behavior, 'Abdullahi suggested that children should be taught to hate pride and love humility. They should not be allowed to brag about their parents' wealth, possessions or livelihood. They should be taught to respect those who associate with them, to be soft in speech, to talk little and avoid unnecessary questions. They should be taught that gentlemanly behavior lies in giving, not in taking and that greed is degrading. They should not spit when in company. They should be attentive when spoken to by older people and offer them a place to sit. At the same time they should avoid people who use obscene speech, curse or insult others.

Mothers have a duty to teach their children to respect their fathers and to give due regard to their teachers and superiors. Children should be taught their duties as Muslims and be told stories of upright men and women. They should be warned against stealing, cheating and lying and be inspired to perform and love good deeds. If they make mistakes they should be corrected and if they repeat them they should be rebuked in secret and made to appreciate the gravity of what they have done. They should conversely be rewarded for displaying good qualities.

As children grow older, they should be made to appreciate that the purpose of eating is to enable them to be strong enough to carry out the injunctions of Allah, and that this world is ephemeral and so a sensible person will only take from it those provisions necessary for the next. The ephemeral nature of this world and the reality and permanence of the Hereafter should be so inculcated into a child's consciousness that it becomes ingrained permanently in their character. When maturity is reached, marriage should be arranged. 'Abdullahi repeated the Prophet's ﷺ teaching that every child is born with a pure natural disposition. It is up to the parents to keep their children on this natural form and not allow it to become corrupted.

Family Obligations

A husband, 'Abdullahi wrote in *Tibyān*, has approximately eleven obligations towards his wife. The first, which arises from the marriage bond itself, is the payment of *sadāqi* or dowry and also the costs of the marriage celebration, provided that it is done as the Prophet ﷺ specified. The second obligation is that a husband should tolerate annoyance and endure injury from his wife and, more importantly, "he should be forbearing, indulgent and understanding when she gets angry following the example of the Messenger of Allah ﷺ." Thirdly, he should stimulate her mind by engaging in lawful fun and games with her but, fourthly, he should be moderate in this regard so as not to lose her esteem or lose the ability to correct her if she violates the *Sharī'ah*.

Fifthly, he is obliged to correct her but is not entitled in the course of this to subject her integrity to suspicion or to change her attitudes or to neglect her or be indifferent towards her.

His sixth responsibility is to maintain his wife fairly though moderately. His seventh obligation is to educate her "in the tenets of the people of the Sunnah and in the injunctions and prohibitions of the law", instruct her in her religious duties and instill the fear of Allah into her if she shows slackness in the practice of her *dīn*. The eighth duty applies to a man who has more than one wife, in which case he has to maintain justice between his wives. The ninth thing is that, if ever she exceeds the limits of tolerable companionship, he should discipline her in the way the Qur'an prescribes, "without violence". The tenth duty is to take pleasure in her children – male and female. Finally, if a divorce does occur, he should continue to please her heart with gifts, guard her secrets and respect her privacy.

As for the rights of a husband, 'Abdullahi explained, "they are many: for instance, a wife should obey her husband in all matters so long as they do not amount to sin, and pursue those things that give him happiness." He quotes the words of the Prophet ﷺ: "Any woman who meets her death while her husband is happy with her will go to paradise."

Finally, servants have legal rights, too. They should be fed with the same food their master eats and be clothed in the same decent and dignified way as their master. They should not be burdened with work that is beyond their capability. Servants should not be subjected to humiliation or blackmail by their employers.

To reiterate, there is nothing radically new in this code of social behavior but it gains special significance when placed in the context of Hausaland at that time and when it becomes an integral part of the growth of a new social movement. The intention behind the code was, no doubt, to create a fellowship of the people who shared a common cause; to establish good and virtuous neighborliness; to build loving and upright homes; and to raise the dignity of even the lowliest of people within the community. On deeper reflection, it would appear that what 'Abdullahi was in fact advocating in *Tibyān* was the transformation of the community into what amounted to a single large family, sharing a single set of values and pursuing a single cause.

The New Culture

In addition to the spirit of fellowship and mutual obligation that was fostered in the *Jama'a*, there was the simultaneous development of a new social attitude, a kind of counter-culture, in the movement. In fact, the cultivation of this particular kind of behavior was an extension of the mutual obligations we have mentioned, which served to strengthen the solidarity of the *Jama'a*, but it was also essential in giving the new movement a sense of identity, a superior spiritual and cultural attitude, that distinguished it from the rest of the community and helped to draw other fair-minded and cultured people towards it. This is the subject matter of Shehu Usman's *Kitāb al-Adab*.

The acquisition of knowledge was the most fundamental characteristic of Shehu Usman's *Jama'a*. Indeed, the emerging ethos and values that were molding the *Jama'a* revolved entirely around knowledge and scholarship. The fact that the eight-page *Kitāb al-Adab*, which dealt with more than fifteen issues, devoted almost half its space to matters relating to knowledge indicates the paramount importance of this matter.

Education, like any other sphere of human activity, should be governed by certain values and ethical principles, all the more so in a society where knowledge is sought primarily as a means to gain wealth or social prestige. For, if knowledge is vulgarized or commercialized, as indeed it was in Hausaland, it will no longer be possible for scholars to raise the moral tone of society or influence it in any positive manner. The reiteration of the ethics of education was therefore imperative, if only to provide the new movement with a distinct sense of direction and purpose.

This meant that the new generation of scholars – the vanguard for the revival of Islam in Hausaland – had to display qualities and attitudes consistent with their role as teachers, guardians of societal values and as the conscience of the *ummah.* So, while remaining humble, they had also to behave in a dignified manner that commanded respect from all. And while it was essential that they show respect to people in general, it was not expected of them to accord honor to oppressors, if only as a mark of their disapproval of criminal, un-Islamic acts. They were to endeavor to be "scholars of the Hereafter" and not scholars of this world. Consequently, they had to seek knowledge that was useful in the Hereafter, knowledge that would facilitate and encourage obedience to Allah.

They were not to be materialistic in matters of food, clothing or accommodation. They were to endeavor to acquire sound spiritual knowledge, strive to combat undesirable innovations in society, and gain insight into the causes of corruption and confusion. In addition, they were required to keep their distance from kings. This, we may add, was essential if these scholars were to serve as the focus of social mobilization and as the symbols of people's aspirations. Indeed, the fundamental distinguishing factor between the generation of *'ulamā'* raised by the Shehu and the rest of the scholars, was that the former saw itself as a distinct body, independent of the existing political order and committed to its overthrow. Such scholars could not fraternize with those they regarded as oppressive rulers, let alone serve them.

The responsibility of the scholars was to their students: to impart useful sciences to them; to urge them to pursue knowledge purely for the sake of Allah; to urge them to learn about their individual religious obligations before embarking on other subjects; and to discourage them from associating with men of evil character. In addition, the scholars had to show kindness to their students, mold their characters and give them good advice at all times. They were not to belittle subjects not taught by them and were to deal with each student according to his intelligence.

The students, on their part, had to pay due respect to

their teachers, give the school the same veneration due to the mosque, and accord to the acquisition of knowledge the same reverence they accorded to the prayer. They should not display any materialistic tendencies and should behave in a dignified fashion. They too had to keep their distance from oppressive kings and strive to preserve their dignity. "Do not," the Shehu advised, "place wealth above honor." The ultimate objective of each of the sciences had to be considered carefully by the students before they made their choice about which disciplines to pursue, remembering, however, that the purpose of knowledge is to improve the character and seek nearness to Allah.

In the area of social behavior, several matters were dealt with in *Kitāb al-Adab*. The Shehu advised his men to display composure, social restraint and common sense in their association with people in general. They should limit their disapproval of the behavior of others but be quick to advise on right and wrong, offering advice, however, only when there was a real hope of it being accepted. They should not plunge into other people's discussions, nor should they pay attention to rumors and lies peddled in public, listen to obscene language, frequent places of ill repute or seek anything from people of low morals. They should be thoughtful and humble and, in their search for a livelihood, they should put their trust in Allah and be content with what they had lawfully acquired.

While it was essential that members of the *Jama'a* should develop maturity by, for example, not eating too much and not tiring themselves unduly during the day, they must at the same time improve their inner disposition, thus strengthening the cohesion of the *Jama'a* and raising their status with Allah. Hence, the mind should be freed from nursing any hatred or enmity towards a fellow Muslim and from being unduly anxious over worldly matters.

The mind should rather be occupied with the thought of the Hereafter, to counterbalance its normal preoccupation with this world. In addition, *qiyām al-layl* (standing for prayer in the night) should be observed on a daily basis, and the mind should be trained to be conscious of Allah, to fear His punishment, and to be ashamed of its moral failures. Over and above this, constant reading of the Qur'an, observing the respect due to it, and making an effort to understand and contemplate it was desirable.

When starting on a journey, members of the *Jama'a*, and in a wider sense Muslims in general, should free themselves first from all moral and economic obligations, so that they could travel with an absolutely free conscience. According to Shehu Usman, they should first amend any wrong they had done, pay their debts, return anything that had been entrusted to them and arrange for the maintenance of those under their care. They should take adequate provision but use only lawful means to acquire it. They should carry items of basic necessity with them. And above all, they should fulfill their spiritual obligations throughout the journey and adhere to the ethics of travel established by the Prophet of Allah ﷺ.

The *Kitāb al-Adab* also touched on the ethics of sleep. The Shehu advised his people to regard sleep not merely as a physical phenomenon but also as a profound lesson which repeats itself daily. They should see sleep "as a form of death" and their reawakening "as a form of resurrection". In other words, the thought of the Hereafter should be paramount in their minds when going to bed. It might, in fact, be their last sleep. Therefore, they should go to bed in a state of purity – teeth brushed and *wuḍū'* performed. They should ask Allah's forgiveness for all their sins and offer the supplication (*du'ā'*) appropriate for going to bed. Their beds should not be excessively soft – either because that would indicate an inclination to luxury, which is hateful to Islam, or because a soft bed might diminish a person's ability to wake for *Ṣubḥ* prayer.

When the Shehu touched on the obligations a man owes to his wife, the wife to her husband and mutual obligations between Muslims, there was no fundamental difference between *Kitāb al-Adab* and 'Abdullahi's *Tibyān*, although the Shehu added several points not included by 'Abdullahi. He advised Muslims to honor the aged and show compassion to the young. He said they should meet each other with cheerful faces, be considerate and fair in their dealings with one another and fulfill one another's needs on a cooperative basis. He instructed them to protect one another against injustice and come to one another's defense and, most significantly, he told them to avoid the company of the rich, associate always with the poor and take adequate care of orphans.

On the matter of the ethics of visiting the sick, the Shehu advised that visitors should exhibit compassion, pray for the sick person as the Prophet ﷺ has counseled and ask as few questions as possible. The sick person, for his part, should be patient, keep his complaints to a minimum and put his trust for recovery in Allah while continuing to take the necessary medication.

It may be said that, on the whole, there was nothing new, either in *Tibyān* or *Kitāb al-Adab*. What was new was that the social and moral rules they contained were being put into practice by a group dedicated to establishing a better and superior social order. The *Jama'a* was nurtured on well-known principles, values and ethics. When these were actualized in a social setting, they assumed added significance and, in turn, made their mark on the emerging social force. As long as the *Jama'a* remained faithful to these values and ethics, there did not exist any force that could weaken them or alter their course towards reviving Islam.

5. Inviting to All that is Good

THE MOST fundamental duty of a *mujaddid*, or indeed any upright scholar, is to call his people to the way of Allah or to enjoin the right and forbid the wrong. For reasons of convenience, we shall refer to it as *amr wa nahy* or simply, "the call". Our discussion in this chapter centers on three issues: the philosophy of the call as seen by the Shehu himself, the preparation of the callers and the methodology of the call as articulated by 'Abdullahi.

The Philosophy of the Call

Our main reference for the philosophy of *amr wa nahy* is Shehu Usman's short treatise entitled *al-Amr bi-l-Ma'rūf wa-n-Nahy ani-l-Munkar*, which we shall refer to as *al-Amr*. The Shehu dealt with three broad matters in this treatise: firstly, he looked at the call as a historical, social necessity, particularly at a time of social decay; secondly, he proposed basic guidelines for discharging this duty; finally, he tackled the issue of armed confrontation as it relates to a movement in the initial phase of the process of reviving Islam.

The duty to call arises as a moral and social response to a prevailing situation of decline and it is fundamentally a function of the learned and the upright. It is necessitated by the very phenomenon of decline itself for, if we agree that there can be no vacuum in the history of a given society, then we may presume that one social order begins its growth precisely at the point when the prevailing one, which has been overwhelmed by spiritual and social disease, is drifting into disintegration. The new social order has two qualities to its advantage: a deeper and more profound perception of human society and the ability to act justly by virtue of its moral superiority. These two qualities distinguish it from the disintegrating prevailing order, which is characterized by an ominous blindness to the course of its own history and an addiction to social, moral and political excesses.

If the call is a historical imperative, it goes without saying that the initiation of the process of calling is justified by the very existence of social decay. There is no need for any additional justification. That is to say, a scholar must call people to Islam even if their response is negative or hostile. The nature of people's response should not be a determining factor in the discharge of this supremely important duty. A scholar should undertake this duty because it is a duty he owes to Allah, a duty for which there is no alternative in a period of social decay, and because a scholar has a responsibility to society, which is to steer it on a course of regeneration when decline has manifested itself. This presupposes a fundamental principle of historical movement. Human society can always direct itself upwards, even at a stage when all hope might have been lost.

Hope, not pessimism, should be the scholar's approach to transformation. But even if hope, in the scholar's estimate, is gone, he must nonetheless go on with his duty of calling people to Islam, for the simple reason that Allah's ultimate judgment on his society is sure to come. We have already noted three elements in society: the symbols of oppression and evil, the victims – that is the mass of people – and those who strive for justice. The last group have two goals before them: either to effect a total transformation of their society to save it from impending collapse or, alternatively, to secure their own safety from Allah's ultimate judgment.

The call is necessary, the Shehu wrote, because Allah made it an obligatory duty for Muslims by saying: "*Let there be a community among you who call to the good, and enjoin the right, and forbid the wrong.*" (3:104) Equally, it is, according to the

Prophet ﷺ, the only certain way by which a Muslim society can ensure its enhancement and survival as a social and spiritual entity, a fact attested to by the history of Islam itself.

Calling people to Islam is, therefore, a means by which the continued existence of Muslim society is ensured, for, by subjecting itself continually to critical self-examination in which everyone is involved in his own way, a Muslim society is most likely to get back on course as soon as it strays. To that end, almost every individual has a role to play. This role, the Shehu wrote, consists of reminding people of those laws of Allah, which most people know about or with which they are supposed to be familiar. The greater responsibility for this duty, however, rests squarely on the shoulders of those the Shehu called *ahlu-l-ijtihād*, that is, those who represent the conscience of society and mold its opinion.

A fundamental problem, however, arises here. Any scholar is well aware of two apparently contradictory sets of injunctions in respect of *amr wa nahy*. The first relates to a condemnation of those who enjoin others to good deeds while they themselves do not perform those deeds. Allah says in this respect: "*Do you order people to devoutness and forget yourselves?*" (2:43) Quoting the Prophet Shu'ayb ﷺ, He says, "*I would clearly not want to go behind your backs and do something I have forbidden you to do.*" (11:88) The Prophet ﷺ indicated that such scholars would suffer punishment on the Day of Judgment.

On the other hand, Ibn al-Hajj is quoted in *al-Amr* as saying that the Prophet ﷺ also commanded those who were present to communicate what he had said to those who were absent because the absentees might take it to heart more than those who had heard it directly. He also said that anyone who concealed his knowledge in a period of social and moral decline was like one who contended with what Allah had revealed. Ibn al-Hajj then added: "Allah has indeed taken a pledge from learned men that they will teach (His message to others) and a pledge from the ignorant that they will learn." In other words, while there is a definite condemnation of those who preach without acting according to what they preach, there is also a definite condemnation of those who maintain silence in the face of social degeneration when the actual need is to speak out.

How are these two contradictory positions to be reconciled? The Shehu, who was obviously well aware of his own society, said boldly:

> "The duty to enjoin what is good and forbid what is evil is not confined only to the pious who do not perpetrate the acts which they forbid others to do. The duty also devolves on someone who perpetrates acts similar to those he forbids because his refraining from sinful acts and his prohibiting of evil are two separate obligations, so it is not proper for one who defaults in respect of the one to abandon the other."

He decided that to perpetrate acts which one asks others not to do is certainly a sin, but to be silent in the face of corruption, decay and prevalent ignorance is an even greater one. Since no one but a prophet is morally perfect, everyone else is bound to sin in one way or another. It is safer, therefore, for a scholar to take one moral risk in the face of an obligation, which is to speak out and teach in an atmosphere of prevalent corruption, than to take the greater risk of remaining silent with the untenable excuse of being likely to succumb to the sins against which he is preaching. In other words, the guiding principle in the face of that moral dilemma is: the perpetration of one evil is better than the perpetration of two evils.

The Shehu's probable intention in taking this position was to disarm the scholars of his time who maintained an embarrassing silence in a climate of political oppression, moral excesses and prevalent ignorance, on the pretext that it was not safe to speak because there was a likelihood that they might commit the same sins themselves. In addition, he called the attention of these scholars to the fundamental historical fact that what had caused the downfall of earlier generations was their persistent clinging to reprehensible and evil customs they had inherited from their ancestors. By maintaining silence, the scholars were, by implication, contributing to the systematic drift of society towards its own destruction.

If a scholar has to wait until he is morally perfect before he can embark on his duty to call, the chances are that he will be overtaken by the forces of decay and perfection will remain an unattainable goal. It is impossible for a person living in a corrupt society not to be affected in some way by it, so the fact that even the most honorable elements in society exhibit certain moral failings should not be turned into an excuse to refuse to undertake the urgent task of social transformation but rather seen as a natural consequence of general decline. In any case, it is virtually impossible for an individual to reach a very high level of piety on his own when the rest of society is corrupt and depraved. *Amr wa nahy* in this situation will have the effect of raising both the individual and society to a higher level of social discipline and consciousness of Allah.

Given that *amr wa nahy* is an absolute necessity, what are the rules governing its implementation? The injunction of Allah regarding it is this: "*Make allowances for people, command what is right, and turn away from the ignorant.*" (7:199) The key phrase here is "*make allowances for people*". It means that, in the effort to transform society, elemental human weakness must not be overlooked, for such a course of action would not only defeat the very purpose of *tajdīd* but would also have the effect of crushing human nature itself. Since no society declines overnight, the process of regeneration is as slow as, if not slower than, the process of decay itself.

We have already noted that the cure for degeneration is the moral and intellectual elevation of society. To raise a person to full moral consciousness involves recognition of his moral weakness from the start. Similarly, if you want to make an ignorant person learned, the fact of his ignorance should be accepted from the beginning. The effort to develop him morally and intellectually then becomes easier and more feasible.

The task, therefore, should be undertaken on the premise that, if people are to be lifted from moral and intellectual weakness to a higher level of consciousness, the process will involve, as it does in the case of physical growth, considerable time and effort. In fact, it is an unending process. To be impatient with the failings of people is to miss the essence of *tajdīd* altogether. To insist that people's attitudes should conform to the highest standards laid down by Islam in a faultless fashion is not only to demand the impossible but also to fail to see the very nature of human society.

The objective of *tajdīd* is not to create a perfect society where everybody always does the right thing at the right time. If that were so then much of the law revealed by Allah, in which there are prohibitions and punishments, would be irrelevant. *Tajdīd* is essentially an effort to renew society's faith in the *Sharī'ah*, whereby it will acknowledge Islam's moral framework – its judgment about what is right and what is wrong – and subject itself wholly to the rule of *Sharī'ah*. It will then reward or punish in accordance with the *Sharī'ah* and strive to preserve its character as a society submissive to Divinely revealed law.

What gives rise to *amr wa nahy* is not simply that individuals commit sins or that society makes errors of omission or commission or judgment from time to time. Rather, the call is necessitated by a collective committal of the act of apostasy, whereby a society subscribes substantially to a system of law other than the *Sharī'ah*, to a judgment in the sphere of social morality other than that of the Most Exalted, and to a set of values other than those of Islam.

Perfection can never be ascribed in its absolute sense to human beings and if no individual can be perfect, how can we expect a human society to be perfect? Man, as Allah himself has testified, has been created weak and that inherent weakness remains with him forever. That weakness remains a fundamental characteristic of human society as well. *Tajdīd* aims at increasing man's positive qualities in such a way that the effects of his frailty are reduced to a minimum, at ingraining the desire for excellence into the psychology of his society, and at raising his moral conscience to a level where he recognizes Allah alone as his Lord, his judge and his ultimate goal.

Thus, the very first rule of *amr wa nahy* is that people should not be subjected to unbearable moral pressures. It should be recognized that the success of the Prophet ﷺ in mobilizing and unifying people was attributable partly to his dealing gently with them, for, as Allah reminded him: "*If you had been rough or hard of heart, they would have scattered from around you.*" (3:159)

Shehu Usman pointed out that in an effort to call people to Islam, a scholar should never condemn them for doing acts which are not expressly prohibited by the Qur'an and Sunnah or by a consensus of the jurists. Similarly, he should not fault the people for failing to do acts which are not expressly made obligatory by the Qur'an and Sunnah or by the consensus of jurists. He should not be quick to condemn the mass of Muslims, or issue a *fatwā* invalidating their worship and transactions, merely on the strength of the ruling of some jurists, without any explicit ruling of the Qur'an or Sunnah, or the definitive consensus of the jurists, to that effect.

This is because it is as bad to repudiate what legally should not be repudiated as it is to perpetrate acts which are prohibited. In other words, many of the moral failings of the people should be overlooked and *amr wa nahy* should be limited to only those matters on which there are definitive rulings in the Qur'an and Sunnah or which the jurists have universally agreed to be obligatory or prohibited.

A second rule concerns a very important problem posed by the duty of *amr wa nahy*: what should someone do if, despite their efforts to transform people, they meet with little or no success? The Shehu's answer was that they should continue with their efforts: "The refusal of the people to do what he enjoins them to do or to abandon what he prohibits them from doing, does not constitute a justification (for a scholar) to abandon *amr wa nahy*." This is because his duty is basically to remind the people of this obligation. If they heed him, the aim has been achieved, and if not, he is nevertheless freed from blame before Allah.

Finally, we proceed to consider the nature of the call. Allah says in this regard: *"Call to the way of your Lord with wisdom and fair admonition, and argue with them in the kindest way. Your Lord knows best who is misguided from His way. And He knows best who the guided are. If you want to retaliate, retaliate to the same degree as the injury done to you. But if you are patient, it is better to be patient."* (16:125-6)

Restraint, then, is the very essence of this duty. Rushing to achieve success through armed confrontation when one is in a position of weakness is ruled out as an Islamic strategy. The call is, therefore, fundamentally a peaceful process and this peaceful stage should be prolonged for as long as possible. For the duty of the scholar is no more than to lay the truth bare and make it available to the people; whoever wishes may accept it, and whoever wishes may reject it. It is not for him to seek to impose the truth on an unwilling people. It is not possible and it is not desirable. As long as there exists the possibility, however small, of a peaceful dissemination of the truth, the scholar is obliged to utilize it. Even if that possibility is blocked, the next course of action is for the scholar to move to another area where he can continue his peaceful efforts.

Recourse to armed confrontation is allowed only when all possibilities for a peaceful education of the people have been exhausted and, moreover, only when the Muslims have gathered sufficient strength to confront the prevailing order. The point being stressed here is that the ultimate conflict between truth and falsehood is not a confrontation between individuals but rather a conflict between two orders: a new order, whose explicit intention is to restore the pure practice of Islam, on the one hand, and a dominant, decadent order on the other. It is necessary, therefore, that the challenging order should first root itself in the hearts of the people and in the fabric of society before it ventures into a confrontation; otherwise, it will be swept away.

The Shehu attributed hasty recourse to armed confrontation to delusions (*ghurūr*), worldly intrigues (*dasā'is dunyawiyyah*), satanic insinuations (*nazghat ash-Shaytān*) and ambition and love of power (*hubb ar-ri'asah*). The Shehu gave three examples of people "overwhelmed by Satanic insinuations", one of whom was the well-known 'Abdul Mahalli who rose in revolt against the Moroccan establishment in about 1610 A.D. and succeeded in expelling Zaidan, one of its rulers, from Marrakech. 'Abdul Mahalli claimed to be a Mahdi and the rule he established lasted for merely two years before it was brought to an end. He was killed, his severed head displayed in the open marketplace, his power eradicated and Zaidan returned to the throne. 'Abdul Mahalli's exploits were seen by Muslims largely as Allah's vengeance on Morocco and not as a *tajdīd,* despite the man's Islamic pretensions. There were several others who met with a similar fate.

As far as the Shehu was concerned, the apparent piety of such people was irrelevant and the significant factor in their case was their refusal to follow the correct procedure in calling to the way of Allah. It is significant that he likened the popular appeal they commanded to the sway which Pharaoh held over his people, for he used the same term, *istakhaffa,* with which Allah described Pharaoh's apparent popularity: "*In that way he swayed (*istakhaffa*) his people and they succumbed to him.*" (43:54) To incite people to armed confrontation without first establishing a concrete power-base, could be construed by "revolutionaries" as the right path, but in reality such exploits are wrong because they lead invariably to unnecessary disorder, corruption and killing.

The fact remains that there is no alternative to exhortation and persuasion in calling the people to the way of Allah. Allah's command was that people should be called with wisdom (*ḥikmah*) and good exhortation (*maw'idhatun hasana*). That requires a deep understanding of the issues involved and a profound knowledge of Islam. The prophets had access to wisdom and knowledge because, in addition to the revelations they received and their intimate association with the angels, Allah gave them insight into the workings of the universe. A scholar has no such advantages. He has to acquire his knowledge himself, which involves great effort over a considerable length of time. He also has to lead others through the same experience. He has to develop a personality which commands respect, awe and confidence.

To sidetrack these essential steps and act like Pharaoh means that one is seeking something other than a genuine transformation of society. If *tajdīd* were merely a matter of political revolution or change of leadership, then there are quicker ways to achieve that than the recourse to the Qur'an and Sunnah. *Tajdīd*, however, involves the transformation of the heart, of the human disposition and of the destiny of man itself. Those things clearly transcend the mere attainment of political power. To believe that a rapid rise to political ascendancy is all that is required to re-establish Islam is to totally misevaluate a sublime system. What Islam requires is an enduring transformation and that cannot be realized by a social hurricane which brings destruction and consumes the very thing it claims it is trying to put right.

Tajdīd, the Shehu seemed to imply, depends on a scholar who is patient enough to establish the roots of faith, Islam and *Iḥsān* firmly in society and who, in addition, has a well-grounded and profound knowledge of the sciences of religion. His cause, in the final analysis, is to establish the good and rule by it, to aid the truth and the people of truth, and to demolish the edifice of falsehood. Once Muslims have found such a person, they are obliged to support him and struggle with him to overthrow an un-Islamic and tyrannical order.

The Callers

If the call is the most important way to transform society,

then it is vital to raise people of the right caliber to assist in the accomplishment of that task. The process of social transformation may fail if the wrong people disseminate its message or, indeed, if the message itself is misrepresented or distorted by those who transmit it. The Shehu tackled this important issue in his *I'dād ad-dā'i ilā dīnu-l-lāh* and also to a large extent in his *'Umdat al-'ulamā'*.

In *I'dād* the Shehu reiterated the importance of *amr* and stated further that this duty devolves almost entirely on scholars. By implication, therefore, anyone who is to be involved in this task must first be trained properly. It is the case, however, perhaps due to the dearth of scholars, that once a person had received even the minimum education needed for calling people to Islam, he became a scholar, at least for the purpose of the *Jama'a*. Because he had got, as the Shehu stated, "a share of knowledge", it was incumbent on him not to keep silent in these times. He was then sent out to teach, preach and call to Islam.

So what was the minimum education needed for a person to qualify as a caller or *dā'ī*? We can only answer by inference, relying on the contents of *'Umdat al-'ulamā'* and *I'dād*. The former was written to provide callers with the relevant verses of the Qur'an and *ḥadīth*s on the subjects they were to teach people. In broad terms, these subjects were firstly, *uṣūl ad-Dīn*, which embraces the unity of Allah, His attributes, belief in the messengers and their attributes, belief in the angels, the Books, the Decree and the Day of Judgment, and several matters pertaining to it; secondly, *fiqh*, which embraces the other four pillars of Islam, *ṣalāt*, *zakāt*, *ṣawm* and Ḥajj, and other fundamental matters of life, such as marriage, business transactions and related issues; thirdly, *Iḥsān*, which embraces all matters relating to the development of character and spiritual purification.

By providing the relevant texts of the Qur'an and *ḥadīth*, the Shehu probably had three aims in mind: to establish the supremacy of the Qur'an and Sunnah in all these matters, so that, with respect to *taṣawwuf*, spiritual development would be possible without belonging to any particular order and, with respect to *fiqh*, implementation of every practice would be possible without necessarily belonging to a particular school; to unify the methods and themes of preaching in his movement; and to provide those who were not yet fully grounded in knowledge with a handy reference for their work.

The callers were told in *I'dād* that in *uṣūl ad-Dīn* they should teach the people about Allah, about the messengers, the angels, and the Day of Judgment. In *fiqh*, they had to teach the people about purification, *wuḍū'*, *tayammum*, *ṣalāt*, and so on, as well as the laws pertaining to marriage and business dealings in general. In each of these, the Islamic rules should be categorized for them as to whether they were obligatory, forbidden or recommended. In *Iḥsān* or *taṣawwuf* the people should be taught first what aspects of human behavior are offensive to Islam and, therefore, destructive to a person, such as self-glorification or self-justification, envy, unjustifiable anger, miserliness or nursing suspicion or rancor against a fellow Muslim. Then, they were to be taught the forms of behavior Islam prescribes for Muslims, such as abstinence, repentance, trust in Allah, entrusting affairs to Him and sincerity in worship.

Apart from these, the people should be made to appreciate the severity of Allah's punishment and also the extent of His mercy. For example, verses in the Qur'an which state that man has not been created in vain and that he will eventually be brought to judgment, were to be quoted and explained. Similarly, verses which highlight Allah's overflowing mercy, such as those which urge people not to despair of His mercy because Allah forgives all sins except that of associating partners with Him and those which state that He has made mercy incumbent on Himself, could be explained to the people.

The Shehu then touched briefly in *I'dād* on the ethics of public education, which is an important element in calling people to Islam. He urged his men to be lenient to people when they call them to Islam. Leniency here possibly means exercising patience with the people because of their coarseness, low moral standards or their ignorance. This, the Shehu indicated, was the practice of the Prophet ﷺ, which made it possible for him to hold people of divergent backgrounds and different moral levels together. Had he been harsh with them, they would have abandoned him completely.

Further, people should not be criticized personally. Criticism should rather be in general terms and not directed at specific individuals or groups. While the callers had to be earnest and grave in their approach and expression, they were not to create an atmosphere of despair and apprehension in the minds of their audience. A fine blend of "fear and hope" was necessary to elicit a positive response. Lecture sessions must not be too long for the Prophet ﷺ had advised that people were not to be overburdened or bored with too much preaching.

It may be asked why there was nothing "political" in the matters which were addressed to the people. There are several possible reasons for this. The Shehu might have felt that there was no need to antagonize the rulers at a stage when the *Jama'a* had not yet gained strength, for that might well lead to the whole exercise being brought to a premature end; or he might have believed that the essence of calling people was firstly to bring about their spiritual and moral transformation. Once this was achieved, their whole attitude to life, including politics, would change automatically. There was no need to jump to a stage which would be reached anyway if the process of mass education was sustained.

Alternatively, the Shehu might have felt that political education fell within the sphere of *mudārah* and was best dealt with more subtly. He might have felt that to generate an uncontrollable, emotive political ferment would not ultimately be in the interests of Islam. It could be hijacked by forces of opportunism. It could also be deliberately misrepresented and crushed before it could take root.

Quite simply, however, the Shehu might have felt that his fundamental role was to improve the moral and spiritual quality of the people and raise their intellectual level. If this effort led to political awareness, all well and good, if not, his duty to call people to believe in Allah, obey His laws and be conscious of the Day of Judgment was nevertheless fulfilled. Or He may have also felt that he needed profound characters, not mere agitators, in his *Jama'a* and that entailed people attaching themselves first to Allah before fighting for His cause.

The Methodology of the Call

Shehu Usman's *I'dād* provides no more than a faint hint of the methodology needed for calling people to Islam. Most probably, at the time it was written, the *Jama'a* was already well established and the duty of *amr wa nahy* had already advanced significantly. Similarly, his *al-Amr*, which we discussed at the beginning of this chapter, might have been written at the time when it was felt within the *Jama'a* that it was strong enough to enter into armed confrontation with the powers-that-be in Hausaland, whereas the Shehu himself, not being convinced of this, felt the need to articulate the philosophy of the call, in order to impress on the minds of his people that the journey had in fact only just begun. He ruled out armed confrontation and urged the intensification of the spiritual, legal and moral education of the people.

Mass education was definitely the cornerstone of the Shehu's method of mass mobilization. His activities at this stage in the process of reviving Islam in Hausaland were aimed first at changing people's attitude towards Allah. He did this by imbuing people with a perspective on life in which Allah is conceived as its fundamental and ultimate focus and the worship of Allah as its main object. All avenues not leading to Allah, all the paths of false worship and false principles, were systematically blocked off.

His activities also aimed at turning people back to the *Sharī'ah* and its prescriptions for worship, social life and economic endeavor. They were also aimed at directing people's social and moral behavior which would bring about their own, and also society's, spiritual regeneration. Once society is reformed, it stirs into action, ready to transform itself socially and politically.

This task fuelled a constant demand for more scholars. The Shehu and his men could not cope with the surging membership of the *Jama'a* nor with the necessity to have, in every mosque and in every village, a scholar to call the people to Islam, as the Shehu himself had demanded. Many scholars were reluctant to join the *Jama'a,* though quite a few of them shared its aspirations for social transformation. To bring those scholars into the mainstream of the process of reviving Islam became, at a certain stage, a fundamental necessity. *Tajdīd* is first and foremost an intellectual and moral process and scholars are the repository, as well as the symbols, of both intellect and morality – the twin prerequisites of a genuine revival of Islam.

It was here that the Shehu's illustrious brother, 'Abdullahi, stepped in. He wrote his well-known *Risālat an-Naṣā'iḥ,* which he addressed to the scholars urging them specifically to "rise up and call to religion" and join in the process of reviving Islam. In particular, 'Abdullahi had in mind people like his teacher, Mustafa al-Hajj. From what 'Abdullahi says of him in *Tazyīn,* he was indeed a formidable scholar: "the mirror of the tribe, the refuge of the poor... the wise man, protector, pillar of knowledge, reviver of the religion among them, of great patience... magnanimous, the mansion of the guests, gentle, friend alike to the humble and the great." To succeed in bringing scholars like this into the *Jama'a* would indeed be a turning point in the struggle for Islam in Hausaland.

The *Risālat an-Naṣā'iḥ* is important to us in more than one respect. It is clear evidence that others beside the Shehu had a role in the mobilization of the people to the cause of Islam. It opens for us a window onto the broad issues to which the Shehu and his men addressed themselves in their social mobilization. It also enables us to understand the growing confidence in the movement itself as to its ultimate victory. Finally, it presents us with a clear insight into the methodology of mass mobilization, or *da'wah* or *amr wa nahy*, depending on which term is chosen to describe it. This last point is our concern here for the *Risālat* is a document of great merit and significance.

'Abdullahi expressed his reason for writing the *Risālat* in these words: "Now when I saw most of the country, the common people and the nobles coming to Shaykh 'Uthman, profiting by his admonitions, becoming influenced by his fine behavior, and entering into his community in throngs, but did not see that happening in the majority of our tribe, though they were most fitted to it, I composed a *qasīdah*... which I called *Risālat an-Naṣā'iḥ*, and I sent it to them in order that they might ponder upon what was in it, and hasten to help the Religion of Allah Most High."

It is clear, therefore, that 'Abdullahi wrote the *Risālat* at a period when the movement had gained considerable influence and some strength. More significantly, its content reveals a practical experience acquired from long years of preaching and mass mobilization. A number of the points raised in it are indications of the practical problems that faced the movement in its strenuous efforts to reach the people, the obstacles it faced, and the bones of contention between it as an emerging social order and the entrenched system in Hausaland. The methodology adopted by the movement and its faith in the rightness of its cause are also revealed.

The Islamic call, or *da'wah*, 'Abdullahi made clear, was the duty of every conscious member of society, man or woman, and it was to be directed towards society as a whole. Both the "common people" and "the great lords" were to be invited to the reform of the faith, to Islam, to *Iḥsān*. But he recognized too that opposition from vested interests was inevitable. There was bound to be opposition from the *'ulamā' as-sū'* (evil scholars), the political leaders and even the common people. 'Abdullahi, therefore, asked the learned men and women of his tribe who constituted, intellectually speaking, the cream of society, to adopt the correct attitude of the true worker in the cause of Allah. They should not fear he said, "the words of one who hates, whom fools imitate... nor the mockery of the ignorant man who has gone astray... nor the backbiting of a slanderer nor the rancor of one who bears a grudge who is helped by one who relies on (evil) customs." They should not be discouraged if they were accused of lying or rejected by the king. For as long as they were working for the cause of Allah, they should be sure of ultimate victory, because:

> "None can destroy what the hand of Allah has built;
> None can overthrow the order of Allah if it comes."

Next, 'Abdullahi acquainted them with the fundamental social issues on which to concentrate in the work of *amr wa nahy*. The first, of course, was the principal source of the decline in Hausaland – clinging to customs that had degenerated into instruments of oppression and social tyranny and were a justification for immoral excesses. It is often posited as a fundamental principle that, in the course of transformation, a society has to be persuaded to approach its customs and traditions with a critical and selective mind. This so that it can discard those aspects of its culture that constitute an impediment to moral consciousness and social growth and so that it will return to justice and fairness.

Islam lays emphasis on the fact that any aspect of culture that is inconsistent with the Sacred Law has no legitimacy and should not be considered binding on society, for it is bound to offend against justice and fundamental moral values. In addition, a given society is responsible for itself alone and not to or for any other society. It is absurd, therefore, for it to seek to justify its behavior by that of its predecessor or to sanctify unjust and retrogressive customs merely because they are old or inherited. The test of the legitimacy of a custom is whether or not it is just and fair, in other words, whether it is consistent with the *Sharī'ah* or not.

In fact Islam does not accept that people should have any

customs or traditions other than religious ones, for if Allah's way is a comprehensive way of life, what room is there for custom and tradition from any other source? What is called custom is either a vestige from the pre-Islamic "days of ignorance", or an aspect of religion itself which, over the years, has become distorted as a result of a weakening of social responsibility. The relics of an ignorant past must be abandoned and forgotten and all aspects of Islam which have been corrupted must be rectified and restored to pristine purity. This is what the call is all about. This was the task which 'Abdullahi had in mind when he told the scholars to explain to the people that "the customs are vain". Society, he said, should return to the Sunnah, which is the natural form of man.

The scholars, 'Abdullahi said, should also address themselves to the youth and let them know that "the market of the pastimes of youth has become unprofitable" and that "there is praise everywhere for the market of righteousness". If we are seeking evidence that the Shehu's movement concerned itself with the crucial issue of youth mobilization and training, here is a piece of it. We do not need to expend any energy in finding out whether the youth at that time were largely immoral, for the character of the youth is mirrored in society as a whole. Considerable progress had been achieved in raising the youth of Hausaland in knowledge and Islamic practices. The *ṭalaba* had grown in number considerably.

Then, said 'Abdullahi, attention should be paid to what he called *ahlu-d-dunyā* (people of this world) and those who were the symbols of worldly power – the pillars of secularism and materialism. This was clearly a reference to the leaders and other powerful men of influence, notably the local merchants who might not have inclined themselves to the cause. Here we are brought face to face with an emerging pattern in the movement, the steady division of people into two ideological camps: the emerging order dedicated to the establishment of Islam and the decadent, crumbling, old order which held on to corrupt customs and traditions. The reference to *ahlu-d-dunyā* in contradistinction to the men of religion, and also to the *munkir*, the denier of religion, as opposed to the *naṣīr*, the helper of religion, all point to that pattern, which 'Abdullahi could be referring to when he says in his poem:

> "And the worldly people, the shadow of their influence has shrunk this day;
>
> And lofty trees cast their shade over our Sunnah.
>
> The measure of one who denies the religion has become light;
>
> And one who makes it manifest, his measure preponderates this day;
>
> And one who helps it has become high among the people;
>
> And one who denies it has become abased in the eyes of the nobles and the common people."

The perennial but crucial problem of women's education was also a central issue in the *Risālat*. In line with the uncompromising stand of the movement that women must be educated and lifted out of ignorance into the light of Islam, 'Abdullahi asked the scholars to give women good education and a sound moral and social consciousness. Women, he said, should be taught how to dress when going out. "Clothing should be seen," he said, "everywhere except on the face and hands."

Women should be educated in *Iḥsān* as well as on how they should maintain their homes. They also had to be told what customs and attitudes were bad and how they should rid themselves of "bad traits" and "how to render themselves pleasing, in a purely praiseworthy fashion."

All this, however, should be seen within the general framework of the movement's methodology of public education. As far as it was concerned, there was no difference between the minimum education stipulated by Islam for both men and women, except that women in fact require additional education, by virtue of their special responsibility for the raising of the family. The content of education in faith, law and business transactions remains fundamentally the same for both men and women.

As for public education itself, 'Abdullahi obviously reflected the activities of the movement:

> "Make them understand what belief makes incumbent on people in the way of religion;
>
> Of those things which the senses make easy – bathing and ablution and prayer and alms;
>
> And fasting; and buying and selling; then how one should marry; and what (in law) is incumbent;
>
> What is exemplary; what is approved; and what is forbidden; it is all in the books, plain to see."

'Abdullahi then turned his attention to two important questions: What should be the personal conduct of the scholar engaged in this task? And what should be his reaction if he gets an unfavorable response from the people? In answer to the first question, 'Abdullahi presented what might be considered as a code of conduct for reviving Islam. His theme, characteristically, was: "Begin with yourself." To be convincing, the preacher must himself be an embodiment of what he preaches. Indeed, much of the success of the Shehu in his work of *da'wah* had to do with his personal qualities, which made people trust and have faith in him. His noble and fine presence commanded respect. We have already said that the man of change wishes to recreate like-minded people so that eventually there will be enough people to bring about the desired change in society.

What the scholar should do, 'Abdullahi suggested, is to begin his struggle from within. The external enemies – the great lords, the ignorant and the denier of religion – are not as potent as the enemy within; and to the extent that the heart harbors that enemy, the heart is the first thing that must be transformed. In other words, the essence of transformation is a change in the moral attitude, in the inner being of the person who desires it. Once this change has been achieved, the change in general behavior is but a matter of time. It is the same for society: once its inner soul inclines to noble virtues the outward manifestation of superior attitudes will follow naturally. 'Abdullahi expressed the point pertinently:

> "Begin with yourself, turning away from the abyss of lust.
> It is in the pastures of lust that you are tending your flocks;
> And verily you set a bad example;
> The most harmful of enemies is one who dwells in your own house;
> Obedient to Satan and loathing Religion."

But how should the enemy within be fought? There are three means to do it. The first is to move closer to Allah, to seek refuge in Him, through the *nawāfil,* which we have already discussed. The second is what 'Abdullahi called "scanty food", that is the training of the body to adapt to austere measures. Allah entrusts civilization to "empty-bellied people" – people whose personal discipline gives them a will and a determination that are decidedly superior to the indiscipline and delinquency of the prevailing order. Men of change, certainly, cannot afford to live the same lifestyle as those whom they oppose. "Scanty food," said 'Abdullahi, "is the medicine which cures diseases of the soul." The third means involves the acquisition of moral and social discipline. In 'Abdullahi 's words:

> "Guard the two small things and the two hollow things;
> And watch over the spies always;
> So that your limbs may obey you."

In other words, the scholar must bring his vital, socially inclined organs under his control, so that he can influence society and also so that he can be safe from society and society safe from him. The scholar should keep his tongue from idle speech, from blasphemous utterances, from condemning people's beliefs and actions without definite authority, and from all slander and abuse. He should also keep his heart from preoccupation with false hopes, base desires, greed, incitement to sin, rebellion, rancor and countless other evil intentions. The tongue and the heart constitute the "two small things" mentioned by 'Abdullahi.

Similarly, the "two hollow things" – the mouth and the private parts – should be firmly controlled, the mouth from taking unlawful foods gained by embezzlement, perfidy, bribery, swindling, theft, and all other forms of unjust enrichment, and the private parts from excesses, from violating the honor and sanctity of women, and from unlawful violation of others' chastity.

The "spies", of course, are the eyes and ears. The eyes should not violate the cherished privacy of others, or look at things disapproved of by the sacred law, or be unduly inquisitive. The ears should not listen to what does not concern their owner, nor eavesdrop on the conversation and intimacy of others. What 'Abdullahi was calling for was a profoundly disciplined personality with dignity, respect and sanctity.

Above all, the scholar must, in his private and public life, and in mobilizing the public, follow the laws laid down in the Qur'an and Sunnah, take the practical examples laid down by the Prophet 🙼 himself, as well as the example of his Companions 🙼, and those who followed them. This, 'Abdullahi said, "is the antidote of the righteous man".

As to the question of what a scholar who finds no favorable response from the people should do, 'Abdullahi's answer was that firstly, the scholar is under an Islamic obligation to enjoin the good and prohibit evil; secondly, he is also under an obligation to undertake the task of conveying the Islamic message. The obligation, as such, stands on its own and so is not subject to the reactions of the people to it, be they favorable or otherwise. Significantly, 'Abdullahi pointed out that people's acceptance of it depends entirely on the will of Allah. If it is His desire that they accept, accept they must, if not, they never will. In the words of 'Abdullahi:

> "The fertile parts of the earth put forth herbage wondrously,
> By the permission of its Lord, if abundant rain pours down;
> But in barren ground nothing will grow, not even the meanest weed,

Even if continuous rain pours down, (without His permission).
The lack of their acceptance will not prevent religious instruction.
The one who makes them enter is the Lord; you are simply the one who opens the door;
And verily, if you have informed them, their excuse is useless.
The Lord gives them to drink, you only mix the draught."

'Abdullahi suggested that the "draught" should comprise a number of books mainly on *fiqh*, *tawḥīd* and *taṣawwuf*, in line with the movement's idea of calling the people to *Imān*, Islam and *Iḥsān*.

"And books which pay heed to the Sunnah like *Madkhal* –
And those derived from it – in these there is sound advice;
And Kiniya, *Iḥyā' as-Sunnah* and *Lubāb Ṭarīq aṣ-Ṣalihīn* (are) advantageous;
Those by al-Ghazali and also those by az-Zarrūq,
And those of lbn 'Ata – by these evil things are cured;
As well as those from Bijai or those similar to them.
One who is enamored of the world, leading a wicked life
Will have nothing to do with them."

'Abdullahi also warned the *'ulamā'* that they had an obligation to support the Shehu's call. If they did not, they would be the losers, while the Shehu would succeed and benefit other people. "The misfortunes of some people are the advantage of other people." In any case, the Shehu's cause was bound to prevail, regardless of his tribe's rejection, so the choice was not for the Shehu, but for them.

"And if relationship alone were of profit in religion,
Then Abū Tālib, the uncle of the Prophet would not have perished or grieved.
It does not harm the sun that blind men deny its light.
It does not harm the pool, that the camels which refuse to drink, decline it.

Whosoever gives thanks, that shall profit him,
And whosoever is ungrateful for blessings and follows lusts
In this world, to say nothing of the next, he shall perish!"

The *Risālat*, according to 'Abdullahi, was received with great enthusiasm by his people. We should not assume that it was sent to ignorant men. The Shehu's tribe contained a substantial number of the most cultured men in Hausaland, whose joining of the mainstream of the movement constituted a landmark in its growth. In the words of 'Abdullahi:

> "When this poem reached the *'ulamā'* of our tribe they received it well and began to make religion manifest among it: men such as al-Mustafa b. al-Ḥājj, Muhammad Sa'ad, Abū Bark b. Abdullah ...and others. And the strongest of them in setting up religion and in toiling for it was al-Mustafa, because he was the first to receive this message, and he read it to the community and ordered them to obedience. Then he tucked up his sleeves, and composed (quintals) on the message, mixing them like water with wine, emphasizing victory for what was in (the message) and acceptance of it. Then our brother Zed al-Athari explained it; Allah have mercy upon them all."

6. Reviving the Sunnah

THE GOAL of *tajdīd*, as we have stressed, is to bring about an all-embracing transformation of society. The means employed include calling people to religion, commanding the good and prohibiting evil, and working relentlessly to demolish the edifices of innovation. They also include establishing, once again, the supremacy of the Sunnah. The *mujaddid*'s ultimate ambition is to establish a society that approximates as closely as possible to the original Prophetic community.

That precisely was the Shehu's ambition and his declared goal. His purpose, he reiterated continually, was to revive the Sunnah and annihilate satanic innovations that had either crept into the social fabric or had been an exotic imposition on its culture and traditions. We have so far examined his concept of *amr wa nahy* and have briefly examined the content of some of his public lectures, seeing the great efforts he expended in educating society in the principles of Islam. What remains for us is to see how he set about reviving the Sunnah and demolishing innovations, thereby reshaping the beliefs, thinking, practices and the very character of Hausa society.

In doing that, we have to take a very close look at the Shehu's monumental work – indeed his *magnum opus* if we agree with Ismail Balogun – which we may consider not only as our basic reference for this matter but also as the summary of everything the Shehu taught and preached. This work is the *Iḥyā' as-Sunnah wa Ikhmād al-Bid'ah*. The book is unique in two respects. Firstly, it is a book of practical, social and moral education, which focuses its attention entirely on Hausa society with the sole object of rectifying its wrongful practices and guiding it aright. There is no theory in it. Everything it deals with was actually practised by the society it was addressing. Secondly, it is a book of protest, albeit of a legal nature and albeit restrained. In a way, it takes the line of al-Barnawi's *Shurb az-Zulāl*, except that the *Iḥyā'* was written by a *mujaddid* and is a textbook of living *tajdīd*.

Its thirty-three chapters deal with the three fundamental issues of the Shehu's message: *Imān*, Islam and *Iḥsān*, with Islam – the regulation of the daily life of society – taking up twenty-seven chapters. Both *Imān* and *Iḥsān* have one chapter each, one chapter is devoted to the Sunnah in its broader sense and one to innovations. It is our intention here to consider ten of the chapters with a view to understanding the state of Islam in the Shehu's society and the methodology he employed to tackle its problems through a peaceful, though vigorously educational, mobilization of society.

Principles of Social Mobilization

The principles he laid down in the introduction to the *Iḥyā'* are so important that we prefer to call them principles of social mobilization, for, if we want to know why the Shehu succeeded where others had failed in their efforts to bring about an abiding social transformation, it is because the Shehu, throughout his active struggle, adhered to certain tenets which facilitated his work and encouraged people to flock to him.

The first of these principles is that the revival of the Sunnah and removal of innovations, that is, the reorientation of society on Islamic lines, rests fundamentally on counseling and sincere advice (*naṣīḥah*) to Muslims. It categorically precludes bringing shame on them or finding fault with them.

"Whoever has as his intention the unveiling of the

> secrets of the people and preoccupation with their faults, Allah, certainly, will call him to account and take him to task, because whoever pursues the weakness of his brother, Allah will pursue his weakness until He exposes him, even if he is in the seclusion of his own house."

Faultfinding and putting people to shame, even under the pretext of seeking a social transformation, constitutes "a grave risk and a tremendous sin" and it is hypocritical. He referred to the *ḥadīth* of ʿĪsā ﷺ: "Do not look at the wrong actions of other people as if you were lords. Rather look at your own wrong actions as if you were slaves."

Secondly, the purpose of striving for the establishment of the Sunnah means, by implication, attracting people to the fold of Islam, reassuring them in their faith and actions, and not rejecting them. Rejecting people is as great a sin as searching for their weaknesses. In any case, the Shehu stated, finding a valid legal justification to repudiate a person for an action he has done is not only difficult but also almost impossible, since, for that to happen, there has to be the unanimous consensus of the great jurists that such an act is absolutely illegal. People should not be reproached except for a violation of the most fundamental principles of religion, concerning which the *ummah* is unanimous as to their binding nature or their prohibition. But this, of course, does not prevent the caller from guiding people by the use of good counsel (*naṣīḥah*) and excellent exhortation.

The Shehu's third principle is that healthy intellectual growth is essential for an all-round transformation of society. Therefore, the view of other scholars on derivative aspects of the law (*furūʿ*) must not only be accommodated but also encouraged, even if they conflict with the opinions of the established scholars, as long as they do not conflict with the Qur'an and Sunnah. Although consensus is to be preferred, a person is perfectly within his rights to choose any opinion he likes in the school of his choice. The reason for accommodating and encouraging divergent views and opinions is to make religion easy and within the reach of every person. Common people, however, should not be subjected to unnecessary burdens in practising religion. Though they must have a certain standard of education in their faith, worship and social life, they should essentially be left with their basic religious duties and occupations, and no more.

The opinions of the jurists, he maintained, are all paths leading to paradise and roads leading to success, therefore: "whoever follows any of the roads, it will certainly lead him to where the jurists have reached, and whoever deviates from the path, it is said to him, 'Away with you!'"

The fourth principle is that it is not permitted for a person calling to the way of Allah – or anyone else for that matter – to hate the sinners among the people of *lā ilāha illallāh* any more than he should hate the righteous among them. This principle is of extreme importance because it lies at the very roots of the philosophy of *tajdīd*. If a movement, which is intent on improving the intellectual perception and moral quality of people, insists on having only those whom it considers good and upright and rejects those it considers immoral, does it not render its work fruitless?

The very essence of *tajdīd* is the raising of people from the abyss of moral decadence they have fallen into and this is lost the moment they are rejected as sinners. Indeed, if everybody were righteous and excellent, there would be no need at all for *tajdīd* to take place. A social movement is judged, not by the number of good people it is able to attract to itself, but by the extent to which it is able to lift sinners out of the abyss of darkness into the light, and the extent to which it is able to transform society from a state of moral decadence into a state of honor and justice.

The sinner, the Shehu explained, may be 'hated' for his sins, but must at the same time be loved for being a Muslim. In addition, a Muslim is under an obligation to give due respect to a fellow Muslim even though he is a sinner. It is by his faith that a believer manifests his relationship to Allah, whether he is pious or not, whether he is truthful or not. This expression of relationship has the effect of conferring dignity and inviolability on him and makes it obligatory for other Muslims to honor and respect him as much as possible and to refrain from either looking down upon him or disgracing him.

The last principle is that the caller must strive for the unity of all Muslims. The people of *Lā ilāha illallāh*, the Shehu explained, have a common bond with Allah, and they are, as such, all close to Him and members of one family. So close, indeed, that if they were to fall into error and commit as many sins as would almost fill the whole earth, Allah would still meet them with a similar amount of forgiveness, so long as they do not worship gods other than Him. It is a grave error, therefore, to nurse hatred for such people, for that is prohibited, and Allah has made known the punishment of such warring against His *awliyā* in this world and the next. Hostility is allowed only against an enemy of Allah – and that is anyone who worships a god other than Allah.

These principles were clearly enunciated in response to a situation which the Shehu considered unhelpful to the cause of Islam. It was a situation in which preaching was merely a barrage of insults and denunciation. This proved to be valueless and counterproductive to the extent that it alienated the scholars from the whole body of Muslims whose attention was ostensibly being sought. The approach to issues of faith and law was narrow and rigid and this stultified thought and reduced the practice of the law to its letter, losing its spirit. It was a situation in which ordinary people were regarded with contempt, being considered sinful and ignorant by those who claimed to be guiding them. The consequence of this was that they were not educated, their lot was not improved, they were not raised morally and they were divided along frivolous, sectarian lines.

That the Shehu did not rely solely on a method such as *da'wah* (calling to the way of Allah) was indeed one of his major achievements. To him what the Muslims needed and what they would always need was *naṣīḥah*, sincere and sympathetic guidance to right conduct, and education in the principles of worship and the transactions of daily life. Indeed, the Prophet ﷺ himself said that religion is *naṣīḥah*. Muslims, as far as the Shehu was concerned, had no need of uncouth or depraved language from the *'ulamā'*, nor does Islam allow that as a means of educating and guiding people.

Similarly, as far as the Shehu was concerned, the generality of Muslims, though ignorant of religion and slack in its observance, did not need to be repudiated, condemned and alienated as sinners. They needed reassurance, understanding and patience from those who sought to guide them, more so when their ignorance and laxity could be traced to the excesses of the very leaders whom the majority of the *'ulamā'* supported.

The correct way to approach the people, as the Shehu quoting Imam Al-Yusi in *al-Amr* noted, is *alā sabīl al-luṭf* – through kindness and friendliness – as one would naturally expect from members of the family of Allah. In the same vein, Muslims do not need to be divided and subdivided into countless fragmentary groups in the name of *da'wah*. Employing a method which leads to that is counterproductive and malicious. The factors which instigate one scholar to plunge Muslims prematurely into a nihilistic war of self-annihilation are the same as those which cause another to create discord and tension among Muslims, keeping them perpetually at war with each other, so that their real enemy gains the upper hand. Differences in opinion are vital, according to the Shehu, for the health of society since "difference of opinion is a mercy", but to quarrel over what is essentially a source of mercy for Muslims is to insist on inflicting a wound on the family of Allah.

Errors in Hausa Society

Islamic society is a society which is governed by the Qur'an, Sunnah and *ijmā'*, and one which safeguards itself continuously against the inroads of *bid'ah* or innovation.

What the *Iḥyā'* sought to do was to re-establish the supremacy of the Qur'an, Sunnah and *ijmā'* in those areas where *bid'ah* had infiltrated. In Professor Balogun's translation:

> "If you have become certain of the obligation to adhere to the Book, the Sunnah and *ijmā'* from what we have said, then let the weight of your deeds conform with them. For every religious duty you intend to perform, ask those who know whether it is Sunnah, so that you may carry it out, or *bid'ah* so that you may shun it."

But what is *bid'ah*? *Bid'ah*, the Shehu said, is what is extraneous to the Qur'an, Sunnah and *ijmā'* – a new matter introduced into religion but not in fact truly part of it, though it has the facade of being part of it either in essence or by resemblance. For a thing to be regarded as *bid'ah*, however, it is not enough that it is just new; it must also constitute a negation of the essence of the three sources. If novelty is consistent with the spirit of the law and advances the cause of Islam it is not considered extraneous. Thus, the *ḥadīth* of the Prophet ﷺ, "Whoever introduces in this affair of ours (i.e. Islam) something that does not belong to it shall be rejected," should be applied only to things which vitiate or nullify religion.

On the strength of this postulate, the Shehu gave us three broad categories of *bid'ah*. The first – the good *bid'ah* – consists of those matters which the *Sharī'ah* considers as either obligatory or recommended, though they were not practised during the lifetime of the Prophet ﷺ. To this category belong the compilation of the Qur'an, the *tarāwīh* prayer, and the establishment of schools and defense systems.

The second category – the repugnant *bid'ah* – is that which the *Sharī'ah* considers either to be prohibited or disapproved of, in addition to the fact that it was unknown in earlier generations. To this group belong such state policies as illegal and unjust taxation, giving preference to ignorant men over learned men in appointments to public offices, appointing leaders on the basis of lineage, and going beyond what is expressly stipulated in worship.

The third category – the permissible *bid'ah* – is that which the *Sharī'ah* permits, though it was not practised by earlier generations. Technical innovations which make life easier, taking delicious food and drink and living in beautiful houses are in this category. This distinction between the various categories of *bid'ah* is essential, the Shehu maintained, so that one knows that not every *bid'ah* is reprehensible or extraneous to the law and that an action should be judged according to the category of *bid'ah* to which it belongs.

Innovations in Faith

We are now in a position to look at some of the specific aspects which the *Iḥyā'* dealt with in the area of *Imān*, Islam and *Iḥsān*, in order to ascertain not only the Shehu's notion of society but also his method of protest and of re-shaping it. We will start with faith.

What it took to belong to the *ummah*, the Shehu said, was a person's affirmation of the faith and whoever did so was considered a Muslim and was governed and protected by Islamic law. He could marry from the Muslim community; he could lead the prayer; his food was lawful; he could inherit and bequeath and be buried in a Muslim graveyard. People are judged in this world according to what is apparent and, therefore, no one's heart should be examined to uncover its secrets. "It is not for us to suspect the faith of any Muslim, be he an ordinary person or otherwise, since the heart is not the place where a person's faith can be scrutinized." The heart is beyond reach of any other than Allah.

It is sufficient for the common man to believe in the essentials of the faith. He is not expected to exert his mind in deducing reasons for them. His faith is in no way impaired simply because he cannot prove it intellectually. It is vital, however, for people of intellect – *ahlu-l-baṣīra* – to reflect on the essence of religion, since "religion is built on clear insight" and this is even more the case when they engage in *da'wah*. The various forms of *bid'ah* which had been introduced into the field of faith included: going to extremes in matters of religion, involving the common people in fruitless arguments on religion, invalidating their faith and plunging into intricate and often irrelevant philosophical speculations. Philosophical speculations about faith – *'ilm al-kalām* – might be justified as a means of protecting the faith from unbelieving or heretical philosophers, and might be useful for the intellectuals, but they are of no use to the faith of the majority of Muslims.

Innovations in the Practice of the Law

The Shehu thought it necessary to stress certain aspects of marriage. A person should marry with the sole purpose of "establishing the Sunnah", in other words, for purely Islamic reasons. People should marry as soon as they can afford it, because the Prophet ﷺ said, "Oh young men! Those of you who can support a wife should marry, for it restrains the eyes and preserves morality." A person should look for a spouse with a religious disposition. No one should seek in marriage a woman whom a fellow Muslim is already intending to marry. The guardians of a woman should not prevent her from marrying a person of her choice who fulfills the Islamic requirements of marriage. And finally, a *walīmah* – marriage feast – should be celebrated.

The Shehu was particularly bitter about a prevalent custom whereby the guardians of a woman took the dowry instead of giving it to her, and the custom for men and women to gather indiscriminately for the *walīmah* and behave in an unbecoming manner. He also condemned the practice of "bed due" – a pervasive custom in Hausaland which stipulated that a husband should pay money to his wife for his first conjugal association with her. To the Shehu, this had a semblance of prostitution. Why should people not do what the Prophet ﷺ suggested: perform *ṣalāt* and pray for Allah's blessing on their marriage?

In the matter of trade, the Shehu stressed that according to the Sunnah, buying, selling and giving credit should all be conducted with gentleness and kindness, and he quoted the *ḥadīth* of the Prophet ﷺ, "May Allah show mercy to a man who is kindly when he sells, when he buys and when he makes a claim!" A debtor should be allowed more time to repay if he is in difficult circumstances. If possible, his debt should be remitted altogether. There should never be deceit or fraud in business transactions.

Certain forms of *bid'ah* had been introduced into trade in Hausaland. One was allowing ignorant men to engage in business for themselves in markets or to serve as agents for others. This was wrong, because such a person would not know the laws governing business transactions. To let him do business was gross negligence not allowed in matters of religion. The next *bid'ah* was the custom of sending women to trade while the men stayed at home, which he likened to habits of Europeans.

Women are not expected, by law, to mix unnecessarily with men and the market place in particular is not a healthy forum for the meeting of men and women. A further *bid'ah* was that women, who out of necessity were forced to transact business themselves, did not acquire the necessary knowledge of the law. A woman has to be taught the rules of trade and business, because this knowledge is as obligatory as the knowledge of prayer and fasting. Once she has learned the law, she can carry on business if she has no one to undertake it on her behalf.

Regarding the administration of the law, the Shehu first stressed that the *Sharī'ah* should be implemented as an act of respect and veneration for Allah. He also emphasized that, in the dispensation of justice, high and low should be treated equally. He made reference to the *ḥadīth* of the Prophet ﷺ who said, when some people wanted to intercede on behalf of a highly-placed woman who had committed theft: "What destroyed your predecessors was simply that when a person of rank among them committed a theft they let him alone but when a weak one of their number committed a theft they inflicted the prescribed punishment on them. I swear by

Allah that if Fatimah, daughter of Muhammad, were to steal I would have her hand cut off."

Judgment, the Shehu continued, should be based on the evidence before the judge and judges should maintain perfect neutrality towards both sides in a dispute and should not give judgment when in the heat of anger.

Other innovations which had been introduced included the substitution of fines, "out of greed for money", in place of prescribed punishments. Ignorant people were appointed as judges in preference to learned people, or incompetent people were given the office because their parents had been judges. Further innovations included giving judgment on tribal lines to promote selfish interests.

In the matter of clothing the Shehu stressed, among other things, the need for a person to wear what was within his means, to have a preference for white clothes, to avoid clothes made of silk, and not to be arrogant in matters of dress. On the question of *bid'ah*, the Shehu disapproved of clothes with long and wide sleeves, the kind worn in almost every part of West Africa, since it is not permitted for a man to add to his clothes what is not needed or necessary, though this was permitted in the case of a woman. Significantly, he noted that, notwithstanding this disapproval, the wearing of flowing robes did, nevertheless, have a purpose. It enhanced the prestige of judges and men in authority, thus indirectly advancing the prestige of Islam.

The wearing of dignified robes, therefore, is allowed when circumstance make it necessary, because "the conditions of Imams and men in authority change in line with the changes in cities, times, generations and situations, so they need to adopt new forms of adornment and new policies which were not needed in the past, and these might even be obligatory in certain circumstances." Thus, what is disapproved of by the law may become imperative for political, diplomatic or social reasons.

This principle became a serious matter of contention in the later period of the movement. A good number of *bid'ah* which were disapproved of or even prohibited could be raised to the status of the permissible, recommended, or even obligatory when circumstances change. It is for this reason that scholars have often been told that they should not be dogmatic or extremist.

A *bid'ah* on which, according to the Shehu, there was a consensus of opinion was that it was forbidden for a woman to have a dirty and unkempt appearance at home but to appear clean and smart when going out.

On the subject of food, the Shehu stressed that meals should be taken with humility; that the servant who prepared the meal should be made to share in it; and that proper hygiene should be observed. The Shehu was concerned about two kinds of *bid'ah* regarding food. One was the earmarking of specific dishes for certain individuals, usually the heads of families, which was prohibited if arrogance or pride was intended; otherwise it was merely disapproved of. It was essential for people to eat in groups, the Shehu emphasized, so that they could benefit from each other's blessings and take care of the poor amongst them.

The Shehu was also concerned about the practice – most common among the wealthy – of giving women "the causes to grow fat". This is prohibited if it interferes in the practice of religion or causes injury to her health – if not it is merely disapproved of but he noted that obesity, which is generally the result of excessive eating, is a violation of the sacred law. It is a waste of money and it could lead to a woman having to uncover part of her body, or worse, it could result in her inability to perform her obligatory duties, such as standing for prayer.

There is disapproval, the Shehu said, of a person eating without placing water at his side, because by so doing he could "cause his own destruction". Similarly, he should not drink water in large draughts nor rush to his meal while it is too hot. A person should not engage in excessive joking while eating for fear that he might choke or cause another person to choke nor should he be too talkative or totally silent.

On the matter of entering another person's house, the Shehu maintained that permission should be sought three times. If none was given, you should leave. You should also seek permission before disturbing another person's privacy and announce your name if asked to do so. On greeting, you are required to greet whomever you meet, whether or not you know that person. The young should first greet the old, someone riding should greet someone walking, someone walking should greet someone sitting and a small company should greet a larger one. Shaking hands is recommended.

The *bid'ah* of bowing to greet another person – the practice of the poor in the community – is prohibited by consensus if one has to bow very low, and disapproved if it is not as low as the *rukū'*. Of course, bowing the head very low to the ground is much more serious, since it has the semblance of prostration, and even the ordinary bowing of the head is prohibited. A person should not remove his hat or cap as a sign of respect during greetings because that amounts to imitating non-Muslims. In this category, also, falls the waving of the fingers or hands in greeting. The former is the custom of Jews, the latter of Christians.

Innovations in *Iḥsān*

We now come to the important question of *Iḥsān* which, the Shehu stated, constitutes living as the Prophet ﷺ lived. And this involves several things. One of them is endeavoring to conquer distraction and absent mindedness in worship and seeking to perfect it by keeping in mind always that you are, in reality, in the presence of Allah.

Iḥsān demands that a person should seek nearness to Allah by diligently performing the obligatory duties as well as the *nawāfil*. The Shehu here quoted the *ḥadīth* in which Allah said, "No one draws near to Me with anything dearer to Me than what I have made obligatory for him." A person should seek nearness to Allah by abandoning what Allah has prohibited and what is disapproved of. Efforts to avoid what is prohibited should be as great, if not greater, than efforts to perform one's obligations, for the prevention of corruption takes precedence over the pursuit of good.

Iḥsān demands that you should never regard yourself as superior to any other person in the eyes of Allah, for no one is sure of what his ultimate end will be. In addition, you should endeavor to develop the qualities of faith within yourself; there are as many as sixty of them.

People punishing themselves, by beating the body with sticks, iron bars or branding it with hot substances is a forbidden *bid'ah* by consensus. Similarly, it is forbidden to seek spiritual perfection by having recourse to ways and methods that are prohibited by law. Good can never be achieved through recourse to evil. Amusements such as beating drums to heighten spiritual ecstasy are forbidden innovations. It is also forbidden to perform a deed on the basis of something seen in a dream, since that would conflict with the *Sharī'ah*. It is, finally, a prohibited *bid'ah* to regard yourself as having reached a station with Allah in which you are absolved of the responsibilities and duties that are enjoined on every other Muslim.

Advice for the *'Ulamā'*

We conclude with an examination of further principles of social transformation outlined in the *Iḥyā'*. We considered five of them at the beginning of the discussion. The rest come now at the end as they do in the *Iḥyā'* itself.

Preaching, or more appropriately the effort to transform society, is essentially a peaceful process, which should not be discordant or create deliberate tension or disorder, for there is no way in which people can ever be changed by force. If there is to be any use of force at all, it should not be initiated, encouraged, or invited by a person whose work requires peace and reasoning.

The scholar has two responsibilities in his search for knowledge and its dispensation. He should seek those aspects of knowledge that are relevant to the needs of his society, because the possessor of such knowledge is "a precious gem". He should disseminate his knowledge with absolute humility, bearing in mind that, like any other human being, he is subject to "error, misinterpretation and digression" and that he alone cannot comprehend everything.

The duty to educate the people, wherever they are, is absolutely binding on scholars. The responsibility for change and transformation is theirs. If scholars fail to perform this duty, they will incur the wrath of Allah.

Know that it is obligatory on every learned person not to keep quiet when innovations have appeared and spread. The *ḥadīth* says: "When tribulations appear and the learned one keeps quiet, on him then is the curse of Allah." Most of the people are ignorant of the *Sharī'ah* and it is obligatory that, in every mosque and quarter in the town, there should be a *faqīh* teaching the people their religion.

A man who intends to strive against corruption and for a better society must start with himself. This is a principle which one comes across at all stages in the thought of the movement:

> "It is incumbent on every scholar to begin with himself and to get used to practising the obligatory duties and avoiding forbidden practices. He should then teach that to his family and relations. He should then proceed to his neighbors, then to the people of his quarter, the inhabitants of his town, the surrounding suburbs of his city and so on to the farthest part of the world... This is the foremost concern of anyone to whom the matter of his religion is important."

Finally, there must be a belief in the mind of the scholar who undertakes the task of social change, that the salvation of the *ummah* lies solely in the revival of the Sunnah. In the past, it was the Sunnah that saved this *ummah* from disintegration, and nothing will save it from such a fate except the Sunnah.

The Shehu ended his book with these words from Abū al-Abbas al-Abyani, one of the Andalusians: "There are three things which could be written on something as small as a fingernail but which contain the good of this world and the next: Imitate, do not innovate; be humble, do not be arrogant; be cautious, do not be too accommodating."

7. The Intellectual War

THE MOST serious obstacle encountered by the Shehu in his efforts to transform Hausaland came from the *'ulamā' as-sū'*, the corrupt scholars. While the challenge posed by the kings was basically political, the *'ulamā' as-sū'* challenged the Shehu intellectually. If he had failed to face up to them, his movement would have lost the moral and intellectual battle – a prerequisite for winning the social and political battles which lay ahead. Conflict with the *'ulamā' as-sū'* raged from the time the Shehu became prominent to the end of his life.

The issues of contention were many. The Shehu listed almost ninety points of disagreement with them in his *Ḥisn al-Afhām*. We shall limit our discussion to four broad issues of contention: the necessity for the mobilization of Muslims, the ideological division of the Muslim community, the mobilization of women and the membership of the Muslim community.

Mobilization of the Muslims

While the debate covered a range of issues, we shall focus on the objections raised about the propriety of mass mobilization and the social and moral dimensions of the debate.

The scholars tried to discredit the entire career of the Shehu. For his part, the Shehu refuted their objections and arguments. The scholars criticized the Shehu's call to the people on several grounds. They argued that the duty to call stands only when people respond favorably to it. The Shehu argued that a person must call to Islam irrespective of whether the call is accepted or not. The scholars remonstrated further that, even if the call were right, silence would be preferable. The Shehu countered by saying that although silence is a praiseworthy habit, silence in the face of corruption and social evil is harmful. He referred to the *ḥadīth* of the Prophet ﷺ, "Hold your tongue except in matters of benefit (to people)."

The scholars stated that customs that had become pervasive and prevalent in society should, as a result of that prevalence, be regarded as Sunnah, and by implication, it would be wrong to attack them, let alone seek to displace them. This was a rather clumsy way of justifying the immoral and oppressive customs of Hausaland and legitimizing a corrupt social order. This claim was also used as an excuse by the *'ulamā'* for their embarrassing silence over tyranny and social injustice. The Shehu countered this by saying: "One of our brothers recalled that he heard one of these *'ulamā'* saying that the prohibition of evil in the land of evil is the real evil and that this was the reason that they did not prohibit any of the evils in society."

The *'ulamā'* maintained that even if, in the circumstances of Hausaland, the duty to call for social change was obligatory, it had nevertheless to depend on an Imam, or at least one who was perfect in behavior, since ordinary people had no share in this function. The Shehu asserted that as long as no fighting is involved this duty devolves on every Muslim. An Imam is only essential when a stage of armed struggle has been reached. And he further maintained that there is no need for an individual to attain moral perfection in order to undertake this task. A scholar who acknowledges his moral deficiency can still raise his voice against social injustice and moral evils in society, since his deficiency does not legally bind him to silence. The common people, moreover, have their own share in this function, since Islamic prohibitions and commandments are a matter of common knowledge.

By saying this the Shehu was implying that a person did not have to be a scholar to know that there was injustice in society, that embezzlement of state resources was wrong, or that forced conscription into the army or oppressive taxation imposed by Hausa rulers was wrong. Nor did a person have to be a scholar to know that Islam commanded justice and moral rectitude, ordained prayer, fasting and *zakāt*, and prohibited theft, adultery, confiscation of property and aggression. Where a matter transcended common knowledge, however, then it should be left to the experts, the Shehu said.

The scholars further objected to the Shehu's call on the grounds that his attacks on social evils amounted to extremism in matters of religion, especially when such evils were common practice. The Shehu replied that the ease, which the Prophet ﷺ recommended, applies to the non-fundamentals of religion and could not therefore be construed as allowing people license to flout the laws of Allah or renege on their fundamental Islamic duties.

Here the Shehu seemed to make a distinction between the need to transform people through a gradual process of moral education – in which the caller has to accept people's moral failings at times, hoping for progressive moral growth – and outright compromise with the evils being perpetrated by society. For if evils in society, especially those threatening the Islamic order directly, were to be condoned and accepted as necessary evils, then society would never be transformed. The *'ulamā'* desired to maintain the status quo precisely because their livelihood was derived from it and they owed their prestige and unearned privilege to it.

Finally, the *'ulamā'* contended that it is wrong to teach *tafsīr* – Qur'anic exegesis – to the masses, since doing this is likely to provoke misfortunes such as drought or social tension. And even if *tafsīr* were necessary, then it should only be taught in the villages and not in the cities, to the old men and not to the youth. They also maintained that it was wrong for a preacher to quote verses of the Qur'an to support his teaching.

In his reply, the Shehu stated that those who believed that the teaching of the meaning of the Qur'an to the people would bring misfortune on society were unbelievers and outside the frontiers of Islam. As for those who claimed that the Qur'an should be taught only in the villages, the Shehu asserted that they were wrong. The Qur'an has been sent to all people. He rebuffed the objection of the *'ulamā'* to quotations from the Qur'an being used by those inviting people to Islam, reminding them that Allah has commanded that the Qur'an should be utilized in inviting mankind to Islam. The contention of the *'ulamā'*, he insisted, implied that the Qur'an was applicable and relevant to the generation of the Prophet ﷺ alone, while in reality it is intended for the whole of mankind and for every age.

Other contentions on the part of the *'ulamā'* offer some insight into the difference between the Shehu and his men on the one hand, and the *'ulamā' as-sū'* on the other. They also give us a glimpse into the respective attitudes of the two groups on a number of issues, especially *da'wah*, intellectual endeavor and moral growth. This category of criticisms was probably directed at the *Jama'a* as a whole and not at the Shehu alone.

The *'ulamā'* branded the Shehu's call to Islam as a censuring of the people and, by implication, as fundamentally un-Islamic. The Shehu countered their criticism by affirming that what he and his people were doing was aimed at benefiting the people and was based on tenderness, compassion and sympathy towards them and a desire for their moral transformation. It was *naṣīḥah* – counseling and good advice – not censure, which is aimed at disgracing, castigating and insulting people.

The members of the *Jama'a* were also branded as power-seekers because of their incessant call to the people. The call, the Shehu replied, was motivated by their love of Allah, their love of obedience to Him and their zeal for Islam. It appears that the Shehu's men dressed in a dignified fashion and the *'ulamā'* were quick to accuse them of being worldly.

However, a person who wishes to exalt Allah and elevate His religion must first dignify and elevate himself. If he appears shabby and unkempt, he dishonors Islam. The *'ulamā'* called this dignified conduct pride (*kibr*) whereas, in reality, it was nothing but respect for Islam.

Humility was an essential part of the training of the men who disseminated the message of Islamic revival. The *'ulamā'* could have interpreted this humility as self-abasement. The Shehu stated that humility emanates from a person's knowledge of Allah, his realization of his own limitations, his finiteness, and the paucity of the good deeds he has performed. This creates in him a sense of utter dejection before Allah, as well as compassion for his fellow men. Abasement, on the other hand, consists in squandering one's honor in order to obtain the fleeting pleasures of this world and humbling oneself before the men of the world – the Hausa rulers to be precise! The Shehu may here have been pointing an accusing finger at the scholars.

Patience was also an essential quality for those striving to bring about transformation. The pseudo-scholars interpreted this as insensitivity and hardness of the heart. The Shehu opposed this with the observation that the essence of patience is to restrain oneself from unnecessary anxiety and to make the heart patiently accept Allah's decree and remain within the framework of the *Sharī'ah*.

The donations that kept pouring in for the sustenance of the *Jama'a* were called bribery by the pseudo-scholars. "No," said the Shehu, "they are gifts freely given." They were intended to strengthen the love and solidarity within the *Jama'a*. Bribery has never been a means of strengthening love and brotherhood but has only ever been a tool used to defeat the truth and pervert the course of justice – an apparent reference to the acceptance of bribery in Hausa society by judges and the acceptance by the *'ulamā'* of gifts from rulers.

And how was it possible for such a large number of people – the scholars around the Shehu in particular – to be so indifferent to wealth and political patronage? The pseudo-scholars had a ready answer: lack of sophistication or even dull-wittedness. The Shehu asserted that it was the moral superiority of these people that accounted for their indifference to an easy and cheap life. They were people whose minds were at peace, free from greed and covetousness, whose consciences were easy and unaffected by evil machinations. Their concern was the Hereafter, which they were striving for in this world.

Finally, the pseudo-scholars argued that, since the books written by earlier scholars were sufficient for society, the books written by the Shehu and his companions were unnecessary. "This is pure jealousy," the Shehu declared. Contemporary scholars, he argued, know more about the fundamental issues facing their own society than earlier scholars could possibly have done and, therefore, their perception of those issues is more relevant to their society than that of earlier scholars.

The Subversive Parties

There was also the debate with the "satanic parties", those sectarian parties or groups the Shehu considered to be undermining the very foundations of society. The debate was fundamentally ideological for it touched on whether the Hausa society which the Shehu had been trying to transform was already Islamic, whether sinners could be considered Muslims, and whether the customs and traditions of Hausaland should be criticized or attacked with a view to replacing them with the true Islamic traditions and values. These were the subjects dealt with by the Shehu in his *Naṣā'iḥ al-Ummah al-Muḥammadiyyah.*

There was a group of scholars who believed that Islam was so firmly established in Hausaland that no one could be considered non-Muslim *ab initio* and, by implication, that the whole of society was therefore Muslim. If this were so, all efforts expended with the purpose of bringing unbelievers into the fold of Islam or of transforming society into an Islamic one would have been rendered meaningless. The Shehu refuted this assertion vehemently. There were in Hausaland people who denied essential tenets of Islamic faith such as the Resurrection, others who derided Islam, others who worshipped idols openly, and yet others who attacked Allah and denied the Prophet ﷺ. Even if such people professed the Islamic faith, they only did so because that was the norm, not out of conviction, for they remained firmly outside the fold of Islam.

At the other extreme, there was another party who denied the faith of the majority of the people and considered them unbelievers because they could not intellectually prove their faith. The Shehu condemned this group for violating the accepted Islamic principle, whereby anyone who declares himself Muslim and performs the rites of Islam is considered to be Muslim. Neither the Prophet ﷺ nor his Companions ﵃ used such exacting standards to judge people's faith.

A third party believed that those who committed major sins were unbelievers. This assertion, in effect, would transform the majority of the people into outright unbelievers and negate all efforts at their moral transformation. The Shehu regarded this declaration as entirely spurious and baseless. It was the stand of the *Khawārij* and the *Mu'tazilī*. Muslim scholars, he said, are agreed that a Muslim cannot be regarded as having become an unbeliever on account of his sins. The Islamic position rests on the *ḥadīth* of the Prophet ﷺ which says, "Leave alone the people of *lā ilāha illallāh*. Do not negate their belief because of their sin, for whoever negates their faith is himself closer to unbelief than they are." Even when groups of Muslims have apparently deviated from Islamic norms and practices, like the *Khawārij*, they should not be termed as unbelievers as long as they do not exhibit any signs of *shirk* (open idolatry).

In saying this, the Shehu overtly disagreed with his revered teacher Shaykh Jibril ibn 'Umar, who branded people as unbelievers for such sins as: marriage with more than four wives, improper dressing on the part of women, unrestrained mixing of men and women and the oppression of orphans. These do not constitute unbelief, the Shehu said, they are sins and no more. He noted that his teacher contradicted himself on this matter and, on the whole, his views were wrong. Short of *shirk* or outright legitimization of what Allah has forbidden or prohibition of what He has legalized, no sin, however great it may appear, could make a believer an unbeliever.

Ahlu-s-Sunnah are agreed, he said, that neither *fisq* (immoral action) nor *bid'ah* (innovation) can nullify the faith of a Muslim. As for his teacher, the Shehu stated that he went to extremes out of a desire to guide the people aright and frighten them away from unbelief, for he had a "vast compassion for this *ummah*". He deserved absolute respect from the *Jama'a* because, were it not for him, the *Jama'a* itself might never have come into being.

One group accepted the *status quo* and thought the customs and traditions of Hausaland were all right as they were, seeing no need for change. Some people, for instance, had virtually substituted *wuḍū'* with *tayammum*. The group raised no objection to this. The privacy of homes and sanctity due to women had been violated. Islamic social and moral norms were flouted. In social functions, people boasted of how much money they had lavished senselessly, thus disrupting the balance of society. Women worked and traded while their men sat idly at home.

Islamic laws of inheritance were not observed, which put children and women at an unjust disadvantage. The Shehu was particularly upset by the fact that women were denied their due share of inheritance. The common people had to bow their heads low to the ground to greet the nobles. The *'ulamā'* told the people sweet things about Allah's mercy but failed to warn them about His punishment, thus indirectly encouraging them in vice. The establishment party did not raise its voice against these evils. Because of all this the Shehu wrote:

> "Do these misled, foolish ignoramuses not know that it is blind following of their leaders and men of influence that caused the downfall of the unbelievers in the past, so that they regretted when regret could no longer be of any avail? The Most High says, concerning what they will say on the Day of Judgment, '*Our Lord, we obeyed our rulers and our men of influence and they led us astray*'."

By believing that everything was right in Hausaland, this "satanic party" was negating the very notion of *amr bi'l-ma'rūf*, and denying the necessity for change in the social order. "Did they not know," the Shehu asked, "that, were it not for continual efforts to bring about social change, the Islamic order would by now have crumbled completely?"

Membership of the Muslim Community

The debate about *Imān* (faith) was the one which was most heated and charged. It raged from the beginning of the Shehu's career to his death but he never flagged in guiding his own followers, persuading others to adopt the opinions of the great jurists and demolishing the "delusions" created by the *'ulamā'* about the faith of the common people. Bello said in *Infāq al-Maysūr* that the Shehu wrote as many as fifty books on this subject alone. Of these, we shall concentrate on two: *Tanbīh aṭ-Ṭalaba 'alā anna Allah Ta'āla Ma'rūf bil-Fiṭrah* and *Irshād Ahlu-t-Tafrīṭ wa-l-Ifrāṭ*.

We shall first of all give the gist of the arguments presented in *Irshād Ahlu-t-Tafrīṭ*, where the Shehu was concerned to guide the extremists to the right understanding of the fundamentals of religion.

All Islamic authorities are agreed on the principle that anyone who is not firm in his belief in Allah, His messengers, His Books, His angels and the Day of Judgment, and wavers with respect to it, is not a Muslim and is bound for eternal punishment in the Hereafter. A person's prayer, fasting or Ḥajj are of no avail if their faith is not absolute and unshakable. Nor would simply being among Muslims and uttering the noble testimony (*shahādah*) be any use, if a person did not know the meaning of what they were uttering.

On this basis someone is considered an unbeliever if they doubt the unity of Allah, the ephemeral nature of the world, the reality and permanence of the Hereafter, or the truth of prophethood. The same applies to someone who believes that Arabs have a share in the prophethood of Muhammad ﷺ or that one of his Companions is associated with it, or act on the basis of what they see in a dream when it is contrary to the *Sharī'ah*, or claim that they have received a revelation from Allah or that they have ascended to the heavens and entered paradise. It also applies to someone who expressly states that the affairs of the Hereafter are mere symbols and have no concrete existence, or denies that faith, prayer, fasting, *zakāt* and Ḥajj are obligatory, or denies that wine, murder, magic and so on, are prohibited.

As long as a person is firm in his belief in the fundamentals of faith, however, he cannot be regarded as an unbeliever, even if he holds wrong views regarding some of the attributes of Allah, provided, of course, that there is no consensus on the part of scholars that such views are tantamount to unbelief. For example, the belief that Allah is corporeal or speaks with a voice like humans, though absolutely wrong, does not amount to unbelief, since there is no unanimity among scholars regarding these things. It is in such scholastic and intellectual details of faith that the common people are sometimes deficient, not its fundamental aspects.

Therefore they need education, not repudiation. Four things, however, should be kept in mind. Firstly, that it is necessary for every Muslim to know the true meaning of the declaration, "There is no god but Allah, and Muhammad is the Messenger of Allah," so that his faith can be preserved from corruption. Secondly, that this is even more urgent when one considers that mere utterance of this testimony does not make one a believer if one's faith in it is not absolute. Thirdly, that this education must, as a matter of necessity, be extended to women and other such underprivileged members of society as servants, slaves and the children of the poor. Women especially should be educated, even if that entails their having to attend the same gathering as men. This is because ignorance regarding matters of faith is one of the things most likely to lead to hell in the Hereafter, whereas knowledge of them brings salvation.

The fourth thing to be borne in mind is that public education does not require the consent of the people concerned as "some devils who indulge themselves with memorizing the Qur'an without improving their own convictions" have claimed. The duty of public education is obligatory according to the Qur'an, Sunnah and *ijmāʿ*. It should also be conducted in a language people understand since the objective is to provide people with an intelligent understanding of their faith.

Those who condemn the faith of the common people do so for evil purposes. They, in fact, want to preclude their learning and understanding the faith. Whoever does so "is a devil, an obstacle in the way of Allah, who wants to leave the ignorant person perpetually impaired in his faith." It is a grave danger on the part of a Muslim to regard another Muslim as an unbeliever or to subject his faith to suspicion, because the Prophet ﷺ said, "When a person calls his brother an unbeliever, it returns (at least) to one of them."

Many pseudo-scholars hastily declare those who disagree with their position to be unbelievers, while, in fact, it is they who fall into unbelief, "because whoever believes that a Muslim is an unbeliever is, in actual fact, saying that his religion, Islam, is unbelief. This vitiates his own belief and so the laws governing an unbeliever become applicable to him." This underscores the true danger inherent in branding people as unbelievers.

The branding of common people as unbelievers by some students is due to their deficient and improper understanding of the books of *ʿilm al-kalām* (theological theory), which they read "without the guidance of scholars". Their conclusions are invariably based on their failure to grasp the import of what they have read. Some of the views they have read are those of Ibn al-Qāsim, Abū Zakariyya, al-Waghlisi, Muhammad Ibn 'Umar, al-Awjali and Muhammad at-Tāhir, who maintained, for instance, that unbelievers can be categorized in a considerable number of ways: the simple, the complex, the doubter, the suspicious and the deluded. They did not appreciate the fact that such classification is basically theoretical, since the actuality of whether a person may or may not be a complex unbeliever, or a simple unbeliever, or indeed some other category of unbeliever, is something hidden in their heart and, therefore, in fact unascertainable.

They also asserted that anyone who does not know the names and attributes of Allah is an unbeliever because of one scholar who asked, "How can you worship One Whom you are ignorant of?" What they failed to understand is that in Islam a person is never required to know the details of the attributes of Allah before worshipping Him. If this were so, then a person embracing Islam should neither pray nor fast nor perform any of the duties of Islam until he has learned every detail about faith. These details are mere intellectual exercises. Nevertheless it is clear that people should strive to acquire the knowledge of *tawḥīd* in order to improve their faith. It is also the case that knowledge about faith should be derived primarily from the Qur'an and Sunnah, rather than books of *'ilm al-kalām*.

Faith is essentially a matter "between a servant and his Lord" and, therefore, anyone who affirms his belief in Allah is adjudged in this world as a Muslim and is bound by all the obligations and rights of a Muslim unless, of course, he openly expresses his disbelief or does an action which amounts to unbelief. This world is not the place for uncovering people's hearts or secrets. This is why the *Sharī'ah* operates on what is apparent not what lies hidden in the heart.

"Whoever openly practices Islam," the Shehu stated, "cannot be termed an unbeliever nor should he be subjected to suspicion, be he a common man or otherwise." There is consensus among the *ahlu-s-Sunnah* that anyone who affirms the two testimonies of belief in Allah and His Messenger ﷺ is protected by the laws of Islam. This is because Allah has not given man access to the secrets that lie in the heart nor has He ordered anyone to pry into them. The order in this world is that people should be judged in accordance with what they state explicitly or do openly.

It is also wrong to investigate the faith of common people by subjecting them to questions and examinations. Ignorant students do this and in the process attribute to Muslims what no Muslim would ever say. All the common people require is *naṣīḥah*. The Shehu observed: "If you want to benefit the people then affirm their convictions for them according to the extent of their understanding and tell them only what they are capable of comprehending, as is stated in the noble *ḥadīth*, and avoid these examinations, hair-splittings and allegories which have never ever been the practice of the men of Allah."

If even the learned find it difficult to articulate the details of faith, how can common people be expected to do so? What they should know are the fundamentals: that Allah exists, is eternal, infinite, absolutely independent, absolutely one in His essence and that there is nothing like Him; that He brought creation into being; that He has will, life and power and knowledge; that He is hearing, seeing, speaking; that the prophets are truthful, trustworthy and have the attributes of human excellence; that they are men subject to human needs such as food, marriage and "buying and selling"; that the angels are sinless, neither male nor female, and that they neither eat nor drink; that the heavenly Books are true; that death is true; that the Rising is true; that Judgment is true; that Paradise and Hell are true; that the vision of Allah by the believers is true; and that all the Messages brought by the prophets are true.

The faith of common people is usually sound according to the consensus of the scholars. This is based on the *ḥadīth* of the Prophet ﷺ stating, "that the majority of the people of Paradise are the simple-minded." They are, therefore, believers, understand about Allah and are destined for Paradise. "Corruption (in society) will not overwhelm their faith until the Day of Judgment." Their faith, regardless of the prevailing corruption, remains sound. The fact that certain individuals exhibit signs of unbelief is not sufficient justification to condemn all the people.

In any case, philosophical understanding of faith is *farḍ al-kifāyah*, meaning that, if it is possessed by some individuals, the rest of society is absolved from having to undertake it. The philosophy and terminology of *'ilm al-kalām* should not concern the majority of Muslims. It was intended to confront heretics and unbelieving philosophers on their own ground, not for common people to grapple with.

The *Tanbīh aṭ-Ṭalaba*, for its part, is the quintessence of the Shehu's teaching on the subject of *Iman*, which is that Allah is known to man inherently. "Know, my brothers," he says, "that Allah, Most High, has made it clear in many verses in His Noble Book that He is known to man by nature. He says in a verse of the Qur'an: *Do not then* ***knowingly*** *make others equal to Allah.*" (2:21)

All human beings know Allah instinctively, because their very beings are molded on the realization of the unity of the Creator, His eternity as well as His creation of all that exists. In addition, Allah Himself says, "*Whoever has iman in Allah - He will guide his heart,*" (64:11) meaning that Allah guides him to the understanding of Himself. Therefore, nothing and no one can be said to be ignorant of their Lord, though the nature of the understanding is as diverse as the creatures themselves. Similarly, Allah created the spirit (*rūḥ*) complete, mature, and fully cognizant of His unity and firmly believing in His *rubūbiyyah* (His being the Creator and Sustainer of all creatures). Such is the natural pattern (*fiṭrah*) upon which every child is formed. Allah is acknowledged therefore without the aid of teaching. Teaching is required for the understanding of existence and ultimately for higher intellectual and moral consciousness.

Mobilization of the Women

The open debate on women was sparked off in Daura in 1201/1786-7 by a scholar named Mustafa Goni. It was he who, according to 'Abdullahi in *Tazyīn*, first openly challenged the Shehu on his allowing women to attend his public lectures. In a message to the Shehu, Mustafa Goni said:

> "O son of Fudi, rise to warn the ignorant,
> That perchance they may understand both religion,
> and the things of this world.
> Forbid women to visit your preaching,
> For the mixing of men and women is a sufficient disgrace.
> Do not do anything that contributes towards disgrace,
> For Allah has not ordered vice which could cause us harm."

The Shehu's immediate reaction was to ask 'Abdullahi to write Mustafa Goni a reply on his behalf:

> "O you who have come to guide us aright
> We have heard what you have said.
> Listen to what we say.
> You gave advice to the best of your ability,
> But would that you had freed us from blame...
> We found the people of this country drowning in ignorance,
> Shall we prevent them from understanding religion?
> It has been said, 'Judgment shall be carried out
> on a people according to the evil they create.'
> Take this as a measure."

The central point in 'Abdullahi's reply is that, even if women's attendance of the Shehu's lectures were a disgrace, their being abandoned to ignorance was a greater disgrace. In the words of 'Abdullahi: "The evil of leaving women in ignorance, not knowing what is incumbent upon them, nay, not knowing Islam at all, is greater than the evil of their mixing with men, for the first evil relates back to religion, which is faith, Islam and good works (*Iḥsān*), and the second evil relates back to genealogy."

The debate, however, did not stop there. The Shehu had to reply several times to the objections and legal issues raised by his contemporaries among the *'ulamā'*. The debate moved from the narrow confines of women's attendance of lectures to the wider issues of their education in general, their involvement in trade and professions and their going out of the house for their needs.

In taking a closer look at the Shehu's replies and examining his views, we shall use three of his works: *Nūr al-Albāb, Tanbīh al-Ikhwān* and *Irshād al-Ikhwān ilā Ahkām Khurūj an-Niswān.*

In *Tanbīh* the Shehu defended his allowing women to attend his lectures, by saying it was justifiable and, indeed, sanctioned by law:

> "I used to teach the men their individual obligations and the women used to attend, staying behind the *ḥijāb* to prevent them from mixing (indiscriminately) with men. I kept on emphasizing in the assemblies my statement that such mixing of male and female is unlawful, so much so that it necessarily became a matter of common knowledge. Then, later, I assigned a specific day for the men and a specific day for the women, since this is better and safer. It is related in *Ṣaḥīḥ al-Bukhāri*... that the women said to the Prophet ﷺ: 'Men have gained an advantage over us in respect to access to you, therefore fix a day for us.' So he fixed a day for them on which they used to meet him, and he would exhort and instruct them."

Women's attendance of open-air lectures, he seemed to say in the *Tanbīh*, was not his own innovation. Other great scholars, who faced similar circumstances of prevailing ignorance, had either allowed it or expressly recommended it. Among them, he said, were the shaykh, the imam, the learned scholar Sidi Aḥmad ibn Sulayman who was "a great saint" and regarded as a "Junayd" of his generation. And no less an authority than al-Ghazali recommended the same. Even those such as Ibn Arafa, who were of the opinion that women should not go to lectures if it involved mixing with men, were referring to lectures dealing with knowledge that is not obligatory. In any case, by "mixing" they meant actual direct contact between men and women and not occasions when they sit separately or when women sit in a separate compartment.

It is obligatory on a woman, he said in *Tanbīh* and *Irshād*, to acquire a full knowledge of her religious obligations such as prayer, fasting, *zakāt*, Ḥajj, as well as the more mundane matters such as trade and transactions. If her husband is not able to supply this knowledge, she is under an Islamic obligation to go out in search of it. "If he refuses her the permission," the Shehu stated categorically in *Irshād*, "she should go out without his permission, and no blame is attached to her nor does she incur any sin by doing that."

A ruler should compel husbands to make sure that their wives are educated in the same way that he should compel them to give the wives adequate maintenance. "Indeed," said the Shehu, "knowledge is superior (to maintenance)."

But in spite of this sound Islamic position, "the devils among men" still believed that women should remain at home in ignorance, knowing very well that ignorance could lead women to Hellfire. In addition, such devilish scholars had remained silent in situations of moral and social decadence in which women freely engaged with men in drumming and dancing, and in which they openly displayed their beauty on festive days. If a woman could go as far as to Ḥajj, why should she not go out to learn about her faith, which indeed, is a greater obligation than Ḥajj, the Shehu asked.

The scholars who opposed women's education, the Shehu postulated in *Nūr al-Albāb*, were merely hypocrites. They abandoned their wives, daughters and servants to ignorance, while they gave knowledge to other people. "How can they leave their wives, daughters and servants in the darkness of ignorance and error while they teach their students day and night! This is nothing but the pursuit of their selfish ends, because they teach their students only for show and out of pride. This is a great error." The education of wives, children and dependants, he said, is an obligation while the teaching of students is voluntary. It becomes an obligation only when there is no one else to do it, and even then it is an obligation that is preceded by the obligation to educate one's family and dependents.

Then the Shehu carried his argument straight to the women themselves. "Muslim women!" he exclaimed in *Nūr al-Albāb*, "Do not listen to those who are themselves misguided and who misguide others, those who seek to deceive you by asking you to obey your husbands without first asking you to obey Allah and His Messenger. They say that a woman's happiness lies in her obedience to her husband. They say this only so that they can fulfill their own selfish ends and fulfill their desires through you. They compel you to do things which neither Allah nor His Messenger has originally imposed on you, such as cooking, washing of clothes and similar things, which are among their numerous wishes, while they do not in the least demand of you to perform the real duties imposed on you by Allah and His Messenger.

"It is true that a woman is obliged by the consensus of the jurists to heed her husband in open and in secret, even if he is of very low social status, or even if he is a slave; and she is prohibited by consensus from disobeying him outright, except if he orders her to do an act which amounts to disobedience to Allah, in which case she must refrain from obeying him, as of necessity, because there should be no obedience to a creature in disobedience to the Creator. In addition, a woman is rewarded twofold for heeding her husband. But all of that is conditional upon her obedience to Allah and His Messenger."

He lamented in *Irshād* the failure of women to demand their right to education in the same way that they would demand their right to maintenance and other basic needs. Women, like men, have been created for the sole purpose of serving Allah, which is not properly attainable without true education. The right to education, he seemed to be saying, has absolute preference over other rights. "If a wife were to demand her right from her husband regarding the affairs of her religion, to take her case to the ruler and demand that either he educates her in the affairs of her religion or gives her permission to go out to learn, it would be obligatory (by law) for the ruler to compel the husband to do that, in exactly the same way that he would compel him to give his wife her worldly rights, since religious rights are superior and preferred."

The Shehu's uncompromising stand on women's education, as opposed to the stand of some of his contemporaries, whom he criticized in *Irshād* for their lack of insight, stemmed from his role as a *mujaddid*. The Shehu's moral and social transformation of society relied heavily on education. To neglect the education of women would have defeated the cause in two ways. Women not only formed an integral part of society but also constituted its larger, more basic and more solid part. As the custodians of the home, which is the foundation of society, they are the most important factors in the stabilization of society.

Secondly, the important role women had to play in bringing up children imbued with the spirit and orientation of the emerging order, which would need at least one generation to take root, could not be over-emphasized. The youth are the pillar of any process of Islamic revival, in so far as it is their energy and zeal that give it the requisite strength and vitality to challenge the prevailing order to the end. And the youth are principally raised by women.

We may also view the Shehu's insistence on women's education from another angle: as a restatement of the principle that education in Islam is not only a right but also a duty. Every human being has been commanded by Allah to gain knowledge. Knowledge is the key to the understanding of Allah and the forging of the proper relationship with Him. It is the key to the understanding of Islam in its true perspective and the understanding of the nature of life, of human relations and of existence as a whole. It is the key to the development of an individual as a complete personality.

In this regard, there is no difference between man and woman. If a woman's spiritual and moral development is in danger of being frustrated by her husband's unjustifiable demands – which obviously stem from selfishness and high-handedness – Islam requires that she assert her rights and take whatever steps she deems necessary to safeguard her moral and spiritual well-being. If that puts her marriage at risk, so be it. For her success in the Hereafter, which is greater and more enduring than the material things she could ever get from this world, should at all times be her priority.

And there is yet another way of looking at this matter. The Shehu was aware that the cause he was advocating could well lead to future hardships for both men and women. Indeed, the hardships could entail exile and loss of life for those who accepted his leadership. Yet it was a cause that rested squarely on conviction, since someone who lacks absolute faith in Allah and in the Hereafter cannot be deemed to have suffered or died in the cause of Allah. It is only fair then that all those who were likely to have to suffer in the cause of Allah should first be inculcated with the right faith and convictions and proper Islamic attitudes. Only then would they be able to gain real benefit from their sufferings and hardships. This was perhaps another reason why the Shehu was absolutely insistent in his demand that both men and women should be properly educated about their beliefs and obligations.

He posed a question in *Irshād*. According to the law, women have to go out in search of knowledge that husbands cannot provide. So should a scholar, who cannot secure separate seating arrangements for men and women, go out to teach Islam, knowing very well that some women are bound to attend his lectures; or should he do so, if he is well aware of the possibility of objectionable things being perpetrated as a result of women's attendance? The Shehu answered in the affirmative, because those issues do not constitute a valid excuse to leave people in ignorance.

He wrote: "No, he should go out but he should prevent

intermixing of the men and women, if that happens in his presence; he should put men on one side and women on the other; and he should let them all know that the intermixing of men and women is prohibited by consensus... Indeed, the majority of the people are ignorant of the law, and if he goes out in order to change what he can of the social evils he sees, his witnessing of other evils which he cannot change will not harm him."

The logic seems to be that if people are not made conscious of the social evils they are required to abandon, by not being given the opportunity to commit some of them in the presence of a teacher, how will they ever learn to abandon them? They need education precisely because they do not know that such things are evil, or if they do know, they lack the necessary moral and social consciousness to appreciate the magnitude of the danger such evils pose to the fabric of society.

Though education was the main theme of the Shehu's writings on women, he dealt with other matters too in his prolonged debate. For instance, should women engage in trade and similar activities? Ideally, he said, a woman's needs should be provided for either by her husband or by other relations, so that there is no need for her to go out to the markets or sit in shops or similar places, but if there is no one to undertake "buying and selling" on her behalf, she is permitted by law to undertake it for herself, but "she should do so without ornamentation (that is, she should observe moral and social restraint when she deals with men), for that is better for her in the eyes of her Lord and is more rewarding."

We can look at this rule from two angles. Firstly, women, like men, are entitled to a decent and dignified life, free from the humiliation of begging and dependence on others. Indeed, a woman is in greater need of economic protection, since economic insecurity could lead her to the kind of life which undermines not only her own integrity but the very foundations of society. If such a possibility exists, it becomes obligatory on her to seek the economic means she needs to preserve her integrity. Indeed, the insistence of Islam that women should have knowledge of some trade is meant to prepare them against such an eventuality.

Secondly, the Prophet ﷺ stated that Allah permits women to go out for their needs. What constitutes these needs is not, however, specified, so it is left to those who represent the conscience of society to determine them from time to time as occasion demands. But of course, some needs, such as education, health and honorable livelihood, are basic and cannot be nullified by anyone.

Another important matter addressed by the Shehu was that of women going out in general. In fact, the Shehu stated in his introduction to *Irshād* that he wrote the book in order to bring the two extreme groups – those who say that women are free to go out at all times like men and those who say they should not go out at all – to the correct and middle course, and acquaint them with the rules formulated by upright scholars. This middle course, he said, implies that it is lawful for women to go out for their needs when it is legally necessary. At times this necessity will be of a worldly nature, such as seeking a livelihood, and at other times the necessity will be of a religious nature, such as going out in search of knowledge of their fundamental religious obligations.

There are a host of other issues dealt with in the *Irshād*, such as women going out to attend the daily prayers, the Friday prayer and for Ḥajj, funerals, visits and so on; and to each of these the Shehu gave a qualified approval in line with his balanced view. We would like to concentrate on his debate about women's attendance at the mosque for daily prayers, for it demonstrates the way he handled the conflicting opinions of Muslim jurists. He writes, for instance: "Al-Ghazali says in *al-Iḥyā'*: 'It is necessary to prevent women from attending the mosques for the prayer if it is feared that men would be tempted by them. In fact 'Aishah رضي الله عنها did prevent them, and it was said to her that (her husband) the Messenger of Allah ﷺ had not prevented them from attending the congregational prayer. She said, "Had the Messenger of Allah ﷺ known what the women would do after him he would have prevented them.'""

Some (jurists) conclude from this statement, as did al-Qastalāni in *al-Irshād*, that women should be prevented outright from attending the mosque. Others, however, have replied that 'Aishah رضي الله عنها was not, in fact, explicitly categorical about this, even if her statement indicates her preference for prevention. It is also argued that Allah knows perfectly well what women will do, yet He did not send any revelation to His Prophet ﷺ to prevent them from going to the mosque. If their behavior necessitated their being prevented from attending mosques, it would necessitate their being prevented from going to other places such as markets as well. In addition, the offending behavior is found among some women only, not all of them. If prevention were necessary it should be confined to those who perpetrate offensive actions. Nonetheless, a woman's prayer at home carries greater merit than her prayer in the mosque.

The Shehu did not really reach any conclusion. He left his readers to make up their own minds. We should however remember his opinion that, regarding any issue about which jurists have made divergent rulings, a person is free to take whichever ruling is agreeable to him, since religion should be easy.

This would be a suitable moment, perhaps, to consider some of the issues that have been raised in this debate on women. The question of education raised by the Shehu relates mainly to women who did not receive education in their childhood. It is they who are being asked to demand their right to education and to gain it by all possible means. The debate is particularly applicable to young girls for, in a proper Islamic order, their education, like that of boys, is absolutely obligatory. Indeed, it is unthinkable that a Muslim society would allow a girl to grow to maturity without having been educated. Universal education for girls as well as boys is the clear rule of Islam and should be known by those with even the most elementary acquaintance with Islam.

The qualified permission for a woman to go out is based on three considerations. In the first place, she is basically responsible for the home and for the upbringing of her children. Whatever else she does is subordinate to this fundamental role. Indeed, she herself derives greater happiness and fulfillment from a stable and successful home than from anything else. Therefore, anything that might distract her from giving her full attention to the family is discouraged, except where it becomes absolutely necessary. In the second place, her own safety has been considered by Islam, since Islam regards the physical, moral and psychological security of women as the responsibility of society as a whole, of which her husband and her immediate relations take a significant share. In the third place, the qualified permission is made with due considerations to public morality.

Since women evoke strong emotions in men, the interaction between the two must always be regulated. For example, the intimacy that exists between a husband and a wife necessitates a considerable display of social, moral and emotional restraint when they deal with other people. If they did not show restraint, discord and malice would result in society. And to the extent that men are almost always the aggressive factor in any situation, it rests upon women to minimize that aggression whenever possible and appropriate. Yet, the same public morality that necessitates greater restraint on the part of women may also require them to go out to assist in society. Who is better than a woman at teaching other women or treating their ailments or solving her emotional and psychological problems?

8. The Concerns of the *Mujaddid*

THE CONTENT of the Shehu's teachings, and his method and response to those who opposed him, reveal his vision of the kind of society needed for the regeneration of Islam and of the type of individual required to bring that about. We shall take another look at his *Nūr al-Albāb* and *Iḥyā' as-Sunnah* and, for the first time, look at his *Wathīqat al-Ikhwān*, which can well be regarded as his social manifesto. The *Wathīqat* contains his views on some of the fundamental issues of his time and how he wanted his students, companions and followers to respond to them.

The nub of his teaching is that both the individual and society should adhere to the *Sharī'ah* – the Qur'an, Sunnah and *ijmā'* – and forsake all *bid'ah*. He deemed Islam to be the one and only means of regenerating those millions of people with whom he lived and to whose education and transformation he had dedicated his life. What he felt it imperative to do as a *mujaddid* was to follow the Sunnah by calling the people to religion, by associating himself completely with their plight and their interests, by serving as a "wing of mercy" for them to shelter beneath and by laying down the foundations for a nobler and greater society.

The Shehu's ardent desire to follow the Prophet ﷺ, his Companions ﵁ and the great jurists step-by-step runs like an unbroken thread through his career. There is hardly any action he took or any major opinion he put forward for which he did not find a justification in the *Sharī'ah*. To him, this was only way to act, since the best of the Companions

– such as Abū Bakr, 'Umar, 'Uthmān and 'Alī ؓ – and the best of the jurists – such as Mālik, Abū Ḥanīfah, Ibn Ḥanbal and ash-Shāfi'ī – did exactly the same.

In both *Wathīqat* and *Iḥyā' as-Sunnah* he noted that Abū Bakr ؓ said that he would never abandon any practice of the Prophet ﷺ for fear of swerving from the right path; that 'Umar ؓ justified his actions by referring to the practice of the Prophet ﷺ; that when 'Uthmān ؓ was allowed to perform the *ṭawāf* by the Meccan chiefs while the Prophet ﷺ was waiting for him at Ḥudaybiyyah, he declined, saying, "I will never do so until the Messenger of Allah has performed it."; and that 'Alī ؓ stated categorically that he would never disregard the Sunnah of the Prophet ﷺ on the strength of anyone else's opinion.

Similarly, the Shehu noted the statement of Imam Mālik that the best aspects of religion are built upon the Sunnah and the worst are based on *bid'ah*; the statement of ash-Shāfi'ī that all that the Sunnah required was its implementation; that of Abū Ḥanīfah urging people to adhere to the established legacy and the virtuous path; and the personal account of Aḥmad ibn Ḥanbal stressing the importance of keeping within the bounds of the *Sharī'ah*.

The case for following the Companions ؓ rests on the premise that they had the advantage of being with the Prophet ﷺ himself and of witnessing the revelation of the Qur'an and its implementation by him; and that they showed their commitment to Islam, first by preserving both the Qur'an and Sunnah for future generations and then by fighting in the way of Allah to uproot and humiliate unbelief, establish the rule of Islam and liberate countries and regions for Islam. Those that followed them also exerted themselves in preserving the Sunnah. They would travel for months in search of a single *ḥadīth* until they were able to master the *Sharī'ah* completely and acquire the knowledge of the rules of Qur'anic exegesis and other essential knowledge directly from the noble Companions ؓ. Those who followed them preserved that vast body of knowledge and developed jurisprudence and other sciences to facilitate the practice of Islam for subsequent generations. They did this so thoroughly that what they did was almost sufficient as a guide for all future generations.

The immediate concern of the Shehu was the moral transformation of the individual. He taught that the way to achieve it was to increase people's knowledge of the fundamentals of Islam, of correct social behavior and of business practices as well, so that each individual could become a true and better worshipper of Allah and a better and worthier citizen. In this way the fundamentals of religion and the basic social and economic responsibilities of the individual would be common knowledge in society. Once the individual was sound in faith, in worship, in dealings with people and capable of enhancing his own economic and social interests – within, of course, the context of the overall well-being of society – the foundations for an all-embracing transformation would have been laid.

The means to achieve that end lay in a vigorous, sustained and systematic public education program or *wa'z*, which should be undertaken in all places – whether through the medium of mosque, public lectures, debates or private discussion – but, of course, there were certain conditions that had to be fulfilled.

First, in the process of *wa'z*, on no account should the faith of the common people, or of any other person for that matter, be subjected to repudiation, contempt or suspicion, because as long as people do not worship idols or openly show attitudes of unbelief, their faith is to be considered sound and healthy. To condemn their faith constitutes an unwarranted act of arrogance and is a hindrance to social transformation. It is a way, as the Shehu would say, of aiding the devil and serving his accursed purpose.

So a person undertaking this task should start with the positive, indeed the correct, presumption that the faith of every Muslim is sound until proven otherwise. This has been the stand of Islam throughout its history and has always been the stand of scholars intent on genuine transformation. It is thus, a false way of preaching to start with the negative presumption that the faith of a person is either weak or unsound, because the reality of a person's faith is known only to Allah.

The second condition to be fulfilled is that the preacher has a basic responsibility to make matters easy for people, to confirm them in their beliefs and to give them good tidings. Therefore, the preacher should not be harsh towards them. Three things are expected of him. He should, in the first instance, try to bring their attention back to the fundamentals of religion and not involve them in frivolous disputation, specious arguments or philosophical speculation. In the second place, the preacher should identify himself completely with the plight of the common people and prepare them for the eventual overthrow of the system that oppresses and humiliates them. He should have nothing but respect and sympathy for them and should dedicate his life to their moral and social advancement.

In the third place, the preacher should impose on them only those responsibilities which Allah and His Messenger ﷺ have imposed on people and no more. He should not admonish them for doing things about which there is no consensus on the part of the great Muslim jurists as to whether they constitute major sins, even though such deeds may be reprehensible; nor should he insist that they do things about which there is no unanimity among jurists as to their being obligatory. Islam requires from the common people only the fulfillment of their fundamental duties, not because they are inferior, but precisely because the nature of their tedious and taxing occupations does not leave them with the time and energy to undertake further duties. Certainly, their work in farms, workshops and markets represents a greater form of worship than many voluntary duties performed by other people.

The Prophet ﷺ left personal examples which we should take as the position of Islam. According to Abū Hurayrah

رضي الله عنه, a bedouin came to the Prophet ﷺ and said, "Guide me to a deed, by the doing of which I shall enter paradise." The Prophet ﷺ replied, "Worship Allah and associate nothing with Him, observe the prescribed prayer, pay the *zakāt*, and fast during Ramadan." He replied, "By Him in whose hand my soul is, I shall neither add anything to this nor fall short of it." Then when he turned away, the Prophet ﷺ said, "If anyone wishes to look at a man who will be among the people of paradise, let him look at this man." This *ḥadīth* was transmitted by both Bukhāri and Muslim, as was the following one.

A poor, ragged-looking man came to the Prophet ﷺ inquiring about Islam. The Prophet ﷺ said, "Five times of prayer each day and night." The man asked, "Must I observe any more than that?" The Prophet ﷺ answered, "No, unless you do it voluntarily." Then the Prophet ﷺ said, "Fasting during the month of Ramadan." The man asked, "Must I observe anything else?" "No," came the reply, "unless you do it voluntarily." Then the Prophet ﷺ mentioned *zakāt* and the man asked, "Must I pay anything else?" to which he ﷺ replied, "No, unless you do it voluntarily." The man then swore that he would do no more nor less than these. When he went away the Prophet ﷺ said, "The man will prosper if he is speaking the truth."

Such is the yardstick which the Prophet ﷺ established and exceeding this measure is futile and does Islam no good. Nobody is helped in his religion if he is overworked and overtaxed, for he will eventually break down and may even lose interest in religion itself. It is precisely for this reason that the caliph 'Umar رضي الله عنه warned his colleagues, "Do not make Allah hateful to the people."

The third condition that the preacher has to fulfill is to turn people's attention away from this world to the Hereafter, from sinful acts to acts of piety. Therefore, he is expected, as the Shehu shows in *Iḥyā' as-Sunnah*, to use relevant verses of the Qur'an to instill fear of the Hereafter, or traditions of the Prophet ﷺ that will serve the same purpose. He is also expected to relate stories of how the prophets suffered at the hands of their enemies to demonstrate that, even though people are Muslims and devoted to the cause of Allah, it does not mean that they will not be subjected to persecution and hardship, for Allah is absolutely independent of His creatures.

He should also impress on people the strong possibility of Divine punishment in this world if society fails to change its ways. Finally, he is expected to let them appreciate the grave consequences of the perpetration of the major sins in Islam. He thus has a wide area to cover and he should have no time for gossip, insults, false tales and frivolous, irrelevant discourses.

That the preacher himself must be a man of learning is the fourth condition. This is necessary because *wa'z* or public education relies for the most part on knowledge. Thus, he must be thoroughly learned in the Qur'an and its commentary. He must be versed in both the Sunnah and *fiqh*. In addition, he should be fully conversant with history, for much of public education needed in the process of social mobilization has to do with history. People should be told of their past in order to reflect on their present and their future. They should be told about the history of other people so that they can see parallels to their own history. They should be taught the process of history – the "days of Allah" as the Qur'an calls it – so that they themselves can have the feeling of being in the mainstream of history and of being part and parcel of the human process. There is, therefore, no room for ignorant people in this field and society should not allow such people to undertake this responsibility.

Thus, the *'ulamā'* are the men and women who should be responsible for public education, for social mobilization and for *tajdīd*. They have a historical responsibility to save society from ignorance, social atrophy, moral degeneration, injustice and oppression, in short, from disintegration. They are, as the Prophet ﷺ said, "the heirs of the prophets", and are charged with the responsibilities with which the prophets, peace be upon them, were charged: to warn, to give glad tidings, to guide, and "to struggle against the people until they testify that there is no god but Allah and that Muhammad is the Messenger of Allah."

There is, when considered from this perspective, an organic relationship between the *'ulamā'* and the people. The *'ulamā'* represent the strength and hope of the people in the face of political tyranny and general uncertainty. They are the light that guides the people and the pillars that uphold the structure of society. The people on the other hand are a source of strength for the *'ulamā'*, the noble instruments of change and the means of reviving Islam.

That organic relationship makes the *'ulamā'* a tremendous force in society, capable of maneuvering society in the direction they choose. This force can also be misused when, for instance, the *'ulamā'* are in alliance with an oppressive political power or have a vested interest which is different from that of the people. Such *'ulamā'* the Shehu called symbols of distraction and lieutenants of the devil. In his *Wathīqat,* the Shehu charged the venal scholars of his time with ruining the laws of Allah, worship and the fundamental duties of Islam in return for money and position, and accused them of assuming an obstinate stance against Allah. It was as if they had never heard the words of the Most High: "*As for those who desire the life of the dunya and its finery, We will give them full payment in it for their actions. They will not be deprived here of their due. But such people will have nothing in the* akhira *but the Fire. What they achieved here will come to nothing. What they did will prove to be null and void.*" (11:15-16)

The underlying direction of the Muslim *ummah*, he said further, is tied to the character of the *'ulamā'*. If they are good the *ummah* will thrive and prosper, if they are evil, the *ummah* will suffer as a consequence. "O my brothers!" the Shehu cries out in *Wathīqat*, "A certain man of God once shed tears in lamentation, saying, 'Truly *'ulamā' as-sū'* sit on the road leading to the Hereafter and cut the people off from Allah'. The people have a binding obligation to shun them and refuse to heed them."

Muslims should seek out upright scholars, the helpers of Allah, the blessings of the world, wherever they may be, so that they can be kept safe from all kinds of unbelief and *bid'ah*. People should form an alliance with these scholars to fulfill the mutual obligations that exist between them. The *'ulamā'* have a duty to teach, warn and preach, and the people have a duty to listen and obey.

Shehu also has a word or two for the upright scholars – the *'ulamā' ad-Dīn*, as he calls them. They should accommodate each other's views, as well as the conflicting opinions of former jurists, and should under no circumstances fall into dispute; and they should distance themselves from *taqlīd* – the blind following of the opinions and rulings of previous jurists. Scholars who call people to Islam also have a duty to look anew at the fundamental issues of their day, to reflect on them and then conclude what is best for their people. That boldness is extremely vital for the success of their undertaking because social mobility follows the pace of intellectual mobility. When the intellect is torpid, society will remain stagnant, filled with the empty and thoughtless prattling of imitators.

During the process of transformation, the attention of society should be concentrated only on the basic moral, social, political and economic issues of the day. And because no one social climate is exactly like another, the priorities and major issues of one society will not be identical to those of any other. Of the issues which the Shehu saw as most fundamental to his society, four may be mentioned here.

The first, of course, was the condition of women, which he considered unsatisfactory and legally indefensible. He called for change in their status and treatment. The starting point for this improvement should be education, which he said was obligatory. Indeed, the Shehu envisaged a time when women would be great scholars, teaching and lecturing not only other women but also men, in accordance with the practice of "the worthy predecessors" (*salaf*). A woman, he maintained, should never sacrifice her right to education for anything else, because her relationship with Allah – the most important thing in the life of any individual, whether male or female – is determined by knowledge alone.

In addition, women have a right to maintenance, the right to seek their own source of livelihood if they are not satisfied with their economic circumstances, and the right to the benefits which Islam accords to every human being. On no account should a woman be treated as a "domestic animal" or "a household chattel" to be thrown away when worn out. She is entitled to dignity and respect, and every effort should be made to preserve her interests, honor and personal integrity. Society should come to her aid if she is abused, the ruler should support her if she is denied education and maintenance, and Islamic law is with her at all times.

The implementation of the *Sharīʿah* was another major issue addressed by the Shehu. He noted that unqualified, and often corrupt, people were appointed as judges and that appointments to sensitive posts were made not on the basis of merit but of blood relationship and questionable patronage. The law of Allah, he lamented, was being substituted by the whims of corrupt and oppressive rulers. What was needed was a return to the proper implementation of the law, whereby judges would be appointed on the basis of merit, and ignorant, corrupt and other undesirable elements excluded.

The condition of markets – and the general economic situation – was also one of the Shehu's focal points. Ignorant people, he said, should not be allowed to sell in markets or to serve as agents for others. The market is as sacred as the mosque and it should be maintained by men of knowledge, as is the case with the mosque. Three principles, among others, should underlie the operation of markets. The first and foremost is the principle of "*lā khilābah*", which means there must be no fraudulent dealings. The second is that there should be no mutual undercutting among the business community. And finally, there is the important principle of *intidhār*, which involves making due allowance for people in adverse economic circumstances until their position has improved or, better still, writing off their debt completely.

These principles underlie the perspective, whereby economic life is seen as a cohesive and integrating force in society, reinforcing other aspects of life, and also as a pillar of social and spiritual well-being like any other great pillar of Islam. If the market is allowed to disintegrate in the hands of ignorant or fraudulent elements, the whole structure of society will eventually disintegrate with it. Thus, to preserve honesty and fair dealing, it is essential that scales and balances should be standardized, and anyone who willfully violates the rules of fairness and equity should be expelled from the market or punished severely.

Finally, the Shehu saw institutionalized magic as an important social problem. *'Ulamā' as-sū'* used it as a means of personal enrichment and had even gone to the extent of incorporating it into Islam to deceive the people. Magic had permeated the entire fabric of society and people employed it on personal quests for luck or when seeking a woman's love. It was also looked to in the treatment of diseases, when recourse was had to incantations, idolatrous concoctions and even witchcraft. People, he said, should look for correct medical treatment and abandon such evil practices.

We are now in a position to evaluate some of the essential features of this remarkable teaching, by asking what the purposes, which the Shehu intended to achieve by it, were. The first purpose – the cornerstone of his teaching – was to spread knowledge very widely, in order to reach as many people as possible and stimulate intellectual activity among them. His intention was to give the pursuit of knowledge, the use of the intellect and recourse to profound thinking the importance and respect which they truly deserved. Indeed, as a *mujaddid*, no other course was available to him, for he was aware that the Prophet ﷺ himself started his mission by appealing to human intellect. True, it takes much time and effort for the intellect to be aroused and stimulated into activity but, because it is the key to human striving and social mobilization, no transformation without intellectual involvement is possible.

We can thus see the reason why the Shehu stipulated the minimum educational levels for every man and woman, encompassing knowledge of the Creator, of the fundamental religious obligations of every Muslim, of social duties and of the laws governing trade and business transactions. Knowledge is the basis of every aspect of social life. A person who wants to barter in the markets – man or woman – should have the knowledge of what is entailed when they do it. A person to be appointed as a judge or a ruler must have a thorough knowledge of what that involves. And a person who wants to preach must be sound in knowledge and thoroughly imbued with piety.

The Shehu's second purpose was to raise the self worth of the common man. He sought, through a painstaking process of education, to impress upon them the importance of cleanliness, modesty and courtesy, so that these could become an integral part of their personalities and consequently an important characteristic of society as well.

His third purpose was to preserve the integrity of society. His insistence that no person should bow his head before another as a mark of respect stemmed from a deep-felt conviction that no one should be dignified at the expense of the humiliation of someone else. His strong opposition to the uncontrolled mingling of men and women and his insistence that women should obey the Islamic rules of modesty in dress, both at home and outside, were intended to protect the moral integrity of society. He asserted the right of every individual to have legal protection against intrusion and against the unwarranted violation of their integrity and privacy.

His fourth purpose was to promote social cohesion among Muslims, which was particularly important because the trend at that time was towards social disintegration. Social cohesion, in his eyes, started with the cultivation of spiritual unity. He accordingly stressed the importance of an internal and external display of this cohesion during the prayer. He called attention in *Iḥyā' as-Sunnah* to the statement of the Prophet ﷺ, "You must keep your rows straight or Allah will most certainly divide your hearts." The closing of ranks, the straightening of rows and the need for serenity and humbleness to be displayed in communal prayer, are all meant to unite the hearts of Muslims and cement their relationships.

The mosque is the most important symbol of that cohesion, being the place that brings Muslims together several times each day and, weekly, on an even larger scale. The proliferation of mosques, unfortunately, divides Muslims spiritually. To avoid that happening, mosques should not be built too close to each other nor should there be so many that the very objective of social cohesion is defeated. If it is clear that a mosque has been built purposely to cause division in Muslim society, it should be pulled down. Allah says in *Sura at-Tawba*: "*As for those who have set up a mosque, causing harm and out of unbelief, to create division between the muminun… Do not ever stand in it. A mosque founded on taqwa from the first day has a greater right for you to stand in it.*" (9:108-9)

The Shehu's stress on honesty in trade and consideration in economic dealings in general was also aimed at strengthening the social integration of the people.

Finally, the Shehu also intended to raise the moral consciousness of the individual in society. In *Wathīqat* he stressed the overriding importance of *jihad an-nafs*, or the struggle against the lower self, and in *Iḥyā' as-Sunnah* he emphasized the necessity for every person to pursue *Iḥsān*, or moral excellence. The concept of *Iḥsān* is rooted in the belief that every individual has a personal, indeed extremely intimate, relationship with Allah and that he is obliged to respect this by raising himself up in his Lord's eyes. The essence of *Iḥsān* is for the Muslim to feel the presence of Allah in his worship, "to worship Him," in the words of the Prophet ﷺ, "as if you see him, for though you do not see Him, He sees you."

In addition, you should feel humble and modest before others, and not regard yourself as superior to any other person for, as the Shehu rightly pointed out, no one really knows what his end will be. Yet, true humility also entails the display of a high sense of self-worth and gives the individual who has it a noble presence, irrespective of their economic or social status. And we scarcely need add that, as has already been said, moral consciousness, along with intellectual elevation, constitutes the key to the overall positive transformation of a society in need of moral regeneration.

9. The Politics of Change

Degel, where the Shehu grew up, had, by the beginning of the third decade of his mission, become an emerging intellectual and spiritual center in Hausaland. It was where the Shehu lived and to it flocked scholars, students, and "waves upon waves" of people for the purpose of studying, seeking guidance or soliciting blessing and approval. Degel had also come to symbolize the new spirit of Islamic revival. It was not only a spiritual university in itself, a community of scholars and saints, it was also, and more fundamentally, the new focal point for the various groups and communities who had been hoping for a positive and profound change in western Sudan.

It was there that the Shehu raised the young teachers who would aid the revival of Islam in Hausa society, hundreds of whom had already become established as scholars in their own villages and cities. They constituted the seeds of the future, upon whom the responsibility for running the new order would eventually devolve. By the time he was forty years of age, he had virtually ceased, or at any rate limited to the minimum, his preaching journeys, so that he could concentrate on raising more scholars and strengthening those who were already established.

His community had grown prodigiously. It was to all intents and purposes a new polity, an *ummah*, headed by scholars who were loyal to a specified leader and who had a direction and purpose distinct from the rest of the people. The *Jama'a* cut across social, ethnic and political lines, and was scattered over all the countries of Hausaland. Their rallying spirit was the Shehu, and their capital was no longer Daura, Katsina, Kano, Birnin Kebbi or Alkalawa; it was Degel.

The Shehu and the Rulers

The Shehu had become the real symbol of an emerging nation, the symbol of the nascent spirit of the revival of Islam in Hausaland and the voice of the people. He was the embodiment of their conscience. What he had sought to do all along, which had now been realized, was to create an intellectual and moral leadership that would eventually displace the present rulers, to forge a new community of scholars who would embody the spirit of an invigorated Islam, and to establish an alternative society with definite goals and aspirations of its own. The roots of this society had already been established in the major parts of Hausaland, principally Zamfara, Kebbi and Gobir, as well as in such distant places as Kano, Zazzau and Bauchi.

We now intend to examine briefly the course of events leading to the formation of this alternative community. The Shehu, 'Abdullahi told us in *Tazyīn*, started his work by extensive travels to the east and to the west, calling people to Islam, instructing them in the fundamentals of religion and discouraging them from following customs repugnant to Islam. In these initial stages, he scrupulously avoided the political authorities.

The Shaykh was not in the habit of visiting rulers or of having anything to do with them, but when the community around him grew larger and his affair became well-known to the kings and others, he saw that he had no alternative but to go to them. He, therefore, traveled to Bawa, the Amir of Gobir, explained true Islam to him and ordered him (to observe it) and to establish justice in his lands.

That encounter with the ruler of Gobir was the first major political activity of the Shehu and it probably took place about eight years after he began his activities. Between this first encounter and the second major one eight years later the Shehu had made considerable progress in establishing himself as the moral and social focus in Hausaland and in endearing himself to a large cross-section of Hausa communities.

When the second encounter took place in 1202-3/1788-9 with Sulṭan Bawa, the Shehu spoke as the leader of a community and as a respected voice of the people. 'Abdullahi reported that the Sulṭan of Gobir called together the *'ulamā'* during *'Id al-Adhā* at Magami and offered the Shehu and the *'ulamā'* "wealth in alms". Shaykh 'Usman stood up before him and said to him, "Indeed! I and my community have no need of your wealth, but I ask you this and this," and he enumerated to him all matters concerning the establishment of religion. The Sulṭan replied to him, "I give you what you ask, and I consent to all that you wish to do in this our country."

Some of the Shehu's requests for the establishment of Islam were noted by Wazir Gidado in *Rawḍ al-Jinān*: that he should be allowed a free hand to call people to Allah; that no hindrance should be placed before anyone who wished to respond to his call; that members of his *Jama'a* – now identifiable by caps or turbans for men and head-covers for women – should be treated with respect; that all prisoners should be freed; and that the people should not be burdened with unjust or heavy taxes. That his requests were granted was indicative of the Sulṭan's recognition of the Shehu as a political force to be reckoned with.

In the next five or six years, the *Jama'a* continued to grow and more scholars were produced. In 1210/1794, the Shehu had a vision in which he was presented with the "sword of truth" to be used to defend the religion. He was left in no doubt as to the inevitability of an ultimate confrontation with the established order. About this time, three other events occurred, each of which was extremely crucial to the *Jama'a*.

The first was 'Abdullahi's *Risālat* to the Fulani *'ulamā'*, asking them to join the movement for reviving Islam in

Hausaland, to which they responded affirmatively. This new influx of *'ulamā'* support marked the turning point in the development of the movement. "When these *'ulamā'* rose up to help religion in our country," 'Abdullahi wrote in *Tazyīn*, "the *Jama'a* increased in fame and its followers became many and the people came in crowds to Shaykh 'Uthman." This development gave new confidence to the Shehu and his companions, widened the appeal for the *tajdīd* movement, and added new strength to it.

The next important event was the visit of Sidi Mukhtar al-Kunti's disciple, Sharif Salih, the only known contact recorded between the Shehu and the Sidi, who was so revered that the three leaders – the Shehu, 'Abdullahi and Muhammad Bello – each sent a separate message to him. The Sidi has a special place in the history of Islam in West Africa. He was the head of the Qādirī *tarīqah* and was considered the epitome of piety in West Africa – the seal of the *ṣufi* personalities who combine *ḥaqīqah* and *Sharī'ah*. In several instances, his voice was crucial in the timing of *jihad* in the Sudan. According to 'Abdullahi the Sidi "roused the people" to the support of the Shehu. Truly, he merited 'Abdullahi's description of him as "the sun of all eastern places and the western places, axis of the time, the adornment of good men".

Yet, another crucial event was the *Jama'a*'s desire to "break away from the unbelievers" and commence the *jihad*. Though the Shehu did not lend his support to this course of action, for he thought it premature, he nevertheless started to have serious thoughts about *jihad*. "He began," according to 'Abdullahi, "to incite them to arms, saying to them, 'Verily to make ready weapons is Sunnah,' and he began to pray to Allah that He should show him the sovereignty of Islam in this country of the Sudan." Yet, another seven years were still to pass before the armed confrontation actually started.

Essential changes took place affecting the political climate in Hausaland. Gobir was at war with Katsina and, according to 'Abdul Qadir ibn al-Mustafa (Dan Tafa) in *Rawḍat al-*

Afkār, the son of Bawa, the ruler of Gobir, was wounded in battle and died shortly afterwards, while Gobir itself was defeated by Katsina. "Bawa," 'Abdul Qadir ibn al-Mustafa wrote, "in grief for his son and full of chagrin at his defeat, also died." That was about the year 1206/1790. The next ruler of Gobir was Yakubu who ruled for just over six years and was killed in a battle against Kiawa. He was succeeded by Nafata.

If the *Jama'a* constituted a threat to Bawa, he did not show it openly nor did he renege on his undertaking to allow the Shehu a free hand in his activities. Yakubu did not oppose the Shehu forcefully either. His successor Nafata, however, sought to destroy the Shehu and his *Jama'a*. The threat posed by the Shehu had become too obvious to be ignored. The Shehu had already cut himself and the *Jama'a* off from the mainstream of the degenerate order. His movement now had a separate leadership and a distinct moral and social identity.

Three factors caused the rulers great alarm. The first was the growing level of social disaffection, due to the scale of social awareness fostered by the *Jama'a*. This disaffection permeated the whole of society and all governmental institutions, including the army. As *ahlu-d-dunyā* (people of this world), as Muhammad Bello called them in *Infāq*, the rulers were for the first time brought face to face with a situation in which "their balance had become light and their market unprofitable" while the Shehu's followers and influence continued to grow.

But a greater cause of fear than this, of course, was the possibility of Islam rising to supremacy in a land where it had been suppressed and where cynical and oppressive rulers had established their power on foundations and principles that were repugnant to it. The Hausa rulers were well aware of the all-embracing consequences of the new order if it were allowed to emerge. Their rule would be swept away, their power broken, their syncretism and opportunism terminated and their whimsical and oppressive laws stamped out.

The third factor that caused alarm was the stockpiling of weapons and the apparent preparation for war on the part of the *Jama'a*. 'Abdullahi wrote in *Tazyīn*: "Now when the kings and their supporters saw the Shaykh's community making ready their weapons, it caused them great fear. Moreover, before that, the numerousness of the community and its cutting itself off from their jurisdiction had enraged them. They made their enmity known with their tongues, threatening the community with extermination, and what their breasts hid was even worse."

The Shehu's Multitudes

It is pertinent to look briefly into the composition of the *Jama'a*. We have already noted that the Shehu had tremendous moral appeal and that large numbers of people attended his lectures. The same pattern repeated itself in every country he visited in Hausaland. Muhammad El-Hajj has suggested further factors, which may account for his massive popular following, and puts forwards a possible reason why the Fulanin Gida (the settled Fulani) supported him.

Although these "settled Fulani" had lived among the Hausa populations for generations and were to a great extent socially integrated, they did not enjoy the same privileges as the Hausa. They did not achieve political power or status and, in some cases, they were even forbidden from carrying arms or owning slaves. At the same time, they were conscious of the long-standing history of their Islamic identity and of their superiority in the art of writing and knowledge of the outside world. Because of this, fear and distrust on the part of their Hausa overlords and a feeling superiority and frustration on the part of the settled Fulani, created unstable conditions within Hausa society which contributed greatly to the growth of the Shehu's movement.

The Bararoji (Fulani pastoralists), according to El-Hajj, were attracted to the Shehu principally on account of their ethnic and linguistic affinity with him and because they had suffered from arbitrary cattle-taxes (*jangali*) and raids on their cattle by Hausa rulers.

The Hausa peasantry joined the Shehu for mainly economic reasons. They had for long been the object of oppression, exploitation and injustice. Eighteenth century Hausaland was feudal. The land belonged to the ruling aristocracy, with an arbitrary system of land tenure open to abuse and exploitation. The peasants were made to pay excessive taxes and their farms were often expropriated. With the conquest of Zamfara by Gobir, much land was expropriated, and its distribution as fief among the ruling aristocracy of Gobir resulted in considerable displacement of the peasant population. They, therefore, joined the Shehu's movement in large numbers, not so much on religious grounds, since many of them had not "smelled the scent of Islam", but rather because the Shehu's attacks on arbitrary land tenure and un-canonical taxes coincided with their own economic grievances.

Slaves also joined the *Jama'a* because of their plight and their being subject to oppression and injustice. El-Hajj concludes: "The Shehu's community comprised, apart from the genuine religious reformers, a number of discontented elements who had specific grievances against the Hausa governments. The Fulanin Gida, the Bararoji, the Hausa peasantry and the slaves were all potential supporters for a movement promising an ideal society in which justice and equity would prevail. From its inception, therefore, the community was a politico-religious body which constituted a potential danger to the State. That it was allowed to grow unhindered for almost twenty years is a great credit to the Shehu's diplomacy and remarkable leadership."

The huge number of the Shehu's followers alarmed the rulers of Hausaland because it was comprised mainly of those who had suffered most from their un-Islamic rule. The *Jama'a* was put under considerable pressure and was left in no doubt that it faced an increasing possibility of annihilation. Finally, and in keeping with the tradition of un-Islamic rulers and tyrants everywhere, Nafata issued his infamous decree, formally proscribing the *Jama'a*. The decree stipulated, among other things: that no one except the Shehu himself should henceforth preach to the people; that no one should become a Muslim except those who had inherited Islam from their fathers; that all those who had embraced Islam should return to the religion of their forefathers, i.e. paganism; and that no man should henceforth wear the turban, nor woman the head-covering. This decree was announced in all public places.

As it happens, this was the last significant act Nafata made. "Allah protected us from his design and strategy," wrote Bello in *Infāq*, "and Allah caused his death shortly after that." It is significant that Nafata could issue such a bold decree and yet be unable to hold his kingdom together. In fact his seven-year rule only served to increase the weakness of Gobir.

It is in the nature of rulers who have failed to save their nations from social decay that they to seek to ruin all constructive efforts to regenerate them and try to eliminate all attempts to do so. It is known that both Yakubu and Nafata were well aware of the Shehu's truth and sincerity. They had sought his blessing on more than one occasion and knew what his intentions were. Their opposition to him illustrates their hatred for Islam, their love of corruption and degeneracy and their attachment to hypocrisy and *takhlīṭ* (religious syncretism).

The year 1217/1803 was an eventful one for the Shehu and the *Jama'a*. Nafata died and was succeeded by Yunfa, who was energetic and ambitious. His immediate concern was to implement the decree of Nafata to the letter and, if possible, to eliminate the Shehu. Consequently, he made an attempt on the Shehu's life. According to 'Abdullahi, the Shehu went to the palace with him and Umaru Alkammu, his trusted companion, at the invitation of Yunfa.

'Abdullahi continues his account: "He fired his *naphta* (gun) in order to burn us with its fire but the fire turned back on him and nearly burned him while we were watching. Not one of us moved but he retreated hastily. Then he turned back to us after a while and sat near to us. We approached him and spoke to him. He said to us, 'Know that I have no enemy on earth like you,' and he made clear to us his enmity and we made clear to him that we did not fear him, for Allah had not given him power over us... Allah kept him back from us, and we went away from him to our house and none knew anything about that (affair) other than we ourselves."

That was, in fact, the last personal contact between the Shehu and the ruler of Gobir. It was clear that there were now two rulers in Gobir: Yunfa representing un-Islamic rule and Shehu Usman dan Fodio representing the nascent Islamic governance. It was evident, too, that there were now two communities: the community loyal to the pseudo-Muslim government and the *Jama'a*, loyal to the Shehu and yearning for a true *khilāfah* (Islamic caliphate). There were now also two orders: the decadent order, which had brought weakness, corruption and tyranny to Hausaland, and the new order, almost ready to explode into *jihad*.

Factors in the Process of Reviving Islam

The first factor was the Shehu's changing relationship with the rulers of Gobir and how he was able to use each situation to the advantage of his cause. In his first encounter with the ruler, the Shehu merely advised him to uphold Islam and be just. He showed neither enmity nor harshness towards him and did not seek to antagonize him in any way. To have been hostile at the outset would have been prejudicial to his cause. Islam always starts in a state of weakness and it is necessary to safeguard its survival in the initial stages by means of diplomacy, courtesy and caution.

In his second encounter – by which time his followers had grown strong and numerous – the Shehu spoke as a public figure worthy of recognition. The nature of his demands showed the nature of his cause. He demanded to be recognized as the leader of a particular cause and that his followers should be respected. Although this demand was specific to himself and his followers, his cause was of a universal nature and embraced all elements in society that were in need of justice. Hence, he demanded the release of prisoners and the abolition of all unjust taxes. Some of those released were not Muslims and a considerable number of the victims of unjust taxes and arbitrary rule were not Muslims either. It is the *mujaddid*'s duty to champion the cause of all those who are oppressed, Muslims or non-Muslims, in the same way that he is duty-bound to seek the enhancement of Islam and its supremacy. Islam's enemy is the oppressor not the victim of oppression.

In the final encounter, when the king tried to kill him, the Shehu did not seek to make a sensation out of it or to capitalize on it in any way. He kept the matter secret and concentrated on safeguarding the *Jama'a*'s well-being and survival. He had grown strong but he was aware that numerical strength was not all that was required for success. He would not, and indeed, had to avoid beginning hostilities. He had to go on with his work of teaching until the enemy attacked first. He did not exhibit open hostility towards the rulers in a way that would provoke them into any early attempt to destroy his cause. In fact, he was almost friendly with Bawa and avoided confrontation with him throughout his rule, simply stressing that he was struggling for justice in society.

The second factor was the nature of the Shehu's appeal. We have seen that different segments of society were attracted to him for different reasons which are all acceptable. Islam is an umbrella for the oppressed, since its purpose is not only to improve the moral standard of the people but also to enhance their social and economic well-being and to establish justice for them. The universal nature of the Shehu's appeal made it possible for a large number of non-Muslims to accept Islam, for nominal Muslims to become committed to Islam, and for society in general to transfer its allegiance from a tyrannical order to genuine Islam.

Islam strives for justice for everyone in this world, and it welcomes anyone who wishes to fight for its cause, because it feels responsible for establishing a just and equitable system for mankind. It leaves the judgment about who is sincere in his faith in Allah and about who is destined for either Paradise or Hell in the Hereafter to Allah alone. Its real enemy, therefore, is not the common people but those who oppress, cheat and manipulate them. It strives to liberate the common people and to remove all political and social obstacles which block their road towards Islam. It is left up to them, when the road has been cleared, as to whether they accept Islam or reject it, but whatever course they adopt, their entitlement to justice is absolute and unconditional.

The third factor relevant to the process of reviving Islam is that of organization. At a certain stage in his career the Shehu recognized the need to settle down in one place and concentrate on organizing his *Jama'a.* Essentially there were three elements involved in this process. The first was the production of teachers and scholars to disseminate his message. The second was intellectual, and he made sure that he himself or 'Abdullahi or others wrote on practically every matter that was of importance to the *Jama'a* in particular and to society as a whole. The third element was political. Delegations that came to him would give him their allegiance and agreed from that time on to place their loyalty to the Shehu above that given to the degenerate governments of the day.

Finally, the Shehu's tremendous patience was also a vital factor. By the year 1217/1803, he had interacted with four different regimes over a period of more than twenty years and, while the last three sought to provoke him into direct, armed confrontation, he had exercised restraint and refused to take any premature step. It is significant that, even when his followers thought they were strong enough to start a *jihad*, he refused to permit such a course of action. He waited for more than a further seven years to start armed conflict and even then he did not instigate it.

The Shehu believed, as he stated in *Amr bi-l Ma'rūf wa-n*

Nahy 'ani-l Munkar, that once an armed confrontation is started it must be carried to its logical conclusion and that, if a movement is not capable of a sustained armed struggle, it should not rush into it unless it merely wants weak and oppressed Muslims to be annihilated. He was not interested in his cause turning into a mere nuisance. He had sought respect and dignity for it and he wanted it to maintain that character until Allah Himself decided on another course of action.

His dealings with the successive regimes suggest that he felt that time was on the side of Islam. If anybody needed to fear that time would run out, it was the oppressor not him. Thus, the Shehu had no cause to panic or to rush into a *jihad* in Hausaland. All that he sought was the right to educate the people. As long as he could preach and take his appeal to the masses he was satisfied. History would eventually take its course.

10. The Ultimate Break

By the year 1217/1803, the *Jama'a* had actually become a nation, an *ummah* in its own right. It had its distinct leader, a political structure, a system of law and an explicit identity of its own. The tension was growing between the *Jama'a* and the political establishment and the Sulṭan, Yunfa, was determined to crush the *Jama'a*. The ultimate break between the Shehu and the political and social system symbolized by Yunfa was at hand. The unfolding of events had made it clear to the Shehu that a formal and physical break with the un-Islamic power structure and an ultimate military confrontation with the Hausa powers were now inevitable.

Because of this, his *Masā'il Muhimmah,* written in 1217/1803, dealt with the fundamental issues that should be understood by the "people of Sudan and those among the brothers whose land is like [their] land in all regions and cities." The Shehu addressed fourteen basic matters and his tone changed sharply from the earlier mild one he had used up until that point, indicating by this that Hausaland had reached the end of an era. A new situation had emerged which required its own approach, method and discourse. We shall consider some of the issues in *Masā'il* within their ideological context.

The Shehu addressed the precept that religion is built on insight and reflection and, therefore, that reflection is one of its underlying precepts. Thus, *tabaṣṣur* – reflection or thoughtful consideration of matters – "is obligatory on every

Muslim" be he a *mujtahid*, a learned man, or an ordinary person. While he may not be required to deduce proofs for his beliefs, the ordinary man is required, nevertheless, to think about what he does and to "stand on what he has no doubt about"; otherwise his religious attitude would amount to no more than mockery and play. This meant that, in the Shehu's view, the days of blind adherence to Islam were over.

From this time on, everyone was obliged to use reason and intelligence in their practice of Islam. This did not grant any license for an intellectual free-for-all, because the *Sharī'ah* remained the yardstick of every opinion and every decision. The intellectual movement fostered by the Shehu had, in his opinion, now come of age, and religion could now be approached on a sensible, thoughtful and intellectual basis, no longer subject to blind and spiritless obedience either to rulers or scholars. The Shehu was thus asking for an enlightened, conscious rejection of Hausa rule in favor of the Islamic leadership offered by his movement.

The second issue dealt with in *Masā'il* was that the need had arisen for Muslims to have a single, recognized Imam, a moral, intellectual and political authority. The question of leadership, in the sense of the appointment of an Imam to whom Muslims should offer their oath of allegiance (*bay'ah*), had not arisen until this time. No doubt the Shehu was accepted as the leader of the *Jama'a* but he saw his role principally as that of a scholar and teacher, someone who calls others to the way of Allah. He had never put himself forward as the Imam to whom allegiance should be offered by all. Indeed, he had consistently asked people to look for their own teachers and scholars and to remain with them – indicating that he was not the only leader or scholar in the movement.

The new developments, however, necessitated formal leadership, a recognized Imam and *bay'ah* (oath of allegiance) – in short a formal declaration of independence from the unbelieving powers and a distinctive and separate political status for the *Jama'a* and Muslims as a whole. This stage was finally reached thirty years after the initiation of the process which had led to the establishment of the *Jama'a*.

Hijrah now became an Islamic obligation if the *Jama'a* was to survive as a spiritual and political entity. In the Shehu's opinion, because of its suppression of Islam, much of *Bilād as-Sudan* had fallen into the category of *Bilād al-Kufr* – the territory of unbelief. The Shehu wrote in *Masā'il*: "I say – and success is from Allah – that *hijrah* from the land of unbelief or innovation or rebellion against Allah is obligatory by *ijmā'* and there is no need for any further explanation than that given by Allah Himself. Allah, Most High, says: '*The angels ask those they take while they are wronging themselves, "What were your circumstances?" They reply, "We were oppressed on earth." They say, "Was Allah's earth not wide enough for you to have made* hijrah *elsewhere in it?" The shelter of such people will be Hell. What an evil journey's end! Except for those men, women and children who really are oppressed...*' (4:96-7)."

In the circumstances in which the *Jama'a* found itself, an immediate uprising against the rulers would have been unwise. As a scattered group, and as yet leaderless in military and political terms, they could not muster sufficient coordinated strength to throw off the tyrants. *Hijrah*, then, was the wisest option and thus became a political and strategic imperative.

So the Shehu insisted that it is obligatory for every Muslim who lives in the midst of polytheists to "flee from them". It is also obligatory for a Muslim to make *hijrah* from a land where he is subjected to terror "to the land of Allah". So flight from a country, in which they fear for their life, their religion and their property, to a place of safety and security is obligatory for all Muslims. Similarly, a Muslim who has no access to proper Islamic education in a particular country should abandon it for a country where he can study Islam and its law.

Islamically speaking, *hijrah* is a flight from *dar al-kufr* to *dar al-Islam*, from *dar al-bid'ah* to *dar as-Sunnah*. It is an escape from a land where the *ḥarām* has prevailed, and flight from potential injury to one's body, family and property. It is thus, a search for justice, honor, safety and the rule of law and remains a standing obligation for Muslims. As long as there is unbelief on earth the obligation to flee from it remains. Such a flight from the land of unbelief to the land of Allah where justice predominates, is, however, only a temporary expedient and Muslims are expected to prepare themselves during the period of respite gained by their flight for the ultimate confrontation with *dar al-kufr*, with the sole aim of establishing a *dar al-Islam* in the area from which they have fled.

It was necessary therefore, for the *Jama'a*, while contemplating the *hijrah*, to review its relationship with the unbelieving power structure with eventual confrontation in mind. In other words, it was essential for the *Jama'a* to view itself as a political entity, indeed, as a state in its own right, and to establish its relationship with others within the framework of a Muslim-*Kafir* dichotomy. There were, in the opinion of the Shehu, three different possibilities of relationship in that situation.

One possibility was to have a friendly relationship with unbelievers and love them despite their lack of belief and their outright enmity towards Islam and the Prophet ﷺ. This is a relationship in which a supposedly Muslim entity is at one with unbelievers and in alliance with them against Islam. This, in itself, is unbelief. Allah disowns such Muslims: "*The believers should not take unbelievers as friends rather than believers. Anyone who does that has nothing to do with Allah at all...*" (3:28)

The second possibility entailed entering into an alliance with unbelievers, which might be detrimental to Islam, for the purpose of economic gain. Although this does not actually constitute unbelief, it nevertheless amounts to disobedience to Allah. Allah says in this regard: "*You who believe! Do not make friends of people with whom Allah is angry.*" (60:13)

The third possibility was to "befriend" unbelievers out of fear for the safety of Muslim life and property and for the survival of Islam. This "friendship" is "with the tongue only, not with the heart." This is permissible in a situation where Islam is weak; but such precautionary friendship ceases to be valid as soon as Islam becomes strong or, alternatively, as soon as Muslims are able to make the *hijrah* from the oppressive situation in which they find themselves.

As long as the relationship with the unbelievers is not positively harmful to the Muslims, that is, as long as it is reluctant interaction rather than the kind of true solidarity with them, which would be against the overall interests of Islam or detrimental to the struggle for justice, then it is permissible. Even then, it should never compromise the status of Islam as the superior religion nor of Muslims as the best of people. A state of humiliation or lowliness, the Shehu insisted, is inconsistent with Islam; Muslims should never humble themselves before unbelievers. However, as in the relationship with unbelievers, there are three kinds of humility.

The first is humility towards Allah and His Messenger ﷺ, and also to Muslim rulers, scholars and parents. This is obligatory. The second is humility towards oppressors and unbelievers. This is unlawful, because such humility is a degradation that has no honor attached to it. It is self-abasement from which one cannot emerge again with dignity and self-respect. The third is humility towards "the servants of Allah", that is the generality of Muslims, and this is recommended. Muslims should be submissive to Allah, humble towards each other, especially towards just rulers, scholars, parents and all those who deserve respect and honor. Towards oppressors and unbelievers, however, toughness and defiance is the answer.

War with the unbelieving powers was in the Shehu's view inevitable and a matter of time only. Indeed, as in all *tajdīd* movements, *jihad* follows naturally after *hijrah* and it was natural that the Shehu should contemplate it, or in fact state it openly in *Masā'il*. Two broad eventualities were contemplated in the book. Firstly, war against the unbelievers, a *farḍ al-*

kifāyah, which included unbelievers by origin, inheritance and apostates. Secondly, war against armed gangs intent on disrupting the Islamic order and against those Muslims who choose to support unbelievers and consciously reside with them and fight on their side. This war is obligatory, and it is a *jihad*.

There was the possibility that the enemy might one day surprise Muslims in their cities and overwhelm them. In that case, recourse to arms in defense of lives, honor and religion would become obligatory for every able-bodied Muslim, including women, and flight would be prohibited under those circumstances. It would also be obligatory for neighboring Muslim communities to come to their aid.

Yet another fundamental issue dealt with in *Masā'il* was the relationship between Muslims and their oppressors, which operated on socio-economic and political levels. On the socio-economic level, the Shehu cast doubt on the legality of the wealth of the oppressors. This wealth, he emphasized, was invariably gained from usurpation, theft or dubious transactions, in which case it was not lawful for ordinary business if it were money, nor was it lawful to eat if it were food, or to wear if it were a piece of clothing, and so on. Since the source of income of an oppressor is largely illegal, business dealing with him is, *ipso facto* – by that very fact – not permissible in law.

On the political level, the Shehu said the *Sharī'ah* did not declare it lawful to associate with the "sons of this world", who constitute the core of the oppressive class, even though the professed aim may be to secure some benefit or protection for Muslims. The Shehu was already too familiar with the class of scholars who frequented palaces ostensibly to defend the interest of Muslims. The truth is that other people, however high they may be, are supposed to come to the doors of the scholar and not the other way round. Moreover, there is the possibility that the scholar might be bought – even if he were honest in his intentions – by the kings, in which case he would fall prey to the strategy of the devil.

More fundamentally, however, association with oppressors leads to "real perdition" because it brings humiliation and abasement upon the "custodians of *Sharī'ah* (scholars) who are the symbols of Islam in every region". Therefore, association with kings constitutes "one of the greatest sins and hypocrisy", and amounts to "warring against Allah and His Messenger". Here again, the Shehu advocated a political and moral boycott of the oppressors.

It is safe to suggest that *Masā'il* was intended to prepare the minds of Muslims for all the possibilities that awaited them and to close the door between the *Jama'a* and the anti-Islamic establishment. Every Muslim should now be thinking about how to appoint the Imam, to whom *bay'ah* should be given, about the possibility of *hijrah* and the *jihad* that would follow, and about the possibility of martyrdom entailed by that.

The Flight

After the threat on the Shehu's life by Yunfa, events followed one another in rapid succession. Some of the Shehu's followers, including scholars and reciters of the Qur'an, who had fled to Gimbana under Abdus-Salām, were murdered by Yunfa's soldiers. Women and children were captured and sold as slaves. Books were destroyed and property pillaged. Yunfa's men were so elated with their success that they openly declared before the overawed Muslims, paraphrasing the Qur'an: "Bring down upon us the divine punishment you had promised if, indeed, you are truthful!" That was in the month of Ramadan.

Yunfa sent a message to the Shehu ordering him to move out of Degel with his family and disperse his community; otherwise, they too would be destroyed. The Shehu replied: "I will not forsake my community, but I will leave your country, for Allah's earth is wide!" Thus the *hijrah* started and the destination was Gudu, just outside the territory of Gobir. 'Abdullahi wrote: "So we fled from their land in the year 1218 A.H. on the 10th of Dhul Qada [Tuesday February 21, 1804] to a place outside Gobir territory. The

Muslims all fled, following us. Many of them joined us with their people; some came with no following at all."

The scale of the mass emigration towards Gudu alarmed the ruler of Gobir. For several months people left to join the Shehu. Efforts to stop this mass movement towards the Shehu by means of intimidation, plunder and slaughter proved unsuccessful. Yunfa then wrote a letter to the Shehu asking him to return to Degel. According to Bello, in *Infāq*, the Shehu sent a reply stating the conditions under which he would call off the *hijrah*: the Sulṭan should repent and purify his religion; he should abandon syncretism and become a true Muslim; he should establish fairness and justice; he should restore all the property he had looted from Muslims; and he should release the prisoners he had taken.

The *'ulamā'* at the court distorted the contents of the Shehu's message and urged Yunfa to reject it. The messenger who delivered the letter was badly treated and left to return to the Shehu through hostile territory. Whatever chances existed for reaching an amicable settlement of issues were shattered by Yunfa's message to the Shehu – the message simply stated that he would be sending an army to crush him.

"Then," 'Abdullahi wrote in *Tazyīn*, the Sulṭan "ordered the governors of his towns to take captive all who traveled to the Shaykh and they began to persecute the Muslims, killing them and confiscating their property. Then the affair came to the point where they were sending armies against us and we gathered together when that became a serious threat and appointed the Shaykh, who had previously been our Imam and our Amir, as our commander, in order that he might put our affairs in order."

The Shehu, now as *Amir al-Muminīn*, hoisted his flag, the flag of Islam, which rose for the first time ever in that region. Now there were two rulers, two governments, two armies and two opposing orders in Hausaland. Islam had emerged. A government had been set up. A formal army had pledged its allegiance. All that remained was the *jihad*.

Putting Theory into Practice

The immediate effect of the *hijrah* was to bring the Muslim community to the threshold of *jihād*. In *Masā'il al-Muhimmah* the Shehu had envisaged, or rather encouraged, the *hijrah*. He thought it was necessary to have an Imam at the head of the community to give sound political and military expression to this nascent spiritual entity. He also envisaged the *jihad* which would follow almost immediately after the *hijrah*. Now "the supreme Imam" had been appointed in the person of the Shehu himself and a *hijrah* from the land of unbelief to the land of Allah had taken place. *Jihad* had indeed started.

Hijrah, Imamate and *jihad* became the dominant themes of the thought and writings of the leaders of the *Jama'a* at this time. The Shehu wrote his *Bayān Wujūb al-Hijrah ala'l-Ibād* some three years after the start of the *jihad*, expounding these themes. In discussing them, we shall use the *Bayān* of the Shehu and the *Tazyīn al-Waraqāt* of 'Abdullahi as our main sources.

The *Hijrah*

The Shehu said in *Bayān* that the Qur'an makes *hijrah* obligatory for Muslims when they are no longer able to practice their religion freely. If *hijrah* is a duty arising out of the conflict between faith and unbelief, between justice and tyranny and between Islam and *kufr*, then the situation in Hausaland had made it an overwhelming spiritual and moral necessity.

What was at stake was not merely the conflict of interests but the very survival of Islam. Therefore, all other human exigencies – "the preservation of the soul, intellect, lineage, wealth and honor" – had to give way to the supreme importance of preserving Islam in Hausaland. All the others would eventually perish if religion were not preserved.

Muslims had, therefore, to undertake *hijrah* from all parts of Hausaland in particular, and *Bilād as-Sudan* in general, to the refuge in Gudu or wherever the Shehu might be. Hausaland and *Bilād as-Sudan*, according to the Shehu, should be divided into three areas for the purpose of *hijrah*. The first was territories in which "unbelief predominates and Islam is rarely found" and included such city-states as Mossi, Busa, Borgu and Yorubaland. The second was territories in which "Islam predominates and unbelief is rare" but where the practice of and adherence to Islam was confined to the masses with the ruling classes disloyal to Islam. This included Borno, Kano, Katsina, Songhay and Mali.

The third area was purely Islamic territories, which do "not belong to the lands of unbelief either as regards the rulers or as regards the masses but belong wholly to the lands of Islam." This type of territory did not yet exist so no one had any excuse to refuse to undertake the *hijrah* from the land of unbelief to an Islamic environment. Failure to emigrate would be a sin because *hijrah* is not merely a political or social command but a spiritual and religious one as well. So long as unbelief exists in the world, *hijrah* from it remains obligatory.

What then would happen to those who remain with unbelievers once the ideological line has been drawn? Those who remain "under the sovereignty" of unbelievers and live "in the manner of polytheists" out of their own volition and not out of necessity or the intention of serving the cause of Islam, would be considered disobedient to Allah and His Messenger. Those in the service of rulers who stay as a result of privileges accruing from their employment or from their sympathies with the un-Islamic system should consider their employment illegal. Only those who remain in order to promote the cause of Islam from within have a valid reason to stay.

There are two factors that make *hijrah* obligatory. The first is the obligation for Muslims to shun unbelievers who mock Islam: "anyone who does this is most unworthy of being befriended and should be taken as an enemy." Enmity towards unbelievers is necessary in order to augment the dignity and supremacy of Islam and to forestall the rise, consolidation and perpetuation of *kufr*. If Muslims enter into alliance with unbelievers they strengthen the power of *kufr* and weaken the power of Islam, with the inevitable corollary of the spread of injustice and corruption. Friendship with unbelievers should be limited to the demands of *taqiyyah* (dissimulation), which should be terminated as soon as the opportunity for *hijrah* has come.

The second obligation on believers is that of befriending other believers. The Qur'an states that, "*The men and women of the believers are friends of one another,*" (9:72) and that, "*The believers are brothers, so make peace between your brothers.*" (49:10) The *ijmā'* of *'ulamā'* restates the same message: friendship entails sincere affection, good counseling, desiring for a brother Muslim what you desire for yourself, "meeting with them and showing them love", and avoiding anything which might create tension, hatred or aversion among fellow Muslims.

The Shehu reminded his followers that *hijrah* has enduring benefits in store for those who undertake it in the name of Allah, and encouraged them with verses from the Qur'an such as: "*Those who made hijrah and were driven from their homes and suffered harm in My Way and fought and were killed, I will erase their bad actions from them and admit them into Gardens with rivers flowing under them, as a reward from Allah. The best of all rewards is with Allah.*" (3:195)

The Shehu urged his followers not to be deterred by the prospect of loss of property or even loss of life, for this would be nothing compared to the ultimate loss of Allah's pleasure if they failed to emigrate. The early Muslims suffered a similar fate. Some were surprised by the unbelievers en route to Madinah, "some of them escaped and some were killed", yet this did not deter the rest from joining their brethren in Madinah. The determination to forsake the domain of evil for the domain of Allah spurred them on.

The Imamate

Muslims, the Shehu said, are bound by law to elect an Imam to direct their affairs and, the moment this duty arises, it takes precedence over all other duties. The responsibility for this appointment rests on the whole community, although it may be exercised by its "pillars" on their behalf. The point to note is that the Imam is elected not imposed. The Imam symbolizes the Imamate, that is the *khilāfah*, which is "an overall leadership embracing all religious and temporal affairs – undertaken on behalf of the Prophet ﷺ."

The Shehu emphasized the supreme importance of the Imam in *Bayān*: "The obligation of appointing an Imam over the Community is based, according to the people of the Sunnah, on divine law, based on the fact that it was the *ijmāʿ* of the Companions, who so emphasized it that they considered it the most important of duties and were even distracted by it from burying the Prophet ﷺ. A similar situation has occurred following the death of every Imam up to the present day. Any disagreement which may have taken place about who was suitable for the office of Caliph does not detract from the general consensus on the obligation of appointing one. None of them said that there was no need for an Imam."

At the time the *Bayān* was written the Imam – in the person of the Shehu – had been appointed by the *Jamaʿa*, so the *Jamaʿa* had discharged that supreme obligation. However, there were further obligations to be discharged by the community, especially as Islam was now faced with the formidable task of defending itself to ensure its very survival. The first of these obligations was obedience to the Imam and his lieutenants. This duty flows from the command of Allah: "*You who believe! Obey Allah and obey the Messenger and those in command among you.*" (4:58), and the statement of the Prophet ﷺ: "He who obeys my *amir* is obedient to me and he who disobeys my *amir* is disobedient to me."

This obedience meant, in a practical sense, that their orders should be carried out, that the community should avoid open conflict or disagreement with them "even if they be perverse sinners", that their shortcomings or weaknesses should be overlooked, and that the community should show kindly disposition towards them, "even if they were to harm you". What was being stressed was not so much obedience but the overriding necessity to preserve the unity of the *ummah* in the face of an open and real danger from the enemy.

The obligation to obey the Imam naturally rules out any attempt to revolt against him, since that would amount to the disintegration of the communal and social order of Islam. Revolt *per se* is not prohibited, rather, if Muslims are faced with the choice of either tolerating a bad Imam, who nevertheless holds the *ummah* together, or of facing the prospect of a total and irreversible disintegration resulting from political and social disorder, they have to take the first choice. "To maintain order is essential," the Shehu said, quoting Aḥmad az-Zarrūq, "and the safeguarding of public interest is an indispensable necessity." For this reason, there was unanimous agreement that it is forbidden to revolt against an Imam by word or deed. This went to the extent that the *ijmā'* of the scholars sanctioned the performance of prayers behind any governor or other (Imam), "be he righteous or sinful".

The Shehu was faced with a practical problem. He was waging a war of survival and, while he was sure that he himself would be just, equitable and conscientious in handling the affairs of the *ummah*, he could not be sure that his lieutenants in distant places would not be harsh, inconsiderate or even corrupt. Yet, the upholding of their leadership was vital to the successful execution of the *jihad* and revolting against them on any minor excuse would definitely jeopardize the success of the *jihad*.

The obligation of remaining loyal to the Imam extends also to not deposing him for committing sins. The sins of a leader could never be as great or harmful as the communal sin of disunity and the subversion of the cohesion of the whole *ummah*. The Imamate is the symbol of the *ummah*, the repository of its power. "It is as a result of this (Imamate)," the Shehu said, "that the power of Islam is maintained, its laws are upheld, and its enemies suppressed." To destroy that symbol because of some minor weakness in the Imam is to destroy the power of Islam and undermine the supremacy of the *Sharī'ah*. Of course, if the Imam reverts to *shirk*, that is if he reneges on his belief in Allah, His laws and the necessity for Islam, it is obligatory on the *ummah* to terminate his rule, for in that case he loses the moral and legal right to preside over the affairs of Muslims.

The *ummah* is, however, obliged to appoint a qualified person to take on the Imamate. Beside the obvious fact that he must be a Muslim, he must also be of "sound mind, one qualified to give independent judgment", and, because he has to defend the integrity of Islam, he should be "courageous, not afraid of facing the enemy and enforcing the prescribed penalties" and, as the Shehu said in *Masā'il al-Muhimmah*, "not be liable to give way under the blows of fate". Moreover, he "should be sound in the realm of politics and diplomacy and astute in his administration, capable of being strict when necessary and lenient when leniency is required", as well as being firm in his decisions and policies.

Once this is the case, anyone who seeks to subvert his authority and divide Muslims should be physically eliminated "no matter who he may be". More than one Imam, however, is required if the authority of one Imam does not extend to other territories. Thus, there is no reason why several *khilāfahs* under different Imams should not exist simultaneously in the Muslim world.

The Imamate should rest on five principles, the most important of which is that the Imamate should not be given to any one "who aspires to it". The Imam should rather be elected "by the best Muslims from among their scholars and virtuous men, a man they are pleased to have as the Commander of the Faithful by virtue of his being the best of them and the most suitable for the office, just as, after the Prophet ﷺ, the Companions chose Abū Bakr, and after him 'Umar and likewise, the other two *khulafā' ar-rāshidīn* (Rightly-Guided caliphs) ﷻ."

The second principle is consultation (*shūrā*). The third is the avoidance of harsh and oppressive measures. The fourth principle is justice, which means, in its political and administrative context, that the Imam "should draw the scholars near to him, since they are the custodians of knowledge (and)... its guardians and propagators who know it thoroughly and show the way to Allah." Moreover, it is the scholars "who uphold Allah's command, maintain the prescribed penalties of Allah and advise His servants." The Imam should not undertake any policy except on their advice. Nevertheless, the Shehu left many options open to the Imam. In addition to adhering to the measures advocated by Islam, he was also free to follow practices of non-Muslim nations "by which they managed their worldly affairs", if these could be of advantage to the *khilāfah*.

The fifth principle is *Iḥsān* which is "the source of nobility of character". In political terms, this means administering to the moral, psychological and spiritual needs of people and, in the material aspects of their life, adding to their livelihood what is above their basic necessities. He said: "Since Allah knows that not everybody prospers through justice alone but also stands in need of charity which is superior to justice, Allah has enjoined them both." *Iḥsān* in this sense means taking particular care of the "old, young and those mid-way between the two" – in other words practically everybody in society. "The sulṭan must treat the old man as his father, the middle-aged man as his brother and the young man as his son. Let him, then, be dutiful to his father, generous to his brother and affectionate to his son."

The Imam, the Shehu stated, should be supported by four pillars. The first pillar is "an upright *wazir*... who wakens him if he sleeps, gives him sight if he cannot see and reminds him if he forgets." The *wazir* should possess benevolent and kindly qualities of his own. The second pillar is the *qāḍī*, the supreme judge, "who is not prevented by anyone's censure from upholding Allah's law." Apart from his ordinary functions of settling disputes it is his duty to "prevent oppressors from taking things by force, or from violating the law" and to "support the oppressed and help everyone to get his due... and to command the good and forbid the evil by word and deed." The third pillar is the chief of police who should ensure that "the weak obtain justice from the strong." The fourth and final pillar is the commissioner of revenues who collects taxes "but does not oppress the subjects." If any of these pillars is weak, the Imam will suffer accordingly.

There are other offices attached to these pillars, each of which is vital for the maintenance of a just and equitable society. Together with the four pillars, they constitute the basis of the Islamic polity. One is the office of *radd al-maẓālim*, or ombudsman, which deals with cases of oppression and usurpation that are beyond the powers of the *qāḍī*. Another is the office of *himah* which, among other things, reserves grazing fields for animals given as *zakāt* and the animals of the poor. There is also the office of *hurūb al-maṣāliḥ*, a special force established to combat apostasy, highway robbery and rebellion – in other words, to maintain unity, social cohesion and peace within the *ummah*.

A further office of the Imam is the leading of public prayer, which "is both an office in its own right and a part of the office of the *amir*." The office of *ḥisbah* is charged with maintaining and overseeing Islamic public policy and social morality. The office of land-grants superintends Islamic land policy and administration. Then there are the offices of *jihad*, records, taxes, *ṣadaqah* and pilgrimage.

Finally, the Imam should appoint governors for the various regions under his governance and other administrators for specific functions. They should be "men of resolution, capability, sincerity and honesty" and their appointment should be made "in pious fear of Allah, not arbitrarily." On their part, the governors and administrators should look after the well-being of their people and should avoid enriching themselves unlawfully. If they are found with wealth not owned previously, the Imam should confiscate it, even if it has been apparently lawfully obtained. "That is due to the fact that, even though what a governor acquires without being bribed may be lawful, he is still not justified in taking it, because he is in a powerful position by virtue of being a governor and on account of that is able to obtain lawfully what others cannot. So his surplus wealth has to be deposited in the State Treasury."

The *Jihad*

Jihad is a term applied to armed struggle but, in its wider sense, it also embraces the spiritual struggle of a person against the promptings and insinuations of the devil, a person's protest against corruption, injustice and evil in society, a leader's war against evil or corruption or disorder in society aimed at reform and justice, and even the hatred which a person nurses in his heart towards unbelief or corruption when he is too weak to raise an armed revolt.

Jihad is an ideological war between believer and unbeliever, or between a Muslim nation and an unbelieving power, which has as its sole purpose, from the Muslim perspective, either the preservation of Islam or the establishment of it. *Jihad*, as the Shehu saw it, is "the fighting of a Muslim against an unbeliever who has no alliance (with the Muslims), in order to make Allah's law supreme... This means that anyone who fights for the sake of booty or to show bravery or the like cannot be considered a *mujāhid*." Of course, this definition of *jihad* is derived from the *ḥadīth* of the Prophet ﷺ in which he said, "the only lawful struggle is the struggle to make the Word of Allah supreme in the land."

Like *hijrah*, *jihad* is a perpetual obligation on Muslims. As long as there are domains of evil from which a Muslim is obliged to make *hijrah*, *jihad* will remain obligatory. The key principle is the verse of the Qur'an: "*Fight them until there is no more persecution and the deen belongs to Allah alone.*" (2:192) Polytheism, which must be completely uprooted, is here equated with persecution since, being a vehement opponent of Islam, it is what is most likely to subject Muslims to persecution.

This struggle should, however, not merely seek to sweep the polytheists from power but also to establish the rule of Islam. So Muslims should carry on with their struggle "until there is no war with the polytheists, because they no longer have any power" and until nobody except Muslims or those in alliance with Muslims are left in the land. The ideal here is a situation in which "all religions will have perished except Islam." In addition, Muslims are obliged to continue putting pressure on unbelievers until their false beliefs are weakened beyond recovery and to defend Islam against all inroads of corruption and disorder.

The duty to undertake the *jihad* devolves on the person of the Commander of the Faithful but, if none exists, on the community as a whole. *Jihad* may be either a collective or an individual duty. It is a collective duty if Muslims are within secure borders and have their own state or territory. If, however, Muslims are in danger of being overwhelmed by the enemy, it becomes an individual duty, incumbent upon every single Muslim man and woman.

Jihad is the extreme outcome of the natural tension that inevitably exists between Islam and *kufr*. To lay down one's life in that struggle is itself the ultimate sacrifice which in turn attracts the maximum divine grace: *"Those believers who stay behind – other than those forced to by necessity – are not the same as those who do jihad in the Way of Allah... Allah has promised the Best to both, but Allah has preferred those who do jihad over those who stay behind by an immense reward."* (4:94)

Of the several traditions of the Prophet ﷺ, the most important one is where a person asked him of any deed that is superior to participation in *jihad*, to which he replied, "I find none." The Prophet ﷺ also emphasized the merits of making weapons, of equipping fighters and looking after the well-being of the families of those in the battlefield.

11. The Declaration of *Jihad*

THE HOISTING of the flag of Islam at Gudu signaled the beginning of the *jihad*. The *jihad* itself was simply the logical conclusion of the process that the Shehu had begun three decades earlier in 1188/1774. Teachers, scholars, sages, soldiers; joined by peasants, slaves and oppressed men and women, all of whom had pledged their lives for the defense of Islam, now clustered around him at Gudu. The seeds that he had sown and nurtured for the better part of his life were now bearing fruit.

The Shehu made a formal declaration of the *jihad* in a twenty-seven-point manifesto, known as *Wathīqat Ahl as-Sudan*. It was addressed to "all the people of Sudan" and, in particular, to "those, whom Allah wills, of the brethren in these countries" of Hausaland. The tone of the *Wathīqah* is terse and the issues are stated in absolute terms.

Stages of the Struggle

In the *Wathīqah*, the stages of the struggle for the supremacy of Islam was referred to as the process of *tajdīd* and the following ten elements were affirmed as obligatory by consensus:

1. The enjoining of what is right
2. The prohibiting of what is wrong
3. *Hijrah* from the domain of *kufr*
4. The befriending of believers for solidarity
5. The appointment of an *Amir al-Muminīn*
6. Obedience to him and to all his deputies
7. *Jihad*

8. The appointment of *amirs* in provinces
9. The appointment of judges
10. Their application of the *Sharīʿah*

It is clear from this that the process of Islamization starts with commanding what is right and prohibiting what is wrong. This constitutes a process in its own right. It is aimed at educating the people, with the ultimate objective of changing their world view and transforming their character and, eventually, their political behavior and allegiance. This is, indeed, the most crucial phase in the entire *tajdīd* process and the rest of the phases depend on whether this initial phase has been carried out successfully or not.

Throughout this preliminary period of spiritual, social and intellectual transformation, the Shehu did not mention *jihad*, or even *hijrah*, in his lessons to his students or in his lectures to the public. Perhaps this deliberate caution was to prolong the stage until he was able to produce as many scholars as possible. His themes at that time were *Imān*, Islam (or *Sharīʿah*) and *Iḥsān*. The People had to know Islam and be committed to living as Muslims before they could be called upon to fight its cause.

If, in the process of public education and transformation, obstacles are encountered, the next course of action is to undertake the *hijrah*, the objectives of which are at least fivefold: to protect the emerging order from being annihilated; to give the cause a time of rest in which to take stock and chart a new course for the next phase; to bring together the children of the new order in one place; to form a concrete force for defense and liberation; and finally, to effect a symbolic break from the opposing order – a step which is absolutely vital.

Once the *muhājirūn* and *anṣār* have been brought together in one place by means of a *hijrah*, spiritual solidarity gains a social and political dimension, and the election of an *Amir al-Muminīn* to head the new community becomes necessary. In this way a new *khilāfah* is born and every Muslim, male and female, is then duty-bound to give the pledge to hear and obey, to fight for the cause of Islam and to obey the *Sharīʿah.*

The appointment of an *Amir al-Muminīn* is in itself a declaration of *jihad* because, as soon as Muslims have become a social and political entity, *jihad* becomes obligatory on them. At Gudu the *Jamaʿa*, after the appointment of the leader, became a state within a state, a tiny *khilāfah* in a sea of *kufr.* The prospect of *jihad* and the sheer necessity of preserving its integrity and ensuring its survival, places on the community the obligation to obey the Imam "in good times and in bad" as long as he holds the banner of Islam aloft and as long as the need for survival, for self-preservation and for the defense of Islam continues. The same obligation obtains in respect of the Imam's deputies, governors and army commanders.

Jihad invariably leads to victory and the expansion of the frontiers of the domain of Islam. Therefore, as soon as new territories are liberated, *amirs* must be appointed to take charge of their affairs and *qāḍīs* are appointed to administer the *Sharīʿah.* The nature and pace of the *jihad* is dictated by the strength of the enemy force and the circumstances that obtain in a given situation.

The Overthrow of the Decadent Order

The ultimate objective of *tajdīd* is the overthrow of the corrupt prevailing order and the establishment of Islam. The Shehu's struggle was one between Islam and *kufr. Kufr* had had its days, decades and centuries and now it was the turn of Islam, the turn of faith, truth, liberty and justice. After reiterating his yardstick for determining the legal status of a country – if the ruler is Muslim the country is Muslim, if he is an unbeliever the country is one of unbelief – the Shehu set forth in the *Wathīqah* the categories of leaders against whom the struggle was being launched. The people of *Bilād as-Sudan*, he said, should know that the following courses of action are obligatory by consensus:

> To fight against an unbelieving ruler who has never in his life declared 'There is no god but Allah' and to take the reins of government from him.
>
> To fight against an unbelieving ruler, who declares 'There is no god but Allah' merely for the purpose of satisfying the established custom of the country but who does not, in reality, profess Islam, and to take the reins of government from him.
>
> To fight against an apostate ruler, who has abandoned Islam and reverted to unbelief, and to take the reins of government from him.
>
> To fight against an apostate ruler, who outwardly remains within the fold of Islam but who, nevertheless, mixes the practices of Islam with the practices of unbelief – like most of the Hausa kings – and to take the reins of government from him.

The Shehu saw his cause as a struggle against all these four types of government. The first was government established from the start on unbelief. Such governments in Hausaland were pagan in the real sense of the word and, in the opinion of the Shehu, had to be swept from power. The second was government by rulers who were unbelievers in their hearts but who, through political expedience, had to manifest Islam and associate with Muslims. They might pray, fast and go to the 'Id with unusual show of pomp and pageantry, but at the same time oppress Muslims, frustrating all genuine tendencies towards true Islam and giving un-Islamic practices and policies supremacy over Islam. The *jihad* must sweep them away, for common sense dictates that if the majority of the people belong to a particular persuasion, the leader should belong to that persuasion as well. It is absurd to have a pagan at the head of a country that is largely Muslim.

The third was government by rulers who had committed

treason by coming to power in the name of Islam and then abandoning Islam once their power was fully established. In most cases rulers reverted to unbelief in order to escape the uncompromising stand of Islam for justice, moral discipline and accountability. Paganism does not offer any serious check on the excesses of kings and aids them by conferring on them a false divinity and infallibility.

The fourth was government by *mukhalliṭūn* (syncretist rulers) who ruled in the name of Islam but whose policies were based on secular objectives, principles and institutions. This category of rulers presented the greatest difficulty because, although they appeared to the people in the garb of Islam, the governments they administered were fundamentally un-Islamic. Secular laws were substituted for the *Sharī'ah*; pagan customs and behavior replaced Islamic social morality; oppressive taxation, usurpation and the confiscation of property replaced the Islamic system of taxation and Islamic fiscal policies; and Islamic inheritance laws were abandoned in favor of pagan whims. The pagan character of such governments also allowed rulers to amass wealth on a colossal scale and to spread corruption and to live their lives without any sense of moral responsibility.

The unmistakable objective of the Shehu's *jihad*, therefore, was to overthrow all those systems of government which were counter to the beliefs, values and systems of their people. The legitimate and logical basis for a government is that it should remain loyal to the ideals of the people, uphold those ideals faithfully and symbolize the people's aspirations, beliefs, traditions and values. *Jihad* requires the solidarity of Muslims and their identification with the struggle, so that they are ready to enter into a state of war when the time comes. Muslims who then identify themselves with the enemy should be considered as enemies. The best course of action is for every Muslim to pledge his loyalty to the *Amir al-Muminīn*.

According to the Shehu, a Muslim group which keeps itself apart from the main body of Muslims under the *Amir al-Muminīn*, should be invited to pledge their *bay'ah* to him and join the main body of Muslims. If they refuse, "to fight against them until they pledge their allegiance is obligatory by consensus" for, if force is required to unite the *ummah* against a real and potent threat, then it must be used. The Shehu went on to state that the following were unlawful by consensus:

> "To declare Muslims as unbelievers because of sins;
>
> To remain in the domain of war;
>
> To remain without paying allegiance to the *Amir al-Muminīn* and his deputies;
>
> To fight against Muslims who live in the domain of Islam;
>
> To devour their wealth unjustly;
>
> To enslave free men among Muslims, whether they reside in the domain of Islam or in the domain of war."

There should be no excuse whatsoever, short of active identification with the enemy, for attacking Muslims, seizing their property or depriving them of their freedom. These principles seem to be aimed at those who joined the Shehu to acquire wealth and slaves and who would bend the laws of Islam in order to enslave free men and legalize their property as booty. The Shehu's objective was to secure the solidarity of all Muslims and safeguard their freedom, well-being and honor.

The Internal Enemy

The Shehu devoted the last part of his *Wathīqah* to the threats that might remain after the completion of the *jihad*. The threat of apostasy had existed at the time of the Prophet ﷺ and immediately after his death when many communities reverted to unbelief. The only course of action, when apostasy arises, is to crush it by force if the apostates do not peacefully renounce their treachery.

Others, who might subvert the new Islamic social order, such as armed brigands, bandits, robbers or subversive armed brigades of any kind, represent a further threat. It is essential to fight them until they are brought into submission, so that peace and security to life, property and honor prevail within the domain of Islam.

Finally, a threat might arise from rebels who have been part of the *jihad* process, but not for the purpose of establishing the supremacy of the *Sharīʿah*. They might have been there for the purpose of gaining territory or in order to obtain political power or acquire wealth and, because they will almost certainly be disappointed in the appointment of leaders and distribution of state wealth, rebellion from such groups must be expected.

That, briefly, was the Shehu's declaration of *jihad*. It was another example of his practice, manifest throughout his career, of following the Sunnah in every step he took, in his public lectures, in the training of his students, in his *hijrah* and now in his eventual resistance to the forces of injustice and unbelief. By addressing his *Wathīqah* to the people of the Sudan as a whole, he may have envisaged a *jihad* that embraced states and territories far beyond Hausaland – a legitimate aspiration for someone who desired to see the justice of Islam prevail over the widest possible area.

The Start of the *Jihad*

The *jihad* started with several skirmishes between the Shehu's Muslims and the forces of Gobir. The *mujāhidūn* achieved some initial successes, notably the liberation of Matankari and Kwonni. These skirmishes were to be followed by what Muslims themselves regarded as their own Badr, the most important battle they ever fought, the greatest in the entire course of the *jihad*.

According to Muhammad Bello, the Sulṭan of Gobir had sent messages to his fellow sulṭans in Hausaland, notably those of Katsina, Kano and Zazzau, asking for their support and assistance in his war against the followers of the Shehu. They gave their blessing and support. "Then the Sulṭan of Gobir, Yunfa, came against us," ʿAbdullahi wrote in *Tazyīn*, "having collected armies of Nubians and Tuareg and those Fulani who followed him such as none knows except Allah." The Gobir forces were efficiently organized and well equipped.

The Shehu prepared an "army" to meet the forces of Yunfa, with his brother 'Abdullahi as its commander. It was poor, ill-equipped and inexperienced, comprised mainly of people driven from their homes for their beliefs, people inspired by love for Allah and His religion. The *mujāhidūn* had one main worry, apart from their weakness in numbers and equipment, which was lack of both food and water, but they received a boost when some of the Gobir army defected to their side and when Shaykh Agale and the son of Shaykh Jibril ibn 'Umar, the Shehu's teacher, joined them.

The two armies met at Gurdam on a lake known as Tabkin Kwatto, on Thursday, 12th Rabī' al-Awwal 1219 (June 21, 1804). The encounter was later described by Bello:

> "Then, as we approached the enemy, we marched in lines. The enemy, too, prepared and took up positions. In truth, about a hundred of them had put on chain-mail and quilted armor. They drew up in line with round shields and square shields and made their preparations. We formed our line of battle against them. We gazed at each other, each man's eyes looking into those of the enemy. Then, we shouted 'Allahu Akbar' three times and charged towards them. They beat their drums and charged to meet us.
>
> "The lines met. Their right wing over-bore our left wing and was mingled with our men and pressed them back into the center. Their left wing also over-bore our right wing and pressed our men back to the center. Our center stood firm. They shot their arrows, and we shot ours. Our horsemen did not exceed twenty, but the Gobirawa had warhorses not to be numbered except by Allah. When our center held firm our right wing, which had been driven back, also stood firm when it reached the center. The fight continued and the opposing lines were intermingled. Allah

broke the army of the unbelievers. They fell back. They retreated, they ran and they scattered.

"The Muslims pursued at their heels and killed them and took their property. Allah alone knows the number of those of them that were killed. Their King fled... Our commander, Waziri 'Abdullahi returned to the lake of Kwatto and halted there and we drank. Then we returned to the camp and halted there and did the afternoon prayer. Then we went on to our houses and passed the night there. '*So the last remnant of the people who did wrong was cut off. Praise belongs to Allah, the Lord of all the worlds!*' (6:46)."

'Abdullahi's depiction of this battle in the two poems he wrote about it could be considered as representing the viewpoint of the *Jama'a* as a whole. He saw it as a war of two ideologies. Yunfa had collected a vast army "to uproot Islam and the Muslims from their country" and his initial successes increased his unbelief and pride. The Muslims of the *Jama'a,* on the other hand, were defending their religion "and we are proud of nothing but that".

Though the two armies were unequal in arms and men, there could be no doubt that eventually Muslims would prevail. Yunfa was but the "he of the she-camel" who instigated the killing of the Prophet Salih's ﷺ she-camel, as a result of which Allah destroyed the people altogether. The combined forces of Hausaland were like the people of 'Ad who were driven into perdition by their arrogance and obstinacy. Yunfa would never again rise to greatness after this battle, for "he has turned back on greatness, hating religion".

'Abdullahi gave a vivid picture of the difference in the spiritual and political outlook of the two forces. The Gobir army was a typical establishment force, enmeshed in luxury and depravity, trusting only in its brute power and superior armor:

"And they had spitted meats around the fire,

And gathered ready in tents,
Fine vestments in a chest,
And all kinds of carpets, with cushions.
And do not ask about wheaten cake
Mixed with ghee and honey among the provisions!"

Yet, in spite of their superior power in weaponry and numbers, "their fire became like ashes" and their arrows were as if they had no heads to them. Their swords were as if they were "in the hands of inanimate things" and their lances as if in the "hands of the blind". Their flight from the battlefield was the inevitable result.

'Abdullahi saw the Muslim victory at Tabkin Kwatto as reminiscent of the Prophet's ﷺ victory at Badr. It therefore heralded the ultimate victory of Islam which would culminate in the liberation of Hausaland and the establishment of the *khilāfah.* This explains his confidence in calling the ill-equipped, uncertain and hungry army "an army victorious in Islam" in the first year of a war that was to rage for several more years. For if the Muslim army at Badr could grow in strength to overcome the whole of Arabia, what could possibly prevent the Muslim army at Tabkin Kwatto from overcoming Hausaland? Yet, in 'Abdullahi's view, the victory was not the victory of Muslim soldiers per se, but of Islam itself.

Shortly after the Tabkin Kwatto encounter, the Shehu moved from Gudu to Magabci. There, according to Bello, he wrote letters to the rulers of *Bilād as-Sudan* in which, among other things, he reiterated the purpose of his *jihad,* which was to secure the victory of truth over falsehood, to revive the Sunnah and suppress *bid'ah.* He then asked them to be sincere in their religion, to rid themselves of those traits against which the struggle was being waged and associate themselves wholly with his cause. He warned them that Allah would punish them if they continued to help the enemy, because Allah has promised to give victory to the Muslims and humiliate the unbelievers.

After a two-month stay in Magabci the Shehu moved to Sokoto, with the intention of sending a force against Dan Gaima. It was here that an attempt was made to conclude a peace agreement with the Sultan of Gobir. The Sulṭan of Gummi had sent a message to the Shehu seeking to make peace between the Shehu and Yunfa. The Shehu accepted the proposal.

Shortly after that Yunfa's *wazir*, Galadima, who had been dismissed from his position because of his sympathies for the Shehu but had now been reinstated, possibly to negotiate the peace treaty, arrived in Sokoto for talks. The Shehu's council met and decided that Yunfa himself should come to Sokoto for the negotiations. The Shehu, meanwhile, offered to refrain from fighting the Gobir forces for a specified time, with the exception of the march against Dan Gaima. The Gobir ruler would have come to the Shehu in person, but his council advised otherwise and the peace initiative came to nothing.

The Laws of War

We will pause here to examine some of the laws and principles that governed the conduct of the *jihad* as articulated by the Shehu. In Islam, all aspects of life must be governed by law, even such emotive and violent acts as war. Our source is *Bayān Wujūb al-Hijrah ala l-Ibād*, which Fathi al-Masri claims to be the Shehu's magnum opus and one of the most outstanding works on the subject of *jihad* in Islamic literature.

The Shehu considered the principles of warfare to be universal and, therefore, of relevance to all people. These principles did not include specific military tactics or strategy, for, as he himself noted, "each nation has its own particular type of maneuver, tactic and stratagem and its own method of engaging, advancing and retreating."

Adequate or maximum preparation must be made against the enemy in terms of weaponry, training and planning. The command of Allah, "*Arm yourselves against them with all the firepower and cavalry you can muster,*" (8:61) implies, according to the Shehu, the mobilization of "all possible resources" for war. Associated with this preparation is the predominant value of strategy. The Shehu elaborated on the statement of the Prophet ﷺ, "War is nothing but strategy," saying: "It is prudent on the part of the ruler not to underestimate his enemy, though he be lowly, nor to be heedless of him however insignificant he might be," and adding, "The enemy is like a fire. If you get to it when it is starting, it is easy to put it out but if you ignore it till the blaze has got a firm hold, it is difficult to extinguish." It is important to gather information about the enemy, principally through spies, and to attempt to break the enemy by infiltrating their ranks.

Another principle, perhaps the most important, is uprightness. "Indeed," he said, "you only fight with your deeds." Ultimate victory lies with the side that possesses superior moral qualities. It is futile, however, to expect every soldier to have high moral standards. What is expected is that the core of the army should possess enough of such qualities to give the entire army that moral superiority.

The commander, in particular, should symbolize those qualities and in addition, should be a man of experience and capability, "a man who has fought in the middle of battles... who has combated his equal and surpassed the heroes." The commander should have maximum security and should not be exposed to the enemy. He should conceal any mark by which he might be known and remove all traces that might betray his tactics to the enemy. "He should not keep to his tent day and night," the Shehu stated, "and should change his garment and his tent and conceal his position lest his enemy should take him unawares." Moreover, he should remain alert at all times.

Finally, there is the principle of victory or rather the observance of rules necessary for victory. The first of these is unity, "for disunity is the beginning of defeat". And unity is achieved through obedience to the commanders and observance of the rules of war. Then comes calmness. Then comes patience. "When battle takes place," the Shehu stated, "fate shows its face. Often a stratagem is more effective than bravery and a word has often defeated an army. Patience is the cause of victory." Then comes justice, both in the process of war and afterwards, for "there is no victory accompanied by injustice". Moreover, the fighting must be purely for the sake of Allah and not for any worldly interest.

To participate in actual combat in a *jihad*, one should be first and foremost a Muslim – though under certain conditions a non-Muslim may be allowed to take part. In addition, all fighters should be mature, sane and sound, physically and financially. Also, they should be male, though if Muslims are surprised within their cities or invaded, the duty to defend the integrity of Islam physically devolves on female Muslims as well.

While undertaking *jihad*, the *mujāhid* is under six obligations: to fight for no purpose other than the exaltation of Islam; to obey the Imam; to remain honest and sincere in respect of booty; to honor the agreements in respect of security concluded with the enemy by the Imam; to remain steadfast on the battlefield; and to avoid corruption.

Jihad is valid only against "unbelievers, either by birth or apostasy, rebels and brigands." Yet, *jihad* is not all killing. The law exempts certain people from being killed: women, children, old men, the chronically ill, the blind, the imbecile and the monk secluded in a monastery, as long as they do not take part in actual combat or in spying and intrigues. Indeed, maximum care should be taken to protect the lives of women and children in particular. Thus, in situations where the enemy shield themselves with children or encamp with their women and children, efforts have to be made, when attacking, to spare them. They should not be attacked at all, unless, by taking such extreme caution, "the Muslims would be defeated, evil would spread, and there is fear that the foundations of Islam would be destroyed, as well as its people and those among them whose example is followed."

The aim of *jihad* is not to take life but to ensure the

supremacy of the *Sharī'ah* and the establishment of justice. Therefore, minimization of loss of life on both sides is a goal to which the *mujāhid* should commit himself. On the Muslim side, although retreat is a grave sin, it is permitted if the survival of the fighters themselves is at risk or if the extent of the loss of life is excessive. "If the Muslims realize that they are certainly going to be killed," the Shehu told us, "then, it is better for them to quit. If furthermore, they realize that they will be of no effect in demoralizing the enemy, flight is obligatory... There is no dispute about that." A Muslim may not flee simply because he fears defeat but he may flee if he fears for the ultimate survival of Islam.

If it is the Muslims who are on the offensive, then they should explore various means towards achieving peace. They should first invite the people to Islam. "Go forth at your leisure," the Prophet ﷺ instructed 'Alī ؓ in a *ḥadīth* the Shehu quoted, "until you reach their *sāhah*, then invite them to Islam and tell them what their duty is towards Allah, for, by Allah, that He should guide a single man through you is better for you than possessing the choicest camels of a herd."

If the enemy accept Islam, then they should be accepted into the brotherhood of Islam. If they refuse, they should be offered another opportunity for peace by coming under the protection of Islam. If this too is rejected, then the matter has to be settled by force. Fighting must also be avoided if the enemy profess Islam on their own accord even if it appears to Muslims that their profession has been motivated by expediency.

The spoils of war encompass the following categories: unbelieving men and women; their children; their property; their land; and food and drink in their possession. The Imam has the choice of putting enemy combatants to death, of setting them free, either by grace or ransom, of making them pay *jizyah*, or of keeping them in captivity. He should exercise this discretion, bearing in mind the overall interest of Muslims. The property, land and other possessions of the enemy are to be used for the benefit of Muslims as determined by law. In particular, the rules regarding the distribution of the booty must be strictly observed.

Yet, *jihad* is not inhumane. Despite the necessary violence and bloodshed, its ultimate desire is a peace which is protected and enhanced by the sacred law. Thus, individuals who are engaged in fighting against Muslims can be given protection, *amān*, within the domain of Islam despite the state of war which exists. This protection can be given by any Muslim and must be respected by all other Muslims and by the state itself.

The Shehu, speaking about this, insisted that: "Such *amān*, when given, binds the Imam and others to observing it, provided it does not cause any harm, no matter whether it produces any benefit or not, whether it is given verbally, or written in any language, or made by some indirect declaration of intent or some indicative sign. And even if an unbeliever has assumed that a Muslim intended to give him *amān* when he actually did not, the unbeliever must not be killed."

The *amān* should also be respected if it is extended to the family and property of an unbeliever: "A man engaged in trading or on an embassy does not need an *amān*, because that mission automatically ensures his protection.... If a belligerent comes to us under *amān* and leaves some property behind with us, it belongs to him and to his heirs after him, and if a non-Muslim is caught on some road and he invents some tale to save his skin, the truth or falseness of which cannot be ascertained, he should be returned to a place where he feels safe if his story is not accepted."

Similarly, the Imam can conclude a peace treaty with non-Muslims on behalf of Muslims, provided that it is to the benefit of Islam and that it is absolutely necessary to do so. He can also conclude a treaty with non-Muslims who are either brought into submission as a result of *jihad* or who surrender before fighting takes place. In either case, they will pay the *jizyah* and are to be treated as free people.

"We must let them settle in our land," the Shehu stated,

"We should leave them in peace and safeguard them with a guarantee of protection for themselves and their property, we should not interfere with their churches, nor with their wine or pigs unless they make them public." They, on their part, must respect Muslims and must not commit an act of treason, such as spying for the enemy, against *Dar al-Islam.*

The *Jaysh al-Futūḥ*

The victory at Tabkin Kwatto greatly boosted the morale of the Muslim forces and enhanced the prestige and influence of the Shehu, but several years of war and enormous hardships still lay ahead. Besides Gobir, the other powers in Hausaland, such as Kano, Katsina and Zazzau, also posed a threat to the very existence of the *Jama'a* and the ultimate success of the cause itself. The prospect of persistent hunger and starvation for the Muslims, as the war raged on, was a further obstacle but there were some significant gains.

The Sulṭan of Kebbi was already an ally and, in addition, the Sulṭans of Mafara, Burmi and Danko had come over to the Shehu – even if their motives were more related to their opposition to Gobir than their commitment to Islam – thus assuring for the *Jama'a* an important source of food.

The Battle of Tsuntsuwa

The next important battle after the collapse of the peace effort was the *mujāhidūn*'s unsuccessful attempt to liberate Gobir's capital, Alkalawa, but their most significant encounter – what might be considered their Uhud from an ideological standpoint – was the setback at Tsuntsuwa. 'Abdullahi was still nursing a wound he sustained at Alkalawa and Bello was sick. Bello advised that, instead of going out to meet the enemy, the *mujāhidūn* should remain on the defensive and stay close to the camp but his advice was rejected. The two armies met. The result was devastating for the Muslims. In all, more than two thousand men were killed, including about two hundred people who knew the Qur'an by heart. The *Jama'a*'s chief justice who was also the

Imam for the prayers, Muhammad Sambo, the standard-bearer, Sa'ad, the *ḥadīth* scholar, Abubakar Binga, and the venerated saint, Sadiq and numerous other men of learning and piety were also among the martyrs.

The *Jama'a* was evidently shaken and the Shehu was overcome. "That day," wrote Waziri Junaidu about the Shehu's reaction to the defeat, "he was angrier than they ever saw him before or after. 'Take me to Alkalawa!' he cried, but his friend 'Umar Alkammu spoke gently to him and brought him back to where the martyrs lay and they buried them." This battle took place in the month of Ramadan in the first year of the Shehu's *hijrah.*

In addition, Shaykh Agale, one of the pillars of Islam, and the Shehu's brother 'Alī, also died within that period. This large-scale loss of the best of their men, and other physical and financial difficulties as well, intensified the sorrow of the *Jama'a.* Bello said that their distress was exacerbated by lack of food and funds, as well as illness; however, the struggle went on.

After the 'Id, the Shehu moved to Sabon Gari in the state of Zamfara. The immediate problem he was faced with was one of the succession there, which he settled by choosing Abarshi, who had been released from prison by the Sulṭan of Gobir as a result of the Shehu's five famous requests. More significantly, however, the *Jama'a* decided to launch an attack on Birnin Kebbi, with the purpose of bringing the Hausa state of Kebbi under the rule of Islam. The first encounter was with the Sulṭan of Gummi who was defeated. "We left no fortress of his," 'Abdullahi wrote in *Tazyīn,* "which we did not conquer." Then, the Muslims marched on Birnin Kebbi, and Allah gave them victory. 'Abdullahi recorded the battle in verse.

While at Sabon Gari, the Shehu wrote again to the rulers of Hausaland exhorting them to become true Muslims and support the cause of Islam. Waziri Junaidu recounted the consequences: "When the letter reached the Sulṭan of Katsina and he saw it, pride took hold of him and he tore it up. So Allah rent his kingdom apart also. When it reached the Sulṭan of Kano he was on the verge of accepting it but then refused and followed the path taken by his brother. When the letter reached the Sulṭan of Zakzak he agreed to repent but his people rejected it and he fought them until he died. After his death they rose against the Muslims, apostatizing."

The Shehu's letters infuriated most of them and increased their determination to crush Muslims everywhere. The Sulṭan of Gobir had already warned his fellow sulṭans that if they did not put out the "fire" of Islam, it would eventually engulf their kingdoms as his had been engulfed. The states of Katsina and Daura were also liberated during the Shehu's stay at Sabon Gari and Kano was embroiled in a turmoil which eventually led to its total liberation two years later. These were far-reaching victories for they set an irreversible trend of liberation all over Hausaland.

The Battle of Alwassa

After a seven-month stay in Sabon Gari the Shehu moved to Gwandu and set up a permanent base there. That was in the second year of the *hijrah.* Soon after the arrival of Muslims in Gwandu, the Sulṭan of Gobir, in league with the Touaregs and several of his fellow rulers, prepared a great force against them. The Muslims were divided as to whether to go out to meet the enemy or to take defensive measures. Both 'Abdullahi and Bello thought it more strategic to be on the defensive. The Commander-in-Chief, 'Alī Jedo, overruled them, however, as did a council held the following day. Disunity was thus apparent on the Muslim side.

One section of the Muslim army comprised a band of undisciplined and irresponsible people who had attacked people obviously sympathetic to the cause, or who were at peace with Muslims, and had plundered their property. 'Abdullahi 's efforts to prevent them failed and Bello was nearly killed when he tried to stop them. 'Abdullahi was greatly disturbed and wished to discontinue the march, being certain that the Muslims with such undisciplined and greedy bands in their midst would face defeat. Again, those who wanted to continue with the march prevailed. In the ensuing battle at Alwassa, the Muslims were defeated and suffered a staggering loss of about one thousand men.

Commenting on this moment of supreme crisis for the Shehu and his army, Johnston has pointed out that this defeat put the fate of the *Jama'a* and the whole future of Hausaland in the balance. The situation was, indeed, desperate but Shehu Usman's decisive moral intervention helped to save the situation and secure the future for Islam:

> "At this moment of supreme crisis it was not the redoubtable Bello nor the gifted 'Abdullahi nor the belligerent Aliyu Jaidu who rallied the demoralized reformers but the frail, devout and unworldly Shehu. It is characteristic of him that even now, with his army defeated, his captains at odds with one another, and his whole cause in jeopardy, he continued to exert his authority by purely spiritual means. Instead of taking personal command, as in the circumstances almost any other leader would have done, he sought to restore the morale of his followers through prayer and exhortation. We have Bello's testimony: 'Shehu came out from the mosque and preached to the people. With loving-kindness he exhorted them to forsake evildoing and turn to the paths of righteousness. He prayed for victory and his words made them eager to fight again.'"

The end result of this intervention was the recovery of the battered Muslim army, even to the extent that they were able, in Johnston's words, "to unleash a fierce counter attack" on the enemy who were forced to retreat to Gwandu. This retreat proved, ultimately, to be the decisive turning point in the struggle, since Muslims were never to face any serious defeat again at the hands of the enemy. As Johnston put it, "If Alwassa brought Shehu's cause to the very verge of ruin, Gwandu certainly sealed Gobir's fate."

In his *Tazyīn,* 'Abdullahi reflected on the indiscipline in the army. As far as he was concerned, it was fundamentally attributable to the loss by the *mujāhidūn* of many of their best and most valuable men in the previous battles: "I have been left among a remnant, who neglect their prayers and obey, in procuring pleasures, their own souls, and the majority of them have traded their faith for the world." Certainly, such people, lacking in discipline and Islamic commitment, could not be expected to fight a *jihad.* Dishonest and ideologically barren warriors may be able to win a war but they will never win a *jihad.*

There was no doubt, therefore, that 'Abdullahi, and indeed several others, knew they were going to war with very many wrong people in their midst: "On the night of ill fortune, I slept at Koldi, confused and defiled by mixing with the rabble of young hooligans... I said – and the daughter of misfortune was amongst us, because of their wickedness – to the morning, 'This morning is dark with adversities.'" On seeing the enemy, these rough men who had been brave in plundering defenseless villages did not have the courage to fight in a battle. So they fled. 'Abdullahi's cry, "O return!" fell on deaf ears, and only the courage of the true *mujāhidūn* prevented a total disaster.

In spite of the setback, however, the cause would eventually prevail because, in 'Abdullahi's estimation, although an uncouth and undisciplined rabble had found their way into the army, those who were committed to the *jihad* were firmly in charge and thousands of others were ever ready to lay down their lives in the cause of Allah. 'Abdullahi believed the Shehu's cause was not in danger but Alwassa did deal a serious blow to the Muslims and their hardships increased. The people of Kebbi, according to Bello, seized the opportunity to turn against the Muslims, and Gobir and other hostile forces went on the offensive once again, perhaps with greater confidence. In addition, famine exacerbated the Muslims' weakened state.

The Meeting at Birnin Gada

The defeat at Alwassa was, however, in the long run a victory for the Muslims, for it turned the tide in their favor. Several successful expeditions were undertaken but the most important event, following immediately after Alwassa, was the meeting at Birnin Gada. The Shehu summoned the leaders of the eastern countries – Katsina, Daura, Zamfara and Kano – to Birnin Gada. Unable to attend himself, the Shehu was represented by his son, Muhammad Bello, who read his father's letter to the assembled leaders.

> "He asked them," Last writes in his book, *Sokoto Caliphate*, "to take an oath that they would not be corrupted or changed by power, as were the Israelites in the desert, but would avoid worldly aspirations, envy, mercilessness, feuds and the pursuit of wealth; that they would avoid falling into the strife that 'finds a man a Muslim in the morning and makes him a pagan by evening.' They took the oaths and dispersed."

The supremacy of Sokoto now began, with the *khilāfah* being recognized by the emigrants and those fighting in the Sokoto *jihad*, and also the Muslims in Zamfara, Katsina, Daura and Kano.

'Abdullahi's Departure from Gwandu

Meanwhile the lack of discipline in the army so worried 'Abdullahi that he left the *jihad* altogether in the fourth year of the *hijrah* (that is, 1808) and moved towards the east to perform the Pilgrimage. "There came to me from Allah the sudden thought to shun my homeland and my brothers and turn towards the best of Allah's creation ﷺ, in order to seek approval, because of what I have seen of the changing times and (my) brothers, and their inclination towards the world, and their squabbling over its possession, and its wealth, and its regard, together with their abandoning the upkeep of the mosques and the schools, and other things besides that... I considered flight incumbent upon me and I left the army, occupying myself with my own affairs, and faced towards the East and towards the Chosen One – may Allah bless him and give him peace."

On arrival in Kano, however, he found that, although the unbelievers had been driven away, the affairs of the Muslims had become confused because of their preoccupation with the world. "I saw among them that from which I had fled in my own country." The people of Kano prevailed on him to discontinue his journey and to write a book on Islamic governance for them. He compiled *Ḍiyā al-Ḥukkām* and read the commentary on the Qur'an to them. They were contrite and put their affairs in order. Significantly, his arrival in Kano actually saved the Islamic revival movement there.

The Shehu was well aware of the army's growing "worldly inclination" but thought that it was a natural process arising from the different capacity each man had with respect to resisting evil impulses. Those like 'Abdullahi, Bello and many others could control themselves, resist the temptations of this world and remain totally uncorrupted, but others could not. It might not be wise to reject those who were fighting for the cause simply because of some moral failing they had. It would be wiser to exhort them to desist from evil and encourage them to improve their moral commitments, leaving judgment to Allah. Thus, while he would not accept those who fought purely to acquire worldly possessions, he was sympathetic to human failings.

In the *Bayān* he says: "I say, that the basis of this definition (of *jihad*) is what is related in *Ṣaḥīḥ Bukhāri* from Abū Musa al-Ashari ﵁ who said, 'A man came to the Prophet ﷺ and said, "One person (may) fight for booty, (another may) fight to gain fame, (a third may) fight to show off his bravery. Which of these is in Allah's path?" The Prophet ﷺ replied, "He who fights to make Allah's law supreme is the one who is in Allah's path."' It is related in *Madkhal*: 'If a man intends to fight for the sake of making Allah's law supreme, he will not be harmed afterwards by anything which may have possessed him during his fighting, whether that is anger, zeal or something similar to that, because all these are whisperings and inspirations from Satan and emotions that are not under our control. Allah has excused us for that.'"

As 'Abdullahi did eventually discover, it is futile to expect everyone to be totally upright. Indeed, he might have been even more disappointed had he reached Madinah, for he would have found that the ideal he was looking for in people did not exist there either. It was enough that people who had never seen the flag of Islam raised before were now giving their lives to make Islam supreme. It was sufficient that the Commander of the Believers was honest, upright, sincere and committed to the supreme cause, and that the core of the leadership – 'Alī Jedo, the Commander-in-Chief, 'Abdullahi himself and the energetic Muhammad Bello and others – was entirely committed and beyond corruption. In spite of the great losses, in spite of the vast forces allied together to destroy them and in spite of the effects of hunger and disease, the army still maintained, fundamentally, its Islamic character, fighting to establish an Islamic order.

'Abdullahi's stay in Kano proved beneficial to the Muslims, for *Ḍiyā al-Ḥukkām* eventually became the manual of government throughout the *khilāfah*. He returned to Gwandu to join his fellow *mujāhidūn* who had continued with their struggle. In the interim, there had been a second unsuccessful attempt to take Alkalawa and many successful expeditions had also taken place. Yan Doto and Yauri had been liberated and the Touareg at Farfara had been subdued. In addition, some of the rebellious groups had been systematically crushed.

The Liberation of Alkalawa

In the fifth year of the *hijrah*, the Shehu decided on a combined assault on Alkalawa, aimed at liberating it totally and irrevocably. He sent messages to all the liberated countries of Hausaland asking them to join in the march against the final stronghold of Gobir power. Bello, his son, was in command.

"After four and a half years of fighting," Johnston states, "the strength had gone out of Gobir and the end came quickly. Bello, as terse in triumph as in disaster, described the final victory without vainglory. 'Allah then opened Alkalawa to us. In the twinkling of an eye, the Muslims hurled themselves on the enemy, killing them and taking them captive. Yunfa was slain and his followers by his side. Thanks be to Allah.'"

The fall of Alkalawa marked the end of Hausa power and the beginning of a new epoch: that of the *khilāfah.* The backbone of unbelief had been broken. The worldly power had at last been humbled and subdued. Islam became supreme.

12. The Vision of a *Mujaddid*

WE SHALL now take our leave from the volatile arena of *jihad* for the quieter, more serene, but equally vital arena of Shehu Usman's thoughts on the new, noble state that had just come into being. How, for example, did he visualize the unfolding of history in the course of the life of this young state? What was his vision of *Dar al-Islam*? In which way, for example, would it differ from the Hausa kingdoms it had replaced and, if decline is inevitable for all peoples and all states, what would be his recipe for postponing such disintegration? Our main sources for this are the Shehu's *Bayān Wujub al-Hijrah*, his *Kitāb al-Farq* and his *Uṣūl al-'Adl*.

The Road to the Revival of the Sunnah

The Shehu saw his role in bringing about the establishment of the *khilāfah* as similar, in many respects, to that of the Prophet Muhammad ﷺ who came to call his people "to profess belief in the unity of Allah and demonstrated to them shining miracles in the face of which no man of sound judgment would doubt that he was the Messenger of Allah." The Messenger of Allah ﷺ, too, was at first rejected and severely persecuted. His followers were killed and forced into exile but he endured and persisted in his mission.

The Prophet ﷺ had an ardent desire to see his people spared the prospect of destruction and eternal damnation, despite the fact that their treatment of him was contemptuous and unjust. "When their persecution intensified," the Shehu recalled, "Gabriel ﷺ came to him and said, 'O Muhammad, Allah has ordered heaven, earth and the mountains to obey you.' He replied, 'I (wish to) grant a reprieve to my community for it may be that Allah will forgive them.'"

The question of rushing to establish a 'state' on the back of the destruction of his people was never contemplated by the Prophet ﷺ. All along, he hoped for one of three outcomes: that his people would be guided to the right path, by which they would be saved from the wrath of Allah and made to live a successful life here and a still worthier and more successful life in the Hereafter; that, in the case of their rejecting his Message, Allah might, in His unbounded mercy, grant them His pardon; and that, in the last resort, He would at least, raise out of them a generation that would accept the Message and be guided rightly.

The Prophet's ﷺ conviction that perseverance was the key to ultimate success restrained any tendency in him to seek an armed confrontation prematurely. "In spite of the offer his Lord gave him," the Shehu insisted, "he was not the first to resort to force against them, on the contrary, he used to present himself to the tribes and during festive seasons saying, 'Who will believe in me? Who will help me so that I can convey the Message of my Lord and thus secure for himself (a place in) paradise?' In the end, Allah opened for him the door of *hijrah* and, through it, the ultimate door to the perfection of religion and the termination of the days of ignorance."

The social order established by the Prophet ﷺ, after his victory over the forces of ignorance, thrived principally on his own "sublime attributes", including his personal discipline and his austere and abstemious lifestyle. This was in spite of the numerous opportunities for an easy and comfortable life which his position as the head of state necessarily opened to him. A leader's self-restraint, his indifference to material wealth and privilege and his selflessness constitute the essence of being an Imam as opposed to a king. It is in this way that a leader symbolizes the spirit that gives birth to a new social order and carries it further, reinforcing it by personal example and commitment.

The Prophet ﷺ also had an absolute sense of humility, both in his personal conduct and his exercise of power. The Shehu noted that when the Prophet ﷺ was given the option of being either a Prophet and a king or a Prophet and a slave, he replied, "Rather a slave!" He noted further that the Prophet ﷺ prevented his people from standing up for him as a mark of respect, saying, "I am only a slave. I eat as a slave eats and sit as a slave sits."

The Shehu also revered his humility in private life: "In his own house, he used to pursue the occupation of his family, in other words serve them. He deloused his own clothing, patched it, repaired his sandals, served himself, gave fodder to the camel used for water-carrying, swept the house, ate with the servant, kneaded dough and carried his own goods from the market, (a job) which he allowed nobody else to do for him... He himself served when entertaining a guest... He used to accept people's excuses, be the first to shake hands with his friends, and he never interrupted anyone who was speaking or made any displeasing remark to anybody. He never avenged himself, save when the holy things of Allah were abused, when he would punish for the sake of Allah."

Another attribute of the Prophet ﷺ was that throughout the entire course of his life he fixed his gaze on the Hereafter, disdaining to take personal advantage of his successes in life lest he should be occupied with it to the detriment of his relationship with Allah. Even as the booty from the battlefields kept pouring into his treasury, even as territories came under his control at a rate beyond his imagination, even as people came to him in complete submission, the Prophet's ﷺ mind was always occupied with the thought of Allah and his own ultimate destiny.

"Nothing could be dearer to me," the Shehu quoted the Prophet ﷺ as saying, "than the thought of joining my brothers and my intimate friends (i.e. his fellow prophets)." One month later, the Prophet ﷺ died, without ever desiring to enjoy any of the material benefits made possible by his lifetime of struggle to ensure the guidance of mankind. He died having never sought anything except the reward that awaited him with Allah.

By speaking about the Prophet ﷺ and the four Rightly Guided *khulafā'* ﷺ, the Shehu perhaps killed two birds with one stone: firstly he described the attributes of the best of all Muslim leaders, the nature of *Dar al-Islam* and the fundamental goals of Islamic governance; and, secondly, he showed the course which the history of his own state was likely to follow, turning from a merciful and compassionate *khilāfah* into a monarchy and then into corruption and tyranny, all of which could easily happen within the short period of only fifty years.

The Shehu's Vision for the *khilāfah*

The *mujaddid*'s vision of his own *khilāfah* was essentially characterized by two fundamental attributes: a commitment to moral values and to an unconditional, universal justice. The *mujaddid* was determined to create a state far superior to, and totally different from, the Hausa states he had just overthrown. The new spirit can be summarized in two words: justice and piety.

The Moral Foundation of the State

Of the ten qualities "commendable both for princes and others", mentioned in *Bayān*, we shall content ourselves with five. These qualities are an expression of the Shehu's concept of the nature of the new social order.

The first quality is wisdom, that moral and intellectual discipline which enables a person to join the company of angels while retaining essential human characteristics. It is the ability to strike a balance between the material and the spiritual in life. Proceeding from the two premises laid down in the *ḥadīth*: namely that "the best men are the wisest" and "wisdom takes one nearer to Allah", the Shehu stated that to be wise means being the master of one's own desires.

Wisdom is therefore acquired not as much from books as from a life supported by an honest and lawful income.

The overriding importance of wisdom to the new order was clearly articulated by the Shehu. "A wise man," he said, "is guided aright by his wisdom and fortified by his sound judgment, so that what he says is sound and what he does is commendable. An ignorant man, on the other hand, is caused to go astray as a result of his ignorance, because what he says is unsound and what he does is objectionable." Further, he says, "The merit of wisdom is that its possessor can judge what he has not witnessed by what he has witnessed. Someone, therefore, who can judge what he has not witnessed by what he has witnessed is called wise."

Wisdom entails the ability to make sound moral judgments and the possession of a keen and penetrating sense of history. The Shehu was, however, quick to add a proviso: "Wisdom is essential but its value can be undermined if it is not freed from its mortal enemies – caprice, envy, arrogance, greed and other desires."

A second quality that should characterize the spirit of the new state is knowledge. The need for the ruler of *Dar al-Islam* to be a man of knowledge is vital for, in as much as the ruler is the symbol of the state, his actions, behavior and character are bound to influence society as a whole. "All people," the Shehu explained, "derive fine qualities from the ruler and are indebted to him for laws, the checking of quarrels and the settling of disputes. So, more than any other of Allah's creation, he is in need of being acquainted with learning and gathering (knowledge) of the law."

The very fact of his being a leader places on him the obligation to be learned. To be successful in government the ruler should not have to rely on aides who might tell him what they think he wants to hear, rather than what he ought to be told. "For a ruler," as the Shehu says, "sets himself up to deal with people's natures, to settle their disputes, and to undertake their government. All of that requires outstanding learning, keen insight and extensive study. How would he get on if he had not made the necessary preparations and made himself ready for these matters?" An ignorant ruler is most likely to be held hostage by his own advisers who will inflate his ego in order to use him for their own purposes. A state will be on a sure path when the love of knowledge, its acquisition and its propagation becomes a characteristic of it.

The role of scholars as administrators, judges, custodians of moral values and ideological guides of the *khilāfah* was also crucial. In fact, the success of the state depended ultimately on the extent to which it was able to draw inspiration and support from its scholars.

A further essential quality of the state is generosity, which operates on two levels: the first level consists of the material support which a state can give to individuals, and that which individuals can give to each other, with the aim of strengthening mutual brotherhood; and the second, which is higher, entails being "so generous with your own self that you wear it out for the sake of Allah, in worshipping Him and in willingly undertaking *jihad* in His path, seeking nothing but His good pleasure." In this respect the *khilāfah* had two tasks before it: the advancement of the well-being of the people through a voluntary mutual support scheme, initiated by the people themselves but boosted by the state, and the development of the *khilāfah* through a continuous effort to defend the state and expand its frontiers.

The quality of patience is also necessary. In the post-*jihad* phase, it acquires a new significance. It means a continuing, unswerving determination to carry out the fundamental objectives of the state and to establish the required institutions, regardless of the material and moral costs. Patience entails a determined resistance to the forces of evil which may well adopt new tactics to frustrate the realization of the objectives of the state.

The last of the five essential qualities is gratitude. How else could Muslims express their appreciation for Allah's support? When they were weak, He strengthened them. When they were scattered, He brought them together. When they were oppressed, He gave them victory and made them rulers. Allah has said, "*But very few of My slaves are thankful.*" (34:13)

There are three degrees of gratitude: gratitude of the heart, of the tongue, and of the bodily members. The first is to recognize that all blessing comes from Allah alone. On this subject there are Allah's words: "*Any blessing you have is from Allah.*" (16:53) The second, which is gratitude of the tongue, is to talk about that, as in Allah's words: "*And as for the blessing of your Lord, speak out!*" (93:11) Its essence is to praise the Beneficent for His beneficence. The third, which is gratitude of the bodily members, is to pay Allah's due with each member and to worship Him with all of them. On this subject there are Allah's words: "*Work, family of Dawud, in thankfulness!*" (34:13)

The Social Edifice of the State

We shall now look at the Shehu's conception of the kind of justice that should characterize the Muslim state. Proceeding from the principle, established in the Qur'an, that Allah is not heedless of the atrocities being committed by oppressors – He is only giving them rope with which to hang themselves – the Shehu postulated two assumptions in his *Bayān*: firstly, that oppression is the main source of a people's demise – "Oppression is the thing most conducive to the withholding of divine favor and the occurrence of catastrophes…"; and secondly, that the oppressed are those most likely to triumph. Allah's statement that He will ultimately destroy oppressors and oppressive regimes is, in the Shehu's words, "a sufficient warning to the oppressor and a sufficient consolation for the oppressed."

Justice, then, was Shehu Usman's recipe for national stability and progress. It is the key to a nation's endurance on the stage of history. The principles of justice put forward by the Shehu and the social and political policies he recommended for the state are the subjects of his *Uṣūl al-'Adl* and *Kitāb al-Farq*.

In *Uṣūl al-'Adl*, the Shehu laid down ten principles of justice, mainly addressed to the overall ruler himself as the symbol of the state. The first of these principles is that the sulṭan should bear in mind the implications of his office. It is, on the one hand, a source of blessing for one who exercises it properly, and on the other, for one who misuses it, it is a source of unmitigated torment and misery. The just sulṭan will have the enviable benefit of being the "dearest of people to Allah", and the unjust sulṭan will have to pay the consequences of being the most hateful of people to Allah.

The essence of justice is that the laws of Allah should be applied meticulously, without fear or favor. Since Allah established His law in a perfect form and for the purpose of realizing a comprehensive justice, it is foolish for a sulṭan to tamper with it, even with good intentions. The ruler should recognize one fundamental principle: Allah knows best how society should be organized and managed and how an abiding and comprehensive justice can be achieved, as set out in the *Sharī'ah*.

An additional principle is that the ruler should endeavor to have upright and courageous scholars as his advisors and should listen to their advice. The scholars, on their part, must advise the ruler in accordance with what is best for both the ruler and the ruled and must, therefore, not hide anything from the ruler for fear of displeasing him. Here the Shehu was stressing the crucial role of the intellectual community in the state. As the conscience of society, they are under a binding obligation to give direction to government. Similarly, as the protectors of the oppressed, they have a duty to raise their voices against injustice and against all tendencies that could lead to permissiveness and luxury.

Their exalted status in society requires them to dissociate themselves from all oppressive policies and to rush to the aid of the oppressed against the oppressor. They must share the people's aspirations, yearnings and, as much as possible, their sufferings, and because the only reason for a scholar's association with the rulers is in order to establish justice, such an association should cease when justice is abandoned by the state. Thus, in reality, the scholar's tent should always be pitched with the people, not with the ruling class, and the intellectual community should not constitute a community separate from the mass of the people.

The Shehu went on, in the third principle of justice, to state that it is not sufficient for only the ruler himself to be fair and just. He must ensure that all the departments of state and all government functionaries obey the rules of justice, so that the whole state is permeated by justice. The ruler must never tolerate any act of injustice committed by any of his officials – be that his personal servants, army officers, civil servants or governors – for Allah will hold him personally responsible for any unjust acts committed by those who serve in his government.

The fourth principle is that the ruler should put himself in the position of his subjects whenever he introduces policies. If he feels that, as a subject of the state, the policy would be advantageous to him, he should proceed with it, but if he feels he might be injured by the policy, he should abandon it; otherwise his actions would amount to a misuse of authority, and even treason against the people.

In addition, as the fifth principle states, the ruler must open his doors to the complaints of aggrieved and oppressed citizens and must beware of the danger of turning a blind eye to them. If he ignores the injustices committed by his officials and strong citizens against the common people, he cannot be helped by his personal piety. His most important task as a ruler is to establish justice and prevent injustice, not to be engaged day and night in acts of personal piety, for "redressing the grievances of the Muslims is more meritorious than voluntary acts of devotion." The shutting of the door against the poor and the oppressed is characteristic of unbelieving rulers, not of Muslim rulers, we are told in *Kitāb al-Farq*.

In three further principles, the Shehu warned against forms of behavior that might undermine the government itself. The ruler must not allow himself to be dominated by arrogance, for pride might kindle in him the fire of anger. Anger, on its part, blots out intelligence. The ruler who is likely to be roused into anger, should remember the words of the Prophet ﷺ: "Woe to him who gets angry and forgets Allah's anger against him." The ruler should treat his people with forgiveness, forbearance and magnanimity. He should avoid treating his people harshly or unkindly by imposing unjust taxes on them or misusing or squandering their wealth and resources.

The state's resources should be utilized in such a way that everyone has his basic needs satisfied and economic and social justice reaches every corner of the state. The ruler should not allow his passions and appetites to get the better of him. The Shehu recounted the story of 'Umar ibn al-Khattab ؓ in which he asked a certain ascetic whether he had heard any objectionable thing about him. The ascetic replied, "I have heard that you have been putting two loaves on the tray for your meals and that you possess two shirts, one for nighttime and one for daytime." 'Umar ؓ asked if there was anything else, to which the man answered in the negative. "By Allah," replied 'Umar ؓ, "both these two things shall also cease." That a Muslim ruler should live sumptuously is offensive.

In the ninth principle, the Shehu turned the ruler's attention to the crux of the matter – the Day of Judgment. He noted that in the Hereafter, there are two domains, Paradise for those who are righteous and Hell for those who have squandered their lives. Real life is that of the Hereafter and, if someone is seeking power, glory, prestige and enduring happiness, the Hereafter is the thing to aim at. It is futile to risk that higher existence for the fleeting and delusive pleasures of this life and even more importantly, it is on the Day of Judgment that every human being will be held to account by Allah.

The ruler will, in addition, have to account for his stewardship: how he tackled poverty and spread happiness;

how he battled against injustice and initiated or facilitated the flow of justice; how far he had curbed the excesses of the rich and powerful and protected the poor and the weak; and how he took care of his people, particularly, the children, the old, the sick and, most important of all, women. In addition, he will have to account for the three most important issues of government and of human society: the blood of the citizens, their property and their honor. In essence, the Shehu was saying just one thing: that the ultimate source of restraint for a ruler in the face of the enormous power at his disposal is his inner self, his conscience, his awareness of Allah.

Finally, in the tenth principle of justice the Shehu reiterated that Allah has sent prophets to show mankind the best way to organize their lives, so that no one can ever have an excuse for following a wrong cause. He sent the Prophet Muhammad ﷺ as the last of the prophets to give glad tidings and to warn people. "He perfected his prophethood," the Shehu said, "in such a way as to leave neither room nor reason for any addition whatsoever, thus making him the Seal of the Prophets." That perfected model, therefore, is the one the leader should follow.

The tenth principle is, in fact, the sum total of all the other principles the Shehu had enumerated. He was effectively telling his own men, if you want to rule with justice, if you want a perfect model for your government, if you want your rule to succeed, your state to survive, your society to be happy, then follow in the footsteps of the Prophet ﷺ. Read the Seerah and retain the essence of it. The Shehu thus returned to his theme, namely that he wanted the Sokoto *khilāfah* to be the nearest approximation to the state established by the Prophet ﷺ himself.

As for specific policies, the Shehu grouped them, in his *Kitāb al-Farq*, into two categories: those geared towards elimination of corruption in both spiritual and mundane matters, and those intended for the well-being of the people. The former include the defense of the state against unbelievers, brigands and rebels, the blocking of all sources of corruption and the prevention of crimes and other social evils. The pursuit of the well-being of the people includes such measures as improvements to mosques, which symbolize Muslim piety and unity, the "commanding of the people to strive earnestly to study the Qur'an", disseminating knowledge with all its ramifications, the improvement of the market system, the relieving of the burden of poverty from the people, and "commanding everything that is good". These constitute the essence of the social and economic policy of a state.

Briefly, the Shehu was saying to the young state, "Defend yourself against all possible enemies, wage war against corruption, crime and oppression, re-establish the purity and sanctity of religion, give education the utmost priority with the Qur'an as its root, establish justice as the basis of the economy, fight against poverty, enrich the people and make them happy, and do whatever Allah has ordered to be done."

Forestalling Disintegration

Is there any way for a state to forestall its inevitable decline or at least prolong its life? We draw from the Shehu's thoughts on this subject in the *Bayān*.

A Muslim state, in the post-*jihad* phase, should endeavor to end disputes, conflicts and divisions by a sustained policy of forgiveness and leniency towards those who might not have full sympathy with its cause but who are, nevertheless, its citizens. "Wise men have said," the Shehu emphasized, "that authority cannot go hand in hand with revenge nor leadership with self-admiration. It is better to pardon wrongly in a thousand cases than to punish wrongly in a single case." Hence, transgressors should be "killed by kindness not cruelty".

In this way, the process of reconciliation can be facilitated in the wake of the turmoil and upheaval inevitably occasioned by *jihad*. If punishment is unavoidable, it should certainly not exceed the limit set by law. Even then, "if just requital against... a wrongdoer may stir up civil strife, or incite a man known to be docile to commit an offense, and the wrongdoer comes to seek forgiveness, then in this case pardon is better." This does not, however, imply giving a free hand to corrupt elements for, "if a wrongdoer publicly demonstrates his wickedness, is uncouth to people and does harm to young and old, it is better to punish him."

The state should not allow the fervor of *jihad* to get the better of its citizens. Those who have lost their power as a result of the success of the *jihad* should not be subjected to ill-treatment or to the confiscation and seizure of their property or land, for the Prophet 🌸 warned that, "Allah has made Hell binding upon anyone who wrongly seizes a Muslim's property," even if such property does not amount to more than a twig of a tree. Assaults on people's honor must be discouraged and prevented. Once the objective of establishing a new order has been achieved, the State must not allow the uncovering of old wounds or the unnecessary slandering of people.

The new state must guard its secrets and not expose itself to enemies. Proceeding from the *ḥadīth* of the Prophet 🌸, "Seek the help of secrecy in achieving your aims," the Shehu counseled, "Know that keeping secrets is a commendable practice for all mankind, a necessary quality for kings and an essential duty for wazirs, courtiers and the royal retinue." 'Alī ibn Abi Tālib 🌸 said, "Your secret is your captive so long as you do not divulge it but if you do, you become its captive." Hence, "He who keeps his secret attains his end and eludes attack. A secret is part of your blood so do not let it circulate in veins other than your own and if you divulge it, it is like shedding your own blood."

A Muslim state has to be conscious of the fact that the complexities of human nature and society are not swept away merely because a *jihad* has taken place. Since, in the Shehu's words, "every human being has in himself some aspects of animal behavior," those complexities are bound to remain. The state, and especially its ruler, must learn to deal with the complexities of human nature in such a way that the prosperity of the state and of the people can be guaranteed and sustained without harming any section of society.

The state must anticipate that there will be those with the nature of leopards, monkeys, donkeys, dogs, polecats, dung-beetles, hawks, wolves, ostriches and jerboa among its people. Caution, therefore, is the key in dealing with different aspects of human nature. For instance, in dealing with the "dung-beetle" among men – those who "delight in eating excrement and are accustomed to the smell of filthy things," in other words people who trade in worldly tales, lies and superstitions – the ruler should throw flowers on them, for "they die when musk or flowers are cast on them".

People like ostriches, "which bury all their eggs in the sand and sit on only one," thereby creating a false impression of what they are doing, should never be believed. "A man of experience... will not be fooled by that first egg but will go on digging until he finds the rest." That is the way to deal with such deceivers. As for people like jerboas, which create two entrances to their burrows, entering through one and emerging through another, thus symbolizing hypocrites, the best course of action is that they should be avoided completely. With "lion" people, a completely different strategy must be employed. "No peace can exist in the face of a lion's roar," so the only answer is all-out defense of state interests.

There has to be the recognition that the state can only be preserved by a rigorous and austere political culture, a profound sense of justice and humility on the part of rulers. Conversely, the state will be toppled by luxury, nepotism and injustice. On luxury, the Shehu warned that, "when Allah desires to destroy a state, He hands over its affairs to the extravagant sons of rulers, whose ambition is to magnify the status of kingship, to gratify their desires and indulge in sins. As a result of that Allah takes power away from them." Nepotism has the effect of destroying a government. Injustice brings the life of a kingdom to an untimely end.

Finally if, despite these precautions and measures, the state finds itself in a state of disharmony, it should question its policies of social justice and equity. If they are not the cause of the insecurity or the trend towards disintegration, then the ruler must return quickly to the roots, "by summoning the scholars and enjoining truth and acting in accordance with it, by upholding the Sunnah, by making justice prevail and by sitting down humbly on rugs to review wrongs." In addition, he should quickly restore honor to whom it is due, abolish unlawful and oppressive taxes and forced labor, and give due respect to scholars and men of piety. "He should not deprive a chief of his chieftaincy, rather he should make sure that every mighty man retains his position and cause everyone to occupy the place he is entitled to. Only then can he be chief of chiefs."

A king will gain victory over his enemies according to the extent he acts with justice towards his subjects and will be defeated in his wars according to the extent of his injustice. Seeing to the welfare of subjects is more effective than a large number of soldiers. It has been said that the true crown of a king is his integrity, his stronghold his impartiality and his wealth his subjects. There can be no triumph with transgression, no rule without the law and no chieftaincy accompanied by vengeance.

13. The Triumvirate

THE ESTABLISHMENT of the *khilāfah* naturally gave rise to a totally different situation from that of the "days of ignorance" which preceded it. Hence, a new role emerged for the Shehu and his companions. In addition to calling people to Islam and striving in the cause of Allah, they now had to administer a state according to the Qur'an and Sunnah and look after the *ummah* in the manner of the Rightly Guided *khulafā'*. The position of the Shehu himself had become crucial. Not only did the mantle of leadership fall on him but he also had to, and did, serve as the symbol of the *ummah*, the guardian of the revival of the Sunnah and the unifying force for the various communities, groups and interests that converged to constitute the *khilāfah*.

When the *khilāfah* finally became an absolute reality, three figures emerged as the principal pillars of the new order. Most of the prominent followers of the Shehu had been martyred in the struggle or had died – many of them from the rigors and strains of a lengthy and gruesome *jihad*. These pillars were, firstly, the *mujaddid* himself, Shehu Usman dan Fodio, the initiator and symbol of *tajdīd*; secondly, 'Abdullahi dan Fodio, the finest and most accomplished scholar the *tajdīd* movement produced and also its philosopher and conscience; and thirdly, Muhammad Bello, the Shehu's son, the energetic, trustworthy leader, destined to serve as the real architect of the new political process and the consolidator of the *khilāfah*.

These three constituted the great triumvirate, the three

men who transformed central Sudan and changed the course of history in *Bilād as-Sudan*. The Shehu divided the responsibilities for the *khilāfah* between his companions and prominent Muslims. The most important of these responsibilities naturally fell on his two wazirs. 'Abdullahi was given the administration of the western parts of the *khilāfah* and Muhammad Bello that of the eastern parts. The Shehu, now at Sifawa where he moved after the liberation of Alkalawa, remained the *Amir al-Muminīn*, though he did not take direct part in the administration; he devoted most of his time to teaching and writing, counseling and guiding the *ummah*.

The *khilāfah* was indeed a complex social entity, bringing together diverse groups, and often, conflicting interests, under one Islamic government. The *Jama'a*, which had initiated the *jihad*, was now, as a social force, no more than a microcosm in the macrocosm of the *khilāfah*. Many communities, scholars and others, who had played no part in the process of reviving Islam in Hausaland, were now part of the *khilāfah* and herein lay the real problems for the new leaders. The egalitarianism, solidarity, brotherhood and high moral standards, which had characterized the *Jama'a*, were now in danger of being weakened, if not overwhelmed, by the larger community. Bello was keenly aware of this problem. His analysis of the larger community, reproduced by Murray Last, suggests the magnitude of the social problems now confronting the leadership. In it, Bello classified the *Jama'a* into ten categories.

The first nine include: those who had joined the *Jama'a* for purely political reasons, because it offered a refuge for the oppressed; Fulani who had joined it out of tribal considerations and had cause to "despise the non-Fulani, even if they were learned, pious or *mujāhidūn*"; those whose reason for membership was no more than "fashion"; scholars whose fortunes had been drained by the momentum of Islamic revival and the *jihad* unleashed by the *Jama'a* and who had no alternative but to join in order to survive; and those who were in the *Jama'a* because it offered material benefits.

There were still others who rode on the prestigious crest of the *Jama'a*, even though they had since been "attracted by the world and the devil" and had abandoned its goals; those who were born within the *Jama'a* and remained in it, not by absolute conviction, but by accident of birth, and who had no interest in learning the values and objectives which the movement stood for; and then there were others swept by the currents of history into the body of the *Jama'a*. They did not know why they were there and did not really belong there, either by orientation or conviction.

The genuine members of the *Jama'a*, who comprised only one out of the ten categories, were those "guided not by the world but by Allah, giving up property, power and family for the sake of the Life-to-come." Last concluded his analysis by saying: "This description of the hangers-on in the Community is probably particularly true of Sokoto, where Bello was living and which had become the center of activity. The emphasis within the community had shifted away from scholarship. Those who had not been attracted by its practice of Islam were now attracted by its success and, under the conditions of *jihad*, army leaders were as important as scholars. While the Shaykh was alive, however, respect for his authority held any serious division in abeyance."

In a state as complex and diverse as the *khilāfah*, where the highly cultured, the ascetic and those who intensely supported the process of reviving Islam had to live side by side with the thoroughly worldly, or where the scholar had to live under one roof with the common man, or where those brought up in an atmosphere of Islamic revival had to share responsibilities of state with outsiders or even opportunists, the problems of maintaining the tempo of the *tajdīd* with regard to preserving the ideals of Islam and implementing the *Sharī'ah* in its pure form was particularly acute. Yet, the leaders had no option other than to face this problem squarely.

This called for a new intellectual, philosophical and legal process aimed at establishing the intellectual basis of the state and its political structure, the formulation of a legal framework within the *Sharī'ah* to deal with the specific complexities presented by the new state, and the articulation of a philosophy of continued *tajdīd* to serve as a guide for subsequent years. This process was spearheaded by the Shehu and his brother 'Abdullahi and continued even after the Shehu's death. Our sources for this discussion are the Shehu's *Miṣbāḥ Ahlu-z-Zamān*, *Sirāj al Ikhwān* and *Najm al-Ikhwān*, 'Abdullahi's *Ḍiyā 'Uli-l-Amr wa-l-Mujāhidīn* and *Ḍiyā as-Sulṭān* and Bello's *Kaff al-Ikhwān*.

Character of the *Khilāfah*

The most important issue was the character of the new state itself: the office of the supreme Imam, the mode of selection, the political institutions and the way authority should be manifested in the light of the specific circumstances presented by Hausaland at that time.

In *Miṣbāḥ* the Shehu wrote that the appointment of a "just Imam" to look after the affairs of Muslims is compulsory by law, irrespective of time or cirumstances. Such was the importance of electing a *khalīfah* (caliph), that the first thing the Companions ﷺ did after the death of the Prophet ﷺ was to appoint one, even before they had buried him. Once appointed, the Imam takes charge of all the affairs of state, both spiritual and temporal.

'Abdullahi added in *Ḍiyā 'Uli-l Amr* that, after his appointment, the Imam has two fundamental tasks. The first is to try to govern solely for the pleasure of Allah and endeavor to improve both the spiritual and economic conditions of the people in accordance with the Sunnah, "so that he may truly become the successor of the Messenger of Allah among the Muslims." He should not govern by "force, seizure of power or by inheritance" for the purpose of amassing wealth or other material benefits. Nor should he run the affairs of state arbitrarily or pursue "delicate tastes in food, clothing and housing", thus becoming a king rather than a *khalīfah.*

The second task of the Imam is to arrange state institutions in accordance with the Sunnah and organize the affairs of the people in ways that will enhance their general interests. This involves organizing the religious institutions, *zakāt*, mosques, roads and water systems properly, encouraging justice and piety among his officials, preventing oppression, sending his armies for *jihad* as often as possible, ordering his governors to apply the *Sharī'ah* in their territories and, above all, making all appointments for the good of his people and not out of self-interest. He should appoint to positions of authority only "men of conscience, knowledge, stature and piety".

'Abdullahi suggested some of the important institutions that should be established to support the office of the Imam. These are, for example, the office of the prime minister, the state governors, the judiciary, the army, office of the *muḥtasib* and the civil bureaucracy. The prime minister shares in the planning and organization of the state, assists the Imam in the management of the state, and serves as "a refuge in the event of a blow of fate".

The governors have to care for the spiritual and material needs of the people in their territories in the same way that the Imam does for the whole of the country. The judges, who must be learned men, are responsible for the upholding of the law and securing the rights of the weak. The commander-in-chief of the army is basically responsible for the conduct of war, defense of Muslim territories and protection of *dhimmis*. He should deal compassionately with his men and consult them in all matters. He should treat Muslims honorably, and "not insult any of them, humiliate the weak, or give preference to the strong, but follow the truth and avoid base desires." The task of the *muḥtasib* is to encourage right conduct and prohibit evil. Finally, the civil servants execute governmental policies and run the state on a day-to-day basis.

The crucial question here, however, was how the Imam should be appointed and, by implication, the other pillars of state. 'Abdullahi was unequivocal in his insistence that, if the state was to be run on the basis of Sunnah and on the pattern of a Rightly-Guided *khilāfah*, it had to avoid a monarchical system with inherited leadership or with leadership confined exclusively to certain families. 'Abdullahi noted that Abū Bakr ﷺ, the first *khalīfah*, recommended 'Umar ﷺ as his successor and by doing that "stopped the *khilāfah* from being a monarchical tradition, in which a son inherits leadership from his father, and made it a caliphal tradition, which relies on careful consideration and choice in the selection of a leader to look after the interests and well-being of Muslims."

In the same way 'Umar ﷺ did not appoint his son to succeed him but left the matter of choosing a *khalīfah* to an electoral college, which then unanimously elected 'Uthmān ﷺ. 'Umar ﷺ acted in that way because the *khilāfah* "is not monarchy". 'Alī ﷺ was the natural choice when 'Uthmān ﷺ was martyred, because "there remained none like him," and so "those who preferred truth to self-interest, the Hereafter to this world, swore allegiance to him."

It was Mu'awiyah ﷺ who turned the *khilāfah* into a monarchy and thus became, in 'Abdullahi's eyes, "the first to corrupt the affairs of the *ummah*." 'Abdullahi stated further that the difference between a *khilāfah* and a monarchy was not only in the mode of appointment but also in the method of government. A caliph takes the wealth of people lawfully and spends it appropriately, while a king usurps people's possessions and shares out state wealth indiscriminately. In short, *khilāfah* represents justice while monarchy leads to corruption and tyranny.

The Shehu agreed fundamentally with 'Abdullahi, stating specifically in *Najm al-Ikhwān* that hereditary kingship was not permitted in the *Sharī'ah*. That prohibition, however, should not necessarily prevent an Imam from appointing, or recommending the appointment, of his son to succeed him, were he to possess the requisite qualifications for leadership. In so far as the Imam is the "trustee of the *ummah*", his judgment should be trusted. The Shehu emphasized that jurists were divided on this matter.

Another crucial question for the triumvirate was that of the way authority should be made manifest. Would it be appropriate, for example, for the new order to make use of some of the titles of the old system? The revivalist stand had insisted on a clean break with the old system in all fundamental aspects of government and policies. 'Abdullahi maintained that the original stand should be upheld. He stated in *Ḍiyā as-Sulṭān* that the use of such titles as "king" automatically connotes "worldly kingship" and that "Islamic titles" such as *amir*, *khalīfah* and so on, should be used instead.

The Shehu, on the other hand, thought otherwise. It was true, he maintained in *Najm al-Ikhwān,* that the Islamic system of government was a *khilāfah* not a kingdom but the distinction related to the nature and conduct of their respective governments and not to the titles of those in office. Moreover, such titles as *mālik* (king), *amir*, *sultān* and *khalīfah* had been used in Islam in varying ways, sometimes depicting a praiseworthy political authority and sometimes quite otherwise. As long as the essential character and conduct of government and its functionaries were Islamic, the titles they adopted would not matter, especially among a people who were all too familiar with such titles.

More serious, however, than this semantic difference was the introduction of certain aspects of the court system of the Hausa kings, such as chamberlains, drummers, praise-singers and the like, the magnificent appearances put on by some of the new governors, and the measure of worldly inclination displayed by them. The importance of these issues lay in the very nature of the new order, which had come into being precisely because its vanguards and symbols were austere and simple in their habits and were distinguished from the rest of the people by their higher moral standards.

The Shehu argued in *Miṣbāḥ* that it was essential for the rulers and principal functionaries of state to present a dignified appearance, since people were more likely to respect authority on the basis of outward appearance than on the basis of its objectives and pursuits. So, while the *khilāfah* had to pursue its objectives and goals as vigorously as possible, it should also raise its prestige in the eyes of those who were likely to be more impressed by a show of pomp and power. The Shehu noted, however, that in the time of the Companions of the Prophet ﷺ, people were respected solely for their higher moral disposition and not for their appearance or any other worldly consideration.

Later, the Islamic order deteriorated, as a result of which people, leaders in particular, were respected for reasons other than their conduct and piety. The need arose, therefore, for leaders to appear in a resplendent manner and introduce certain aspects of court protocol for the purposes of the *ummah* to be achieved. Even though such practices contrasted unfavorably with the pure Islamic standard exemplified by the Companions ﷷ, their introduction was nevertheless an appropriate innovation, in that it enabled the rule of Islam to be extended and the laws of Allah to continue to be implemented.

The Shehu advised his men in *Miṣbāḥ* to be "content with the basic necessities in your food, drink and dress" and to make a habit of wearing white, without, however, harboring any prejudice against other colors, since the Prophet himself ﷺ used to wear clothes of many different colors. Further, they should dress well when receiving foreign diplomats and when sitting as judges in courts "for the Prophet ﷺ used to order prominent *Ṣaḥābah* ﷷ to wear fine clothes when meeting with foreign emissaries and he constantly urged them to do this." The Shehu seemed to be trying to strike a balance between the austere demands of *tajdīd* and the practical necessities of statecraft and diplomacy.

'Abdullahi agreed that the pressure of changing circumstances could force an Islamic political authority into adopting alien customs and manners in order to safeguard the interests of Muslims but that adoption, unless there was an acute necessity, could not be regarded as consistent with the *Sharī'ah*. 'Abdullahi's assessment of the *tajdīd* that had taken place was that it was largely a success. It had established the basic foundation and had the necessary men and women to enable it to mold itself completely on the pattern of the Rightly-Guided *khilāfah*, without having to introduce "kingly customs" to support their rule.

The Shehu restated his arguments in *Najm* and then proceeded to propound an important principle of law. The thrust of his argument seems to imply that respect for authority was essential for maintaining the order of Islam and that, in spite of all the efforts that had been made, the *tajdīd* and *jihad* had not managed to re-establish the state of Madinah in its entirety. Moreover, the wearing of expensive clothes is not prohibited in Islam, even though it may be frowned upon. When, however, the purpose of wearing them is to achieve a fundamental objective of Islam, it becomes in fact imperative to do so.

To support his argument, the Shehu related another incident in which 'Umar ⬡, in one of his visits to other countries within the *khilāfah*, saw some Companions dressed in silk and wearing embroidered materials. 'Umar ⬡ was so enraged that he threw stones at them but, on being told that such materials protected the body in war, he said, "In that case it is excellent!" In other words, the rulers, judges and administrators of Sokoto were only adopting such an awe-inspiring appearance to protect the order of Islam by preserving its prestige and intimidating any potential enemies.

The Shehu agreed with Ibn Rushd that there is no universal dress for Muslims. Allah has created different peoples and dispersed them throughout the earth, so it is absolutely natural that their mode of dress should differ from place to place. "There is no necessity for anybody," he said, "to abandon their own mode of dress for another." At the same time Muslims are not prohibited from dressing in the manner of other people. The Prophet ⬡, he said, used to wear clothes known to be of Roman origin and the *Ṣaḥābah* ﷺ in other regions used to wear the clothes of those regions. The clothing worn in Hausaland was natural to its people because they lived in that region and there was no reason why they should adopt the clothing of another part of the world.

More fundamentally the Shehu argued that not all non-Muslim behavior is prohibited in Islam. Muslims are free to follow any custom provided that it serves the purpose of Islam and does not contravene the *Sharī'ah*. "After all," he said, "the Prophet ﷺ built a trench around Madinah at the Battle of Khandaq, thereby imitating the foreigners." Perhaps the Shehu was urging his brother to take a broader view of the world, to adopt a more pragmatic approach to the evolution of a polity that would be distinctively Sudanic, while at the same time remaining essentially Islamic. If, therefore, certain aspects of Hausa tradition could serve the purpose of Islam, they should be regarded as assets to Islam and adopted as part of its heritage.

It should be borne in mind, however, that the Shehu's sanction for rulers to introduce the new policies and government structures they deemed necessary did not mean that he himself indulged in extravagance of any kind. Indeed, the Shehu remained completely above such things. The learned author of *Rawḍ al-Jinān* tells us that throughout his life the Shehu lived an austere and simple life, most often restricting himself to the bare minimum he needed to survive. Even after his appointment as *Amir al-Muminīn*, the Shehu retained his former lifestyle. "The storehouses of the Kings of Sudan were captured but he did not accept anything given to him from them." His only ambition was to establish those sound policies of state which would ensure the survival of the *khilāfah*. Indeed, he himself urged his men to observe *wara'*, that is, care and caution with respect to what they consumed.

The Shehu advised the citizens of the new *khilāfah* that they must obey their rulers and not seek to humiliate them in any way or to rise against them. Rulers are "Allah's door to the fulfillment of the needs of the people on earth" and were, therefore, a great source of benefit to men irrespective of any minor faults they might possess. As symbols of the community they constitute a source of unity and cohesion.

The nub of this argument was carried further by the Shehu in *Najm*. Political authority, he said, symbolized the unity of Allah. "Just as there can be no two Divine powers in the universe, so there can be no two authorities in one city." Authority is vital to the preservation of order in the world. This is because people without a ruler are like fish in the sea – the big swallow the small, the strong devour the weak. Without political authority, people's affairs will not be properly organized, nor their livelihood sustained, nor is it possible for them to enjoy the good life.

"For this reason," the Shehu emphasized, "one of our forebears said that if authority were withdrawn from the earth, Allah would disown it completely." A just government spreads benefits, protects human life, honor and property and augments the economy. The decline of authority provides a profitable market for evil and corrupt men, warmongers, hypocrites and thieves. Only an ignoramus or a profligate would desire the fall of an upright government. Both this world and the Hereafter are secured through the agency of a just government, hence, it is essential that government should be pleasing to Allah and be esteemed by the people.

Leaders should, therefore, be accorded due respect, for if Allah could command his Prophet, Musa 峩, to speak leniently to Pharaoh, even though he was an unbelieving tyrant, "how much more will that be the case with a man to whom Allah has given power, guided to the true faith, and made him disposed to justice and excellence?" Respect for rulers is even more imperative when they uphold the *Sharī'ah*, make Islam manifest, prevent oppression and fight corruption.

The new leadership must be respected and criticism limited to what is necessary and useful because, if the new order were to fail, the Muslim community would go down with it.

"Islam," he said, "is like a foundation and political authority is like a guard. Whatever has no foundation will eventually collapse and whatever has no guard will eventually be lost." If the leaders fulfill their obligation to maintain the order of Islam, ensure justice and combat evil, all other faults of theirs should be overlooked. As long as they protect the property, honor and well-being of their people, Allah is likely to excuse any minor moral lapses on their part.

Principles of Legislation

Something which engaged the attention of the Shehu and his brother, 'Abdullahi, was the issue of the principles of legislation. Their views on new policies, particularly those introduced by the Shehu, some of which apparently contradicted the letter of the *Sharī'ah*, generated debates about the process of legislation and the nature of the evolution of Islamic society and legal norms. The Shehu's views stated here are contained in *Najm al-Ikhwān*.

The most important of principles is one that rests on the premise that "religion is ease", implying that the purpose of legislation is to lighten the burden of the people, improve their lot, and allow them, albeit within the framework of Islam, sufficient leeway in their social, economic and political behavior. Thus, enacting laws which may prove too taxing on the people or which tend to restrict them to the narrow confines of law or which imprison them in one particular school of law would not, the Shehu thought, prove conducive to the running of the affairs of the *ummah*. It is imperative that differences should exist among jurists, or those with legislative responsibilities, so as to provide options within the framework of the *Sharī'ah*.

These differences are an integral part of the divine purpose, "so that if one scholar is severe, another is lenient; for Allah's religion is ease." Even so, all scholars are advised to take a lenient approach, for "a person of sound knowledge and depth of understanding... is lenient to the people."

Restrictive laws should be curtailed as far as possible so

as not to overstretch people's power to comply with the law or overtax their endurance. The laws should not stray far from the fundamentals. The Shehu noted that the Prophet ﷺ used to be apprehensive that his *ummah* might become burdened by too many laws, which implies that he would rather have less legislation as a matter of principle. By way of warning, the Shehu noted the statement of Sayyid 'Alī al-Khawass, that any scholar who imposes on people duties which are not stated clearly in the *Sharī'ah,* will be subject to blame on the Day of Judgment.

The principle of ease does not, of course, mean that Islamic injunctions and prohibitions should be abandoned just to please the people. The scope of severity, the Shehu said, is well known. There are duties established in the Qur'an and Sunnah and these are binding on all Muslims. There are prohibitions and these must be observed by all Muslims. On this, there is no disagreement among scholars.

The principle that "differences of opinion constitute a mercy" indicates that diversity should be deliberately cultivated. Those who are aware of this principle, the Shehu said, should not repudiate any person who holds divergent opinions within his own school nor should he repudiate any person with views from a different school. He should not be strict on matters over which scholars are in disagreement. In other words, the existence of valid differences of opinion necessitates an element of freedom of choice for Muslims in the legal sphere and this freedom must be respected by every Muslim.

The Shehu raised matters of fundamental importance based on the principle that "all the schools of law lead to Allah". Even though Muslims generally accept only the four schools of law and confine themselves to them, other schools exist which are equally valid. Thus, Imams like Sufyan ath-Thawri, Hasan al-Basri, 'Abdullah ibn Mubarak, Dawud aẓ-Ẓahiri, Laith ibn Sa'd, Ibn Muṣayyab, al-Awza'i and others are all "*mujtahids* in Allah's religion, and their schools are roads leading to Allah." Indeed, the Shehu went as far as to say that there could be as many as three hundred schools, all of them within the bounds of Islam.

There is no obligation on any Muslim to bind himself to one particular school or another, nor is there any blame attached to a Muslim adopting the views of different schools on certain issues, provided that he does not seek to cheapen or vulgarize the practice of Islam. A Muslim should adopt a universalistic approach to the schools and take all of them as his own. Quoting al-Qarāfi, the Shehu said, "Jurists are agreed that a Muslim is obliged to follow an opinion of a scholar of his choice without any hindrance whatsoever and the *Sahābah* 🌸 were agreed that anyone who sought the opinion of Abū Bakr or 'Umar 🌸 and followed them should also seek the opinions of Abū Hurayrah or Mu'ādh ibn Jabl or other Companions 🌸, without any restriction whatsoever." In short, whoever follows one school must necessarily follow the others.

All actions flowing from authentic opinions and rulings of accepted schools of law must be accepted as valid by all Muslims. This is necessary for at least two reasons: firstly, to avoid invalidating the worship, transactions, and marriages of Muslims as not being sanctioned by the *Sharī'ah*, in keeping with the injunction of the Prophet 🌸 that Muslims should be handled gently; and secondly, to avoid subjecting Muslims to suspicion and treating them as if they were outside the fold of Islam.

In a debate between the Shehu and 'Abdullahi, the principle was formulated that, in its efforts to rid society of evil, the state should be lenient to people. The Shehu laid down two conditions. Firstly, that the state should only be severe regarding those things that all jurists agree should be prohibited or in respect of behavior capable of "causing the collapse of worldly and religious affairs", such as the perversion of justice, political repression, usurpation of people's property, armed robbery and so on. Secondly that the state should be lenient regarding behavior about whose prohibition scholars are not in agreement or which generally does not disturb the order of Islam, such as drumming, music, and the mixing of men and women.

The Shehu argued in *Miṣbāḥ* that there was no consensus among scholars about the prohibition of certain forms of drumming, music and singing and so they could not be banned outright. Ibn al-ʿArabi, for instance, justified drumming in battles on the grounds that "it raises the morale (of Muslim fighters) and overawes the enemy." Drumming and singing on days of festivity are allowed in law since sports and displays of happiness on such occasions "commemorate the delight of the people of Paradise" and because they lift the general mood. Music during marriage ceremonies is even recommended by the Sunnah.

There are, of course, objections to these things. Some forms of music are objectionable because they distract people from Allah and lead to lust and frivolity. These are absolutely prohibited. But we are told in *Miṣbāḥ* that if "music is free from this, a little of it is allowed in periods of happiness, such as marriage ceremonies and ʿId days, and when undertaking difficult tasks, as happened at the digging of the trench during the time of the Prophet ﷺ."

The Shehu noted that there is nothing in the Qur'an nor is there any order of the Prophet ﷺ which directly prohibits these things. In fact, the Prophet ﷺ seems to have sanctioned some forms of merriment and condoned others. The Shehu observed, for example, that, when the Prophet ﷺ passed a group of girls singing, they sang out his name and the Prophet ﷺ said to them, "Allah knows that I love you!" Moreover, on festival days drums used to be beaten in his presence and, on one occasion, two girls went right into his house to sing. Abū Bakr ﵁ wanted to stop them but the Prophet ﷺ prevented him, saying that it was an ʿId day.

ʿAbdullahi raised some objections to this in *Ḍiyā as-Sulṭān*. He queried the legitimacy of the *ḥadīth* quoted by the Shehu about drums being used on ʿId days, declaring it unsound, abrogated or subject to different interpretations for, if it were sound, then the majority of scholars would not have held a contrary opinion. It was the view of the majority of scholars that drumming and music are not permissible, which implies that they should be banned outright.

The Shehu returned to this question in *Najm al-Ikhwān*. The fact that the majority of scholars prohibit it did not constitute a sufficient reason to ban it outright in Sokoto. It was sufficient that some scholars had no objections to music provided it was not vulgar. If a scholar did proffer an opinion prohibiting singing and drumming, such a scholar would be right, in the opinion of the Shehu, provided he did not condemn those who held the opposite view because, as he said, "the majority of scholars in all the four schools prohibit it, as stated by Abdur Rahman as-Suyūti." Nevertheless, the Shehu insisted, scholars were divided on this matter. Some had forbidden music outright, some had legalized it and some had laid down conditions under which it became legal.

Music falls into the category of issues which do not necessarily constitute a danger to the order of Islam and which should therefore be handled with leniency. The Shehu said of it in *Najm al-Ikhwān* that it has no significance in religion and so a person cannot be indicted for engaging in it and such matters should not unnecessarily absorb the attention of the state. Part of the reason for this lengthy debate on music was its implication for the *ṣufi* orders. The *ṣufis* had legalized it and believed that there were benefits to be derived from pious music and singing. The Shehu respected their opinion.

The last of the principles we shall examine is the one relating to the choice of the lesser evil when faced with two unavoidable evils. The operative effect of this principle is that, if a state is confronted with a situation in which its application of a particular piece of legislation might bring an amount of harm greater than the benefit for which it is intended, that particular legislation should be shelved for the time being in favor of a more beneficial ruling, even if that ruling had less legal force than the former.

The new *khilāfah* was faced with two conflicting situations:

on the one hand, it had to protect the property and honor of its citizens; and on the other, it had to close all the doors to corruption and social tension, in order to have sufficient time to lay the necessary foundation for the post-*jihad* era.

A case in point was the question of the property of Muslims who had fled their homes in the wake of the *hijrah*. After the *jihad*, they naturally wanted to claim their property back. The Shehu ruled that the fall of Alkalawa should be the cut-off date for claims arising from losses during the *hijrah/jihad* period. 'Abdullahi, in *Ḍiyā as-Sulṭān*, objected to this ruling on the grounds that there was nothing special about the fall of Alkalawa as far as the application of *Sharī'ah* was concerned. He was particularly dismayed by the fact that, in several instances, the operative effect of this ruling was that some Muslim men and, more particularly women, were left in the hands of non-Muslims or corrupt elements of society.

But the Shehu carried a greater burden. The fate of the *khilāfah* as a whole rested on him. He was just as sensitive as his brother to the suffering of a section of the Muslims and to a possible violation of the honor of some of the Muslim women. Yet, his duty lay not in securing the rights of a few citizens but in ensuring the security of the *khilāfah* itself. Thus in *Najm*, he agreed with 'Abdullahi that the choice of Alkalawa was arbitrary, but, he said, the policy was necessary to prevent greater harm, "since investigation into people's property leads to corruption".

Moreover, because of the previous oppression in Hausaland, the complaints were so numerous that, if everything were to be investigated, there would be no time for the matters of the moment or for matters of crucial importance on which the very future of the *khilāfah* depended. The Shehu noted that, in pursuing this policy, he was following the injunction of the Prophet ﷺ to adopt the lesser of two evils.

Means of Social Integration

We now move on to examine the means adopted by the Shehu to maintain the unity of the *ummah* and strengthen the cohesion of the new state. Here again there are several principles of fundamental importance which were the outcome of a debate with 'Abdullahi and possibly other scholars as well.

The Shehu consistently curbed all tendencies towards extremism in matters of law and policy and established the golden mean as the basis of governance and legislation. He said in *Miṣbāḥ* that the purpose of writing the book was to, "caution people against tilting towards permissiveness, that is against being overindulgent with respect to sins and innovations, and to caution others against tilting towards extreme strictness, that is repudiating as unlawful those things about which scholars have expressed disagreement." Allah describes His servants as being those "*who, when they spend, are neither extravagant nor mean, but take a stance mid-way between the two.*" (25:67) People should not be driven to despair of the mercy of Allah nor be made to feel secure against His punishment.

The Shehu had a word or two for the men in charge of the affairs of the *khilāfah* whom he usually addressed as "my brothers". First of all, they should cultivate in themselves true consciousness of Allah and adhere strictly to the Sunnah. This entailed maintaining "goodwill towards every servant of Allah". They should never undertake any task except for the sake of Allah and in compliance with His commands. He added, "Let your desires be in agreement with the dictates of the *Sharī'ah*, in compliance with the word of the Prophet ﷺ, 'None of you is a true believer unless his wishes are in complete agreement with the Message I have brought.'"

Finally, they should never seek to uncover the secrets and weaknesses of others. They should rather leave people to their Lord's judgment and accept their excuses and sympathize with their weaknesses, for "a believer accepts excuses while a hypocrite seeks out human failings". They should bear in mind that no one is free from imperfections and failings. It is safer, therefore, for a person to occupy himself with his own defects rather than to busy himself searching for the faults of others.

Continuing his recipe for the integration of the new order in *Miṣbāḥ*, the Shehu urged his men to, "know... that the Companions, their immediate successors and the immediate generation following after them exerted themselves beyond measure in adhering to the Sunnah and shunning *bid'ah*. Therefore, follow in their footsteps, so that you can reap the good of the two abodes."

In short, the Shehu desired to unify the people on the grounds of common understanding and shared values. Yet, problems could arise where differences of opinion led to tensions and damaging squabbles. Hence, his refrain in *Miṣbāḥ*, repeated more than eight times: "Beware and again beware, my brothers, of holding Muslims in suspicion and repudiating as unlawful things about which jurists are in disagreement." Unity could be achieved, but only provided that Muslims tolerated in one another matters over which they differed.

In *Najm al-Ikhwān*, the Shehu was clearly trying to tackle two basic problems which had developed in the *khilāfah*: the involvement of ignorant people in debates which were clearly beyond their competence and dissatisfaction about the *jihad* among some of the leading men. He, thus, wrote the book with the aim of preserving the cohesion of the *ummah*, forestalling confusion and ending disputes.

The Shehu admitted that the involvement of ignorant people in arguments and debates between scholars was injurious and could lead to the validity of some of the schools of law being questioned. Only scholars "acquainted with all the schools" should enter the debates. The ignorant should not regard the debates as the creation of conflicting groups within the *ummah*. They should see them as the mercies which they were meant to be.

As for those who criticized the pace of the efforts being made to revive Islam in Hausaland – notably 'Abdullahi – the Shehu's words for them, in *Najm*, can be analyzed as follows. Firstly, it was imperative for them to give thanks to Allah "for all He has conferred on us in the spheres of both religion and this world" because "giving thanks is imperative" because it is what entitles you to more favors from Allah. Secondly, they should remember that they were living "at the end of time" and that the world had deteriorated.

Because of this they should rather compare the situation then existing in the *khilāfah* to the state of affairs previously existing in Hausaland, which had been characterized by all sorts of evils, such as the worship of idols, perpetration of sins, oppression and arbitrary usurpation. Moreover, they should not forget that this universal, continuous deterioration had affected religion, intellectual life, livelihoods and leadership everywhere and that the world had changed beyond all recognition.

The Shehu then depicted the problems they had to contend with by quoting 'Abdul-Wahāb Sharāni: "Men themselves have undergone so many changes in their character. Some are wolves today dogs tomorrow... devils today unbelievers tomorrow, hypocrites one day believers the next, righteous some of the time and so on. I have witnessed these changes in myself before I even saw it in other people and it should be sufficient for you that you are like those people, in word and deed. However, you will have nothing to worry about if your heart is safe for the heart is the center of all activities." To turn the tide in favor of truth was not, therefore, an easy task, for the world had continued to grow in complexity.

The fourth point recognized that every age has its own unique conditions, fortunes and men. It is, therefore, futile to try to judge one's own age by the yardstick of another age. It is worse still to judge a people living in the twelfth Islamic century by the standard of the *Ṣaḥābah* ﷺ, and, what is more, if the *Ṣaḥābah* ﷺ had lived in that age "they would have fallen into the same state as we have fallen, in confirmation of what the Prophet ﷺ said when he made it clear that the world would continue to deteriorate morally."

The Shehu's fifth point was that the best course of action for the men in charge of the *khilāfah* was to confront the situation which actually existed. Since affairs had changed out of all recognition, the only course was to move with the times and not remain ossified in the past. People should be dealt with as their behavior demanded. "If they appear to you as wolves, then be a wolf yourself..., if they appear as foxes, be a fox yourself, if they stand up against you, stand up against them until you obtain your rights." The Shehu was quick to add that this did not mean going outside the framework of the law; it only implied the rejection of evil.

The Shehu was telling his somewhat dissatisfied people that the only way to judge the *jihad* was to weigh its achievements against the system it had replaced and, perhaps, against the prevailing systems all around it. People would then realize that, in spite of the enormous moral, material and social difficulties they faced, and in spite of their distance from the age of the Prophet 🕌 and the *Ṣaḥābah* 🕌, the men and women of Hausaland had created something which truly approximated to the pattern of the Prophet 🕌 and the Rightly-Guided *khilāfah* 🕌 and had in fact achieved many of the objectives of Islam.

A negative approach to the *jihad*, the Shehu cautioned, would not bring any benefit; it would merely waste the energy of the best elements in society. Nothing would result from such efforts except the tiring of people's minds and tongues. It was imperative to give thanks to Allah and adopt a positive attitude to the *jihad*, for that was more akin to dignity and more likely to bring about peace of mind, freedom from anxiety, confidence in the people and, because of that, a greater desire to stand by them and strive for their interests and aspirations.

Islam would continue to be a living reality, truth would continue to be made manifest and there would always be men and women to rise to defend Islam until the Day of Judgment. The Shehu assured them that, even at that stage, Islam had changed the reality of Hausaland, perhaps forever. "Our era," he declared, "is an era of light and of banishing darkness from the world." Further, it was "an era of victory, an era of defeat for the unbelievers in their entirety, and an era of glory and happiness for all Muslims." "And if we give thanks," he said, "we will achieve even greater things."

Muhammad Bello's Role

For his part, Muhammad Bello seized the opportunity in his *Kaff al-Ikhwān* to raise issues he considered fundamental to the process of establishing and consolidating the new Islamic order and, at the same time, to defend 'Abdullahi from charges of extremism, disassociating him from the actions and utterances of ignorant students and pseudo-scholars who took the opportunity of the disagreement between the Shehu and 'Abdullahi to foment tension in society.

In his introduction, Bello quoted extensively from two of 'Abdullahi's works in order to prove wrong those who considered him harsh and extreme and to show that he had always followed a course advantageous to the *ummah*. He quoted 'Abdullahi as saying that commending the good and forbidding evil should be conducted with due respect for the feelings and sensitivities of people and by way of giving good counsel and not through rough treatment, exposure or bringing shame upon them.

On the issues themselves, Bello reiterated the Shehu's warning that unnecessary arguments and fanaticism are damaging to Islam and should therefore be avoided. He noted that people have varying abilities and interests in the practice of Islam. Some are inclined, as Imam Mālik is said to have observed, more to prayer than fasting, some have certain qualities and lack others. Those who find it easier to engage in supererogatory prayers have no right to claim superiority over others who find fasting easier. People should direct their attention towards more fundamental things, such as the *jihad* at hand and spiritual and moral development.

Bello also raised the issue of true and venal scholars. Corrupt scholars, he said, fall into two categories: those who have knowledge of Islam but act contrary to what they know, and those who are lacking in knowledge but who, despite their ignorance, still give legal opinions. The latter mislead the people for they themselves are misled. True scholars, on the other hand, are those who fear no one but Allah in their dissemination of the truth and whose knowledge increases them in fear of Allah and makes them shun the world. Moreover, they maintain an intelligent and reflective attitude towards their own moral failures. Their knowledge is useful because it has a direct impact on their behavior, as opposed to the superficial, ineffectual knowledge gathered by venal scholars.

Bello warned his comrades against self-justification or nursing a sense of purity in themselves, while looking down upon others. Allah, he said, has condemned such attitudes in the strongest terms, quoting the Qur'anic verses: "*Do you not see those who claim to be purified? No, Allah purifies whoever He wills. They will not be wronged by so much as the smallest speck. Look how they invent lies against Allah. That suffices as an outright felony.*" (4:48-9)

This attitude, Bello noted, is bound to lead to denigration and insult or even to cursing fellow Muslims and seeking to uncover their faults, whereas Allah has prohibited such kinds of behavior. No matter what his faults, a Muslim, Bello insisted, has an absolute right to respect and dignity. Bello returned to his father's familiar theme that a particular action cannot be considered actually wrong unless it is categorically prohibited by the *Sharī'ah*. It is only the perpetration of clearly prohibited actions that should be repudiated. Even then, the purpose of 'repudiation' should be the moral uplifting of the person concerned and this necessarily demands leniency and consideration. If Allah asks His Prophet, Musa ﷺ, to speak in a mild manner to His enemy, Pharaoh, how much more must that be the case when a Muslim speaks to a fellow Muslim?

Bello referred to an incident involving a youth who came to the Prophet ﷺ asking for permission to commit adultery. The people were indignant but the Prophet ﷺ drew him near and said gently, "Would you like your mother to be involved in adultery?" The man replied in the negative.

After one or two similar questions the Prophet ﷺ told him that other people feel just the same about their mothers, daughters and sisters, and placing his hand on the youth's chest, the Prophet ﷺ prayed, "O Allah, purify his heart, forgive his sins and preserve his chastity."

In reality what Muslims need, Bello continued, is good counsel because, as the Prophet ﷺ said, religion consists of good counsel. The community's leaders need advice on how to carry the burden of the *ummah* conscientiously and efficiently. The advice concerning the masses is to show compassion towards them, taking care of the old, being merciful to the young, helping them to solve their problems and inviting them to what is beneficial to them as a whole. Insults and faultfinding are not part of good counsel. It should be a lesson to anyone concerned with the moral failings of people that although Allah knows very well the evil and corruption of mankind, He nevertheless forgives their sins and provides them with sustenance.

Muhammad Bello urged the closing of the ranks of the new leadership, so that the Islamic order could be preserved. True, the *ummah*, as it stood in Hausaland and elsewhere, had its faults and failings, but it also had great prospects. As a whole it was preserved from error, for the Prophet ﷺ had said that his community would never be united on an error. Its prospects lay in the fact that a party of the *ummah* would always stand up for truth and regeneration, whenever its social body was undergoing decline. Its future, in other words, was perpetually assured.

The common people, in particular, had a great many faults, Bello agreed, but, at the same time, they also had great merits. The common man lives by the sweat of his labor and is generous towards others with the fruits of his work. He has a pure and lawful income which many others cannot claim to have. He sees himself as the most despicable of people in the eyes of Allah – a sense of humility treasured by Allah. He is least bothered either by thoughts of wealth or by intellectual doubts in his worship and is, therefore, a better worshipper than many who are of a higher class than himself.

The best course of action is to handle the affairs of the people with patience and the leaders should hold on to what is already "in your hands of religion and this world, even if it is only a little". The struggle for Islam, Bello assured his comrades, is an on-going process which will never cease despite people's failings and weaknesses.

Finally, Bello urged his fellow Muslims to maintain a good opinion of Allah, and of all Muslims as well, and to have faith in their basic integrity. One generation should not be judged by the standards of another. "Let the hard, ignoramuses know," he said quoting al-Yusi, "that this *ummah* is purified and exalted. It is like rainfall – no one knows whether its beginning or its end is the most beneficial." People would continue to fight for the cause of Islam in the future, just as they had in the past.

It is interesting that these thoughts, arguments and concepts about the rights and obligations of people, the need to treat them compassionately, to give them due respect or even veneration, to cater for their good and to avoid inflicting hardships on them, were all coming from the rulers themselves! This was, perhaps, the real strength of the *jihad* leaders, and of the Sokoto *khilāfah* as a whole: that those who ruled also defined their own limits and confined themselves entirely within the rule of law. The natural tendency of people in power to oppress the weak, overstep the limits set by the *Sharī'ah*, or in any way to take undue advantage over the people under them, did not exist in these rulers. As far as they were concerned, every citizen was a sacred individual, more sacred than the Ka'bah, and so his life, his property and his honor were sacred and inviolable to them as rulers, to the state and also to his fellow citizens.

The Shehu regarded this process as absolutely vital for the *khilāfah*. There had to be differences of opinion if the Islamic law was ever to be developed in the *khilāfah*, so, in *Najm al-Ikhwān*, he advised his people to read the books of the three pillars of the movement – 'Abdullahi, Muhammad Bello and himself – because their works were mutually complementary and because any differences that they might find in them were simply part of Allah's mercy to the community.

Taken together, the surviving works of the triumvirate do, indeed, complement one another, illustrating the different roles each of the three men played in responding to Shaykh 'Uthman's call for the establishment of a true Islam. They are a good and a true record of the emergence and formation of the *Jama'a*, the conducting of the *jihad* and the establishment and expansion of the *khilāfah.* It is impossible to avoid reflecting on how opportune it was that these men were there together at that time with all those abilities and that zeal to serve – despite their differences of character and, occasionally, of opinion – the common cause.

14. The Shehu's Legacy

By the year 1227/1812, when the Shehu gave the responsibility for running the *khilāfah* to 'Abdullahi and Muhammad Bello, he was already in the twilight years of his illustrious life. Several years had passed since Allah "completed the victory of the Muslims" and gave them a nation, a social order and political power of their own. From the start of the *jihad* to the establishment of the *khilāfah* and to the handing over of responsibilities to trusted scholars and administrators, the Shehu himself had also undergone a transformation. His tone had changed considerably. He was no longer the protester, the challenger, the aggressive reviver of Islam, but rather the father, guide, teacher and symbol, fully conscious that his parting with his companions, students and the millions who adored him was drawing near.

There is no doubt that, at this time, the Shehu's sense of commitment to the *ummah*, his love for it, and his desire to guide it rightly and leave for it an abiding legacy, had grown stronger and deeper. In examining precisely what the Shehu left as a legacy for posterity, we will use three of his works. *Naṣīḥat Ahlu-z-Zamān*, written as advice for the people of the Sudan, will be our basic reference. The others are *Miṣbāḥ Ahlu-z-Zamān* and *Najm al-Ikhwān*.

The Legacy on Policy Making

The first aspect of this legacy was the Shehu's advice to the *ummah* to heed Islam's call for the fulfillment of a tripartite duty: to cultivate the consciousness of Allah – *taqwā*; to adhere to the Sunnah; and to follow the course of diligence and scrupulousness – *wara'* – especially on the part of rulers and scholars in their handling of the affairs of the *ummah*. These duties are interrelated and mutually indispensable. *Taqwā* is the gateway to Islam; the Sunnah is Islam in history and in practice, constituting its moral order and social values; while *wara'* constitutes the political and social policies necessary to preserve the order and supremacy of Islam.

When translated into concrete political and social terms, *wara'* embraces far-reaching legal and governmental policies, ensuring that they are characterized by tolerance, accommodation and broadmindedness on the part of Islamic government, jurists and law-makers. For example, for a jurist, *wara'* implies being strict on oneself by having stringent moral standards for oneself, while remaining lenient and tolerant towards other people.

When we go back to *Miṣbāḥ Ahlu-z-Zamān*, we see further implications of *wara'*. There is a duty on scholars and leaders to be tolerant of one another's views and actions and to be fair in their criticism of one another. They should temper their zeal to eradicate evil in society with the corresponding need to protect the well-being of the people, so that if the eradication of a particular social evil is likely to defeat the aim of the *Sharī'ah* – which is, in every case, the enhancement of the people's welfare – then the eradication of such an evil should be put on hold.

Furthermore, scholars and jurists should bear in mind that, according to Imam Shafi'ī, the Sunnah embraces whatever is consistent with the *Sharī'ah* and is not specifically rejected elsewhere by the Sunnah. By implication, the Shehu advises Muslims to amplify the definition of the Sunnah to embrace deeds and policies which enhance the purpose and objectives of the Muslim *ummah*, even if they have no precedence in the practice of the early generations of Islam and even if the Sunnah is silent about them.

In political terms, *wara'* implies that rulers should be compassionate in dealing with the affairs of the *ummah*, for the Prophet ﷺ beseeched Allah, "to be compassionate to a ruler who handles the affairs of Muslims with care and to be hard on a ruler who is hard on them." Where society at large is concerned, *wara'* imposes on them the responsibility of remaining united and of fostering brotherhood and solidarity among themselves, in Allah's words the duty of being: "*Hard on the unbelievers, merciful to one another.*" (48:29)

On Legislation and Administration of the Law

In the sphere of legal order, the Shehu's advice to the *ummah* was to accept the principle that differences of opinion among scholars are a mercy as an article of faith. In practical legal terms, it implies that whatever the *'ulamā'* have not unanimously agreed to be unlawful should be accepted as permissible and whatever they have not agreed to be obligatory should not be imposed as a duty. The operative effect of this policy is the minimization of restrictive laws and the giving of comfort and considerable leeway to ordinary people.

To legislators, judges and those in charge of public morality, the Shehu advised that they should not force people to accept their personal view of right and wrong. Any wrong, which was not unanimously regarded as such by the *ummah,* should not be regarded as wrong in state policy, in law courts or as a basis of legislation. Similarly, no one should be censured for not doing a duty or fulfilling an obligation over which there is no unanimity among scholars. This meant that the law enforcement agencies, legislators and judges should confine themselves to matters about which the Qur'an and Sunnah are categorical or about which there is an accepted general consensus. To go beyond this, the Shehu warned, would be tantamount to a deliberate attempt to create confusion in society and to open the door to disputes.

It is best for those in authority to realize that, since Muslims have accepted the orthodox schools of law as valid and correct and the *mujtahids* as upright in their decisions, no one who follows any school or opinions of any *mujtahid* can be considered as doing wrong. The most that can be done is to advise someone to do what is better. Repudiation or rejection is out of the question. The actions of the *ummah* must be respected and treated as generally acceptable to Islam, in that they rest on the Qur'an and Sunnah and are "founded on the life pattern and moral behavior of prophets and saints".

No behavior should be repudiated outright unless it is in direct conflict with the Qur'an, Sunnah or the universally accepted practice of Muslims. This advice was expanded in *Miṣbāḥ*, where the Shehu urged leaders to endeavor to "discern the real objectives of the *Sharī'ah*" when they legislated or made decisions. The Shehu specifically warned jurists and law-makers not to go beyond their competence or jurisdiction in their zeal to "Islamize" society.

"Beware," he warned, "of looking down on any matters permitted by the Legislator." Many a scholar has gone beyond the bounds of his competence. He gets exasperated with people for doing what he considers as reprehensible, even though such things are not categorically forbidden and, as a result, "Allah deliberately causes [such a scholar] to stray." It is wrong, therefore, for a scholar or jurist to attempt to anticipate Allah in matters of law, saying that if such a thing had happened in the time of the Prophet ﷺ he would have forbidden it.

"We know," the Shehu said, concurring with ash-Sharāni, "that the ultimate Legislator is Allah, Most High, Whose knowledge is absolute and all-embracing. If He had permitted or forbidden something for one particular group of people to the exclusion of others, He would have communicated that to us through His Messenger." If that did not happen, whatever is permitted to one generation is permitted to all others. Human interference in a province that is the exclusive preserve of Allah is the real source of corruption, because Allah's purpose in His law is to enhance the overall well-being of the people for all time.

On the Process of Reviving Islam

On the weighty issue of the Islamic revival that had taken place, the Shehu indicated in *Naṣīḥat* that he was leaving it as an abiding example to posterity. His satisfaction with the ten "great favors" that constituted the essence of his achievement shows that he regarded them as being all that Muslims can be expected to achieve at "the end of time". And, more importantly, the Shehu indicated the various stages through which the process of reviving Islam must go if it is to succeed.

> "Know then, my brothers, that the ordering of what is good is obligatory by consensus and this is what has happened in this time; that the forbidding of evil is obligatory by consensus and this is what has happened in this time; that *hijrah* from the domain of unbelievers is obligatory by consensus and this is what has happened in this time; that the appointment of an *Amir al-Muminīn* is obligatory by consensus and this is what has happened in this time; that the acquisition of weapons is obligatory by consensus and this is what has happened in this time; that defending one's life, family and wealth is obligatory by consensus and this is what has happened in this time; that *jihad* is obligatory by consensus and this is what has happened in this time; that appointing provincial governors and administrators is obligatory by consensus and this is what has happened in this time; that appointing judges is obligatory by consensus and this is what has happened in this time; and that the application of the *Sharī'ah* by judges is obligatory by consensus and this is what has happened in this time. These are ten matters for which the people of this time must be grateful to Allah because, added to faith, they are among the ten greatest favors of Allah and all of them have occurred in this time."

This comprehensive list introduces us to the four stages of the process of the revival of Islam in Hausaland: the stage of preparation, aimed at molding public opinion and attracting people away from their oppressors and the oppressive system they operate towards allegiance to Allah and confidence in His religion; then the stage of *hijrah*, which is withdrawal from the domain of oppression in search of the domain of justice; then the stage of preparation for confrontation, defense and armed struggle aimed at overthrowing oppression; and finally the stage of the establishment of *Dar al-Islam* with all its institutions and objectives.

The establishment of *Dar al-Islam* is, therefore, only one phase in this progressive struggle against evil and so any tendency to rest on its laurels displayed by a *Dar al-Islam* is a misunderstanding of the process of Islamic revival and must be resolutely resisted. The spirit of Islamic revival must be constantly maintained and *Dar al-Islam* must always seek to extend its frontiers, continue to defend the interests of Islam, reduce the power of evil and break the backbone of oppressors wherever they may be. Hence, the Shehu repeated in *Naṣīḥat* the points he had made earlier in his declaration of *jihad*, which included, among other things, that it is obligatory for Muslims to fight against unbelieving rulers and remove the reins of government from them; and that it is obligatory for all Muslims to identify themselves with *Dar al-Islam* and emigrate from the domain of evil to it.

Although there was certainly cause for satisfaction and thanksgiving on the part of Muslims, there was no cause for them to be unduly exultant over their achievements. The Shehu advised the men in charge of the new order to remember the past. They would find to their dismay that there was in their behavior certain things that pertained to *jahiliyyah*. As a reminder, the Shehu enumerated a number of evils, considered unlawful by jurists, all of which had been perpetrated during the course of the struggle.

Some people had aligned themselves, at one time or another, with the oppressors and refused for a time to pay allegiance to the *Amir al-Muminīn* and his deputies. Some had fought against their fellow Muslims. Some had usurped the property of or enslaved their fellow Muslims. Some had anathematized other Muslims and declared them unbelievers simply because they had committed sins. Others had fought unbelievers who were under the protection of *Dar al-Islam* and usurped their property or enslaved them, despite the fact that these unbelievers had been under the protection of the law. These were just some of the unlawful things that had occurred.

"I caution you," the Shehu advised, "against treachery, for Allah has forbidden it to us saying: '*You who believe! do not betray Allah and His Messenger, and do not knowingly betray your trusts.*' (8:27) And I also caution you, my brothers, against prying into people's secrets and private affairs and being preoccupied with their failings, because whoever goes after the people's nakedness, will find Allah going after his nakedness even if he locks himself in his own bedroom. A believer accepts excuses whereas a hypocrite searches for faults. In the *Muwaṭṭa*, the Prophet ﷺ says, 'Do not engage in searching for people's faults as if you were lords, but rather look at your own faults as slaves of Allah.'"

In addition, they should cultivate brotherhood among themselves and avoid sowing seeds of enmity. Individual faults should be overlooked, jealousy and scandals repressed. Love should be fostered, for it is the very essence of Muslim solidarity, and Muslims should know that love for their fellow Muslims is the price of admission to paradise.

On Education and Scholarship

The Shehu's advice on intellectual endeavors is that every age is duty-bound to look at Islam afresh and must try to solve its problems by itself without necessarily relying on earlier generations. While noting in *Najm al-Ikhwān* that all generations are mutually dependent on one another and that a given generation is "a mercy" to the one which follows it, he nonetheless advised against relying on past generations to solve contemporary problems. Contemporary scholars, he said, "are more learned in the fundamental issues of [their] time" than their predecessors and for this reason their works are of greater relevance to their community than the works of earlier scholars, who could not have anticipated the exact form that future problems would take.

Contemporary scholars, therefore, have a duty to write their own books in the light of their own particular situation, even if books of earlier scholars may have in fact provided all that they require. They have to make their own additions and improvements to the intellectual heritage of Islam. The people on their part should read the works of contemporary scholars rather than being totally preoccupied with writings of the past. The Shehu and his men wrote books on practically every aspect of Islam in response to the needs of their people, even though there were books of earlier scholars dealing with those matters.

On the Need for Piety

Finally, the Shehu left to posterity four matters by means of which, as he said, "Allah will illuminate your hearts with the light of faith." These were: the cultivation of direct awareness of Allah; sustained study of the Qur'an; the study of the Sunnah and Seerah of the Prophet ﷺ; and the study of the biographies of the men of the past – the Rightly-Guided *khulafā'* ﵃, the *Ṣaḥābah* ﵃, and the founders of the *madh-habs*, saints and others who have made their imprint on Muslim history.

The Shehu Passes Away

The Shehu moved from Sifawa to Sokoto in 1230/1814-15. In the words of Waziri Junaidu:

> "He settled there and organized the town. It became the center of Islam in this country and will remain so, if Allah wills, until the Day of Judgment. After his arrival in Sokoto, he asked his daughter Fatima how old she was and she told him twenty-eight. That made her think that the time of her death had been revealed to him but he denied it, saying instead that when she had completed thirty years

> an important event would take place. When she reached thirty the Shaykh himself died, may Allah have mercy on him. That was in the year 1232, three days into Jumada al-Akhir (April 20th, 1817). He had held the *khilāfah* for thirteen years and died at the age of sixty-three."

Thus, ended an active, lofty and truly remarkable life – a life whose absolute devotion to Allah and unrelenting struggle for His cause finally brought into being the noblest phase in the entire history of Hausaland and, indeed, one of the finest periods in the whole history of Islam. The Shehu saw himself as endowed with "the sword of truth". He fought relentlessly to make Allah's word supreme and to abase unbelief and tyranny. He fought falsehood and conquered it. He fought tyranny and conquered it. He fought ignorance and conquered it.

Achievements of the *Mujaddid*

Perhaps, if Shehu Usman were asked to comment on his achievements, he would point to his struggle against ignorance and the intellectual revival of Islam that he had brought about as his greatest accomplishment. This intellectual revolution – "the extraordinary outpouring of Arabic writing" as 'Abdullahi Smith refers to it – was one of the greatest events ever to take place in Hausaland and its impact, not surprisingly, was stupendous. Indeed, the *khilāfah* itself could not have come into being without this intellectual awakening, for it is this copious flow of thought and ideas that constantly fed and enhanced the spirit of Islamic revival and brought together the great body of scholars who made the struggle for Islam their ultimate goal.

"Here was a political revolution on a remarkable scale, but the movement represented much more than an attempt of a few under-privileged and determined men to seize political power for their own benefit. In origin, it was also an important intellectual movement involving, in the minds of the leaders, a conception of the ideal society and a philosophy of *tajdīd*...

In their search for the ideal society and the just ruler, they looked back to a previous golden age in the history of *Dar al-Islam* and their aim was to re-create in the Western Sudan the society of the Rightly-Guided *khilāfah*."

The end result of that intellectual renaissance was a *khilāfah* run entirely by scholars. There was not a single aspect of state organization or institution, be it political, economic or military, which was not placed under the charge of a scholar. Gone was the old order in which rulers wallowed in ignorance and the state was run at the whim of tyrants. Now the *Sharī'ah* reigned supreme and who else but scholars knew the *Sharī'ah* or how it should be applied? And more fundamentally, the intellectual revival of Islam gave birth in Hausaland to fresh values, a different attitude to life and a new worldview. For the first time, the world became evaluated in purely Islamic terms. Its transitory nature and its deluded hopes and deceptive pleasures were contrasted to the abiding nature of the Hereafter with its infinite hopes, its stability and its certainty.

It is better to seek a stable place of residence, abiding comfort and a lofty, everlasting life than to fall prey to the temptations of a world that deceives, an abode that is ephemeral. To achieve that abiding home of the Hereafter, you must, in the conception of the leaders of the Islamic revival movement, set yourself on a new course with its own goals, priorities and purposes. The goal is not anything that is earth-bound or world-oriented. The goal is Allah Himself. As the Shehu was wont to say, human beings only fulfill the ultimate purpose of life when they gain the acceptance and pleasure of Allah.

Once the goal is Allah Himself, then man's perception of life and his priorities in it are completely transformed. The priorities, like the goal itself, become heaven-bound, and not only lofty in themselves but elevating also. In a three-page treatise, *Qawā'id Ṭalabi-l-Uṣūl ila-Llāh*, the Shehu indicated priorities that would be bound to change not only people's characters, but also society itself.

The first of these priorities is the attainment of a knowledge, defined in *Qawā'id* as the essential knowledge. It embraces the knowledge of Allah and of His law, and also the means of self-purification and the discipline needed to achieve it. In other words, man's first priority in life is to know his Lord, Creator and ultimate goal, then to know the proper way of living and dealing with his fellow human beings, and then to know the way to obtain the ultimate acceptance and pleasure of Allah.

Associated with this first priority is a second: the twin-objective of personal intellectual development and social restraint. The Shehu stated that a person who wants to gain nearness to Allah must strive "not to be dull-witted, because dull-witted people cannot grasp the real implications of any issue." Nor should he be obsessed with the love of leadership or political office, because anyone so inclined is bound to be "absolutely inclined to the world". In short, to gain the pleasure of Allah, one must use one's intellectual ability to the full and not pollute one's desire to reach the ultimate goal with a petty desire for fame and glory.

The third priority is physical and spiritual exercise (*riyāḍah*). Its purpose is to equip body and mind with the ability to withstand the moral pressures of a corrupt society, endure the physical hardships and strains of a *jihad* and resist the temptations of power and wealth when the *mujāhid* eventually achieves political authority himself. Here we may recall 'Abdullahi's prescription of "little food" as the medicine that "eliminates" the diseases of the mind. *Riyāḍah* is thus, a process of spiritual fortification, a preparation to face a corrupt world, and a means of securing the requirements needed to bear the responsibilities of an improved world when that comes about.

The fourth priority is meditation, the opportunity for which should be provided by periodic retreat (*khalwah*). The Shehu said that a person should occasionally withdraw to a place where he is not likely to be seen by anyone and where he sees no one else; where he hears no speech and speaks to no one else. This gives him the possibility of turning completely to Allah, meditating on created existence, reflecting on the prevailing conditions in society and coming up with the framework and means for bringing about change or improvement. *Khalwah* may, in fact, be seen as a kind of *hijrah*. In a way, it is a protest against a society that is hell bent on proceeding on a ruinous path. It is a symbolic withdrawal from the existing order. It is a flight from a world dominated by evil. It is thus, a means of gaining moral refreshment and intellectual rejuvenation.

The fifth priority is to give the Messenger of Allah, Muhammad ﷺ, one of the things owed to him. The Shehu stated that invoking blessing on Muhammad ﷺ is one of the surest ways of gaining Allah's pleasure. We may here recall one of the numerous references to this matter in *Mishkāt al-Maṣābīḥ*: "Ubayy ibn Ka'b ﷺ said that he told Allah's Messenger ﷺ that he frequently invoked blessings on him and asked him how much of his prayer he should devote to him. He ﷺ replied, "that he might devote as much as he wished" and when Ubayy suggested a quarter he said, "Whatever you wish but if you increase it that will be better for you." He suggested a half and the Prophet ﷺ replied, "Whatever you wish but if you increase it that will be better." He suggested two-thirds and he ﷺ replied, "Whatever you wish, but if you increase it that will be better for you." Ubayy then suggested devoting all his prayer to him and he ﷺ replied, "Then you will be freed from care and your sins will be expiated." It is good to seek nearness to Allah through the "medium" of His Prophet ﷺ by praying, for example, for Allah's good pleasure, invoking the esteem with which Muhammad ﷺ is held by Him.

Finally, one should cultivate the proper relationship with one's shaykh by giving him the respect due to him, while at the same time appreciating all that one learns and experiences from one's mentor of the Qur'an and Sunnah. Here the entire relationship is based on the student's quest for knowledge and moral elevation. So the priorities start and end with knowledge, illustrating the absolute primacy of knowledge in the scale of the Shehu's all-embracing transformation.

The Advancement of Women

These priorities, which were all geared to serving the ultimate goal, transformed a whole people. The old order, characterized by ignorance and depravity, caved in under the sustained pressure of the "extraordinary outpouring" of knowledge and the elevated standards of morality. Women were great beneficiaries of this transformation. The Shehu insisted on their education and moral progress and withstood all pressures to reverse his unyielding stance. He reserved the harshest words for those scholars who encouraged the abandonment of women to ignorance and an ignoble life. At the start of his career, he lamented the appalling state of ignorance to which women were condemned. At the end of it, he was satisfied that, as far as possible, he had mobilized women through education, brought them into the mainstream of life and, above all, produced women of a sufficient caliber to take pride of place in Islamic history.

The most prominent of these women was the Shehu's own daughter, Asma. This noble lady grew up to become a scholar in her own right, a teacher who educated not only a generation of women but, through these women, also educated many children as well. She was indeed a torch that lit up the path of Islamic revival in Hausaland and a pillar that supported Islam in even the most trying periods.

Jean Boyd, who has pioneered research into this remarkable woman, suggests that she managed to step out of her role as simply "a teacher of women" and enter the world of politics, "boldly campaigning to keep the idealism of the Shehu alive." In any event, it was Nana Asma's role as a teacher and ideologue more than anything else, that has left her indelible imprint on the history of the Sokoto *khilāfah* and indeed of Nigeria as a whole. She says: "Asmau has a place in the history of the (caliphate) and when a history of the ideas of the *Jama'a* is produced – how they were nurtured, metamorphosed, sustained and propagated – Asmau's role will be shown to have been of significance... Her influence which, in the Islamic context, is unusual in its scope, was found acceptable in Gobir and Zamfara, while her scholarship and her commitment to the perpetuation of the memory of the Shehu and his ideals find ready acceptance in the *Jama'a*."

Her merit lay principally in combining the education of women with looking after the well-being of the poor and deprived. Her husband was responsible for public welfare in the early days of the *khilāfah* but Asma herself eventually came to symbolize both the aspirations of women for education, respect and justice, and the yearning of the poor for justice, health and comfort.

One can only wonder at the scale of the change in men's attitude to women brought about by *tajdīd* and wonder too at the rapid rise of women. Before it women were seen as mere chattels. After it they were spoken of with respect and even reverence:

> "The tireless lady who excels in everything
> She has to do or has already done.
> East and West, near or far, she is known for her wisdom,
> Meritorious work and scholarship, which
> resembles a river with outspreading waves."

When the venerated lady died, a great sense of loss overwhelmed the *khilāfah*. It was as if the last pillar of the *tajdīd* and *jihad* – the *Sayyidatunā*, as she was reverently addressed – had been lost.

Asma showed the extent to which a determined and well-bred woman can influence society. She showed the height a woman can reach in knowledge and moral consciousness and how she can use these to keep a society involved in the process of *tajdīd* on its feet. Successive *khulafā'* looked to her for guidance. Indeed, her influence on the general course of the *khilāfah*, enhanced by her stature as a saint and the daughter of the Shehu, might yet prove more decisive than we read in books. Up to today, her poems on religion, history, politics and military activities of the *khilāfah* can still be heard coming from the lips of women all over Nigeria and she is still a living presence in the minds of many people.

The Ascendancy of Islam

Beyond the singular achievements of Shehu Usman during his life, lie even greater posthumous ones. When he came onto the scene, religion was in decline but at his death, Islam was the dominant force in Hausaland, ready to stir the whole of western Sudan with the spirit of *tajdīd* and *jihad*. For a man who had devoted his life to this single cause, there could have been nothing more satisfying to him, when he was dying, than that realization. He had no fear of leaving a weak legacy to posterity. He was confident that Islam had gained the upper hand and was bound to make further triumphant inroads into the domain of *kufr*. The *khilāfah* was not a dormant political structure but a state that took its responsibility for the defense and enhancement of Islam very seriously.

In the philosophy of *tajdīd* articulated by the Shehu, the state, as much as the individual Muslim, had to commit its energy, resources and its very life to the propagation of Islam. It was by its very nature dedicated to the expansion of *Dar al-Islam*, the abasement of unbelief and to ensuring that the perpetual conflict between Islam and unbelief would be resolved in favor of Islam. "In general," Smaldone observed, concerning the extent of the ongoing wars fought by the *khilāfah*, "it would not be very inaccurate to estimate that there was at least one major military expedition conducted per amirate per year. Such a record of intensive and frequent warfare can be matched by few states. Sokoto and its subordinate amirates must be numbered among the most militant states in history."

Finally, the Shehu showed clearly that the life of the Prophet ﷺ can be recreated by Muslims at any age and in any place. The Shehu's life was, in a very fundamental sense, similar to the life of the Prophet ﷺ reconstructed in the twelfth century *hijrah* in Hausaland. This testifies to the universality of not only Islam itself but also of the process of *tajdīd* necessary for its re-establishment in every age. "Shaykh 'Uthman consciously emulated the Prophet," Professor Ismail observes, "and in many respects his actions were made to approximate those of the Prophet ﷺ, who was his ultimate example. The similarity in the development of their careers should not be overlooked."

Smaldone made the observation that, "one cannot fail to be impressed by the historical parallels between the development of military organization in Arabia in the seventh century and the evolution of military organization in the Sokoto *khilāfah*." The two armies, although separated by a thousand years or so, maintained "a striking resemblance in their tactics and strategy". The same comparison can be made between the war conducted from Sokoto after the Shehu's death and that fought by the generations which immediately succeeded the Prophet ﷺ, a fact which convinced Smaldone that, "it was the Islamic content of these two societies that explains many of their common military doctrines."

Thomas Hodgkin, on the other hand, noted that the predominant objective of the Shehu's movement was to establish a state on the model of the Prophet's – a state totally committed to social justice, guided by the *Sharī'ah*, and ruled not by despots, but by God-fearing people. In this enterprise, Hodgkin implied, there was a conscious effort on the part of the Shehu and his lieutenants to follow closely the historical examples set by the Prophet ﷺ. Hence, says Hodgkin, "the conscious parallelism between 'Uthman's mission and that of the Prophet. His withdrawal to Gudu was described as 'the *hijrah*' and dates in the history of the *jihad* were calculated from it. Thus, the original Islamic drama was, in a sense, being re-enacted in the central Sudan."

The scale of the Shehu's success and achievements, the sheer force of his character and the parallels between his life and that of the Prophet ﷺ impelled many people in central Sudan to believe that the Shehu might, after all, be the Mahdi or, at least, one of the most perfect saints. The Shehu dismissed these speculations. But how, in fact, did he actually assess himself? M.A. El-Hajj has translated the *mujaddid*'s assessment of himself in *Taḥdhīr al-Ikhwān*.

> "Know also, my brothers, that I am not the Imam al-Mahdi and that I have never claimed the *mahdiyyah*, albeit that is heard from the tongues of other men. Verily, I have striven beyond measure in warning them to desist and have explicitly rejected their claim in my Arabic and *ajamī* writings. For example, I said in one of my Arabic compositions, namely *al-Khabar al-Hādī ilā Umūr al-Imam al-Mahdi*: My purpose in writing this book is not to affirm that I am the Imam al-Mahdi. My purpose in writing it is to explain to you that Allah the Exalted has favored me with states (*aḥwāl*) similar to some states of Imam al-Mahdi, which the *'ulamā'* have mentioned in their books. My aim was to comply with the command of Allah: *And as for the blessing of your Lord, speak out!*
>
> "After mentioning these states, I said: 'The Imam al-Mahdi, however, has certain secret attributes which nobody else can possess. Truly, there is a vast difference between the faint whirring of a fly and the loud buzzing of a bee!' In one of my *ajamī* compositions, for example, I mentioned thirty-three characteristics which I shared with the Mahdi and then said: 'I am not the expected Mahdi, though it is his garment that I wear. I am the clouds that precede the awaited Mahdi and it is for this reason that I am linked to him.'"

In a poem he attempted to silence speculation about this matter:

> "This is a poem to refute the long-standing lies which people spread about me…
>
> They say that I have been to Makkah and Madinah, and

they have no doubt about it.

They say that I can fold up the earth, walk on water and fly through the air.

They say that I meet with people hidden in the Unseen Worlds (*ahlu-l-ghayb*).

These qualities are attributed [to me] by many people, and I must say that they are wrong.

Yet if you chide them for doing it they manifest much resentfulness.

Having seen a minor quality or characteristic, they refuse to believe that I am nothing.

Truly, I am nothing but a stream of light, emanating from him ﷺ who is the source of blessing (*barakah*)..."

Conclusion

What, then, are the fundamental issues stemming from the revival of Islam in Hausaland that may serve as guiding lessons for contemporary Muslims? For answers to this question, we will turn to three scholars of the *tajdīd* movement. The learned *wazir* Usman Gidado Dan Laima, one of the architects of the *tajdīd* and *jihad* who later shouldered its heavy responsibilities and assessed the *tajdīd* movement in his *Rawḍ al-Jinān*, which may well be the most authoritative text available to us. An eyewitness of, participant in, and tireless defender of the *jihad*, his keen sense of history, his full understanding of the purposes of Islam and of the philosophy of *tajdīd*, and his piety, give his assessment an unassailable merit. His son, Abd al-Qadir, is the second scholar who assessed the *tajdīd* and *jihad* in his *Anīs al-Mufīd*. Finally, Waziri Junaidu, who was one of the greatest contemporary authorities on the Sokoto *khilāfah* and the one person in our time who still symbolized some of its finest elements, left his assessment in his *Ḍabt al-Multaqaṭāt*.

To begin with, the Shehu was confronted with a political situation in which the destiny of Muslims was in the hands of a political class that was either unbelieving or sinful. They were backed, unfortunately, by a class of *'ulamā'* that was basically fraudulent. The Shehu's solution was to initiate a powerful process of mass education with political, social and moral dimensions. "The Shaykh," Waziri Gidado said, "exerted himself in elaborating this matter and brought them back to the truth." Part of this elaboration was to erode the political base of the ruling class. Part of it also was to expose the fraudulent *'ulamā'* and to show that their unqualified support for a tyrannical political power elite was a blatant violation of Islamic principles.

The Shehu was faced also with a people who derided any efforts at reform. Perhaps some saw corruption as being already too deep-rooted in society to be eliminated. Others might have looked at the Shehu himself with utter cynicism, for what could an itinerant preacher with no strong social standing, whose tribe was underprivileged, do in a society that was firmly rooted in tradition and had a powerful political culture? Others might have thought his followers were too few to create any impact on society.

Within the context of Hausaland, there was no historical tradition of *tajdīd* from which the Shehu might draw lessons. This made his task all the more difficult, since his people might not grasp the issues at stake easily nor see any reason why he should single-handedly, and without any precedent, attempt to confront the Hausa establishment. However, the Prophetic example was there and several others too, particularly that of the Askia. The Shehu went on, despite the obvious historical difficulties, and, in the words of Waziri Gidado, "undertook to fight them all [i.e. the people of the Sudan] and cared not [for the consequences]." It may well be said that the reason he did not care was because he was sure of the ultimate victory of truth over falsehood, and that of justice over tyranny.

Another reality faced by the Shehu at an early stage was a personal matter. It was the choice he had to make between serving Islam wholeheartedly and the attractive requirements of a normal lifestyle. Should he take a job at court as other *'ulamā'* did? Should he settle for an occupation as an *'ālim* which often was lucrative? Should he stay permanently in one place, build a school, and pursue a contented life? Or should he give up personal pleasures and comforts for the sake of uplifting his nation? He chose the last alternative and as a result, "he had no settled home", as Waziri Gidado told us, "and he derived no means of livelihood [from his activities]".

He could thus afford to reject the offer of gold from Bawa, which the other *'ulamā'* who depended on him could not, and to demand, instead, justice for the people. He could afford also to move from country to country before the *jihad* in his bid to educate the masses and to move during the *jihad* from one region to another in response to military and political developments.

Finally, the Shehu faced the choice of either trusting entirely in Allah or believing in the efficacy of his own designs and abilities. The course of reviving Islam in Hausaland depicts the Shehu as an unassuming personality who never displayed inordinate ambition or any desire for power and glory. Indeed, many of the political and military developments – such as the liberation of Kano, Bauchi, Adamawa and other distant places – might have come as a surprise to him. Even in his immediate surrounding, he refused to call on the people to rebel against their rulers; rather he said that he would not be a party to sowing dissension between the people and their rulers. The Shehu seemed to believe that, since he was serving the cause of Allah, it was not befitting for him to take opportunistic advantage of any situation but to let Allah decide which way matters should go.

The Causes of Success

Waziri Gidado discerned five reasons for the Shehu's astounding and overwhelming success. "The first was that Allah chose for him a good generation whose hearts were soft and who listened to him and obeyed his command." What could the Shehu have done if the people had refused to listen to him or respond to his call? In other words, the

Shehu was raised by Allah at an opportune time. He himself displayed no noticeable desire to hurry the people because he knew that the process of reviving Islam in Hausaland could not be rushed. When the time came society exploded of its own accord.

Waziri Gidado thought that the profusion of Qur'an reciters, scholars and students who were his assistants in all matters were the second reason. A thorough intellectual preparation was a necessary condition for the *tajdīd*. The Shehu took pains to build a formidable body of scholars, jurists and saints – both men and women – on whom he depended almost totally for the dissemination of his message, for his contact with the masses, for the conduct of the war and eventually for the running of the *khilāfah*. The process of reviving Islam in Hausaland was built almost entirely on an intellectual foundation which perhaps explains its depth and its resilience.

The third reason for the success of the *tajdīd* , according to Waziri Gidado, was that his call had distinct phases. The Shehu did not force one stage into another. He patiently disseminated education and moral consciousness among the people for almost three decades without seeking any occasion to provoke the rulers. Throughout this period, he never mentioned *jihad* in any of his open air preaching but rather sought to purify people's faith, enlighten them about worship and transactions and initiate them into the *tarīqah*. He attacked un-Islamic customs but did so without any reference to those in power or any attempt to provoke the masses against the rulers.

When the Shehu had brought about the desired transformation, Allah permitted the social and political transformation of the region as a whole to take place, and, as soon as *jihad* started, the Shehu's emphasis shifted and he began to speak of *hijrah/jihad*. This went on for several years. When victory came and the *khilāfah* was established, the Shehu again changed his themes in response to the new historical and political contingencies. The emphasis now was on how to run the *khilāfah*, strengthen the solidarity of Muslims, apply the *Sharī'ah* and generally how to preserve the order of the *ummah*.

This gradualist, systematic approach is the natural one known to have been adopted by prophets and all genuine *mujaddids*. The Shehu believed in the victorious nature of Islam, that no one can preserve Islam better or love it more than Allah Himself, and that time has never been against Islam. He had confidence in Islam, confidence in Allah's judgment and confidence in the eventual triumph of his cause. The confidence paid off and the result was an *ummah*, an Islamic order, a true *khilāfah*.

The fourth reason, according to Waziri Gidado, was that the Shehu took his appeal directly to the masses – the women, the poor, the slaves and all other groups of the underprivileged and dispossessed in society. The *'ulamā'* he trained helped him to reach them. He lived like them, shared their aspirations and endeavored to know and experience personally their plight and their grievances. He identified with them completely and championed their cause unconditionally.

It is Islam's abiding responsibility to defend the poor against the oppressive rich, to protect them from a tyrannical social order and government, and to secure their interests for them. It is Islam's duty and commitment to work for the overthrow of any government or social order that denies to the poor their rights, or seeks to tilt the socio-economic balance in favor of the rich.

The fifth reason for the success of the Shehu's *tajdīd* "was that the body of his consultants and those who worked with him and migrated to him were keen and obedient." More important even than this, perhaps, was the very existence of this body of consultants. What appears clearly throughout the course of the movement was that the Shehu was not working alone. Indeed, he hardly ever took any decision unilaterally. For example, the need for the election of an *Amir al-Muminīn* was suggested to him and he left the matter to his advisors. Throughout the *jihad*, decisions on the conduct of war were left to the council. When these advisors became rulers, they were left to follow their own initiatives, for the Shehu withdrew to occupy himself in teaching and training. The movement was not a one-man affair but a collective undertaking, which rested very much on mutual consultation.

In his *Anīs al-Mufīd*, Waziri Abd al-Qadir added other reasons for the success of the movement. Firstly, as a whole, the members of the *Jama'a* preferred the Hereafter to this world and so were ready to forego their homes, property, families and other personal considerations in order to undertake the *hijrah*. They preferred knowledge to ignorance, causing them to strive to acquire it and act by it. They also preferred consciousness of Allah to moral degradation, which made them able to reject whatever was contrary to the *Sharī'ah*. And finally, they preferred social transformation to the corrupt situation which confronted them.

The *Jama'a* worked as a single body and were clear about their objectives and goals: that they were working for a cause the reward of which lay in the Hereafter; that they had to acquire knowledge and live enlightened lives; that the triumph of their cause depended on their relationship with Allah and not on the pleasures of this world; that they were involved in a process of *tajdīd* and could not accept anything which was likely to corrupt them. This keen consciousness of a common goal, a defined mission, a noble cause and a unique identity helped to weld the *Jama'a* together and gave it the strength to work for many years and to fight continuously for more than a decade.

A vital factor in the success of the Sokoto *jihad* was, of course, the personality, characteristics and methods of the Shehu himself. The author of *Anīs al-Mufīd* listed ten qualities of the Shehu, which are also endorsed by the author of *Ḍabt al-Multaqaṭāt*. Our concern here is not so much to give the list of qualities as to categorize them and consider their implications.

With regard to methodology, the Shehu trained his men by personal example and not by theory. His own life was the embodiment of Islam and that involved his going out to preach. Indeed, that was the main activity of his life. We are told that his preaching was excellent and that he followed to the letter the Divine command in the Qur'an: "*Call to the way of your Lord with wisdom and fair admonition, and argue with them in the kindest way.*" (16:127)

His training of the men around him and his call to people were both soundly based on his comprehensive knowledge, meaning that the Shehu fully utilized all the relevant "sciences" (*'ulūm*) in his efforts to transform his society – the science of *tawḥīd*, the science of *ḥadīth*, the science of *tafsīr*, the science of *fiqh*, as well as the sciences of medicine, astronomy and mathematics. Any aspect of knowledge which was thought to be of benefit to the community was taught and acquired.

Political strategy was as important and crucial to him as his training and preaching activities. One of his qualities was his possession of *ḥusn as-siyāsah* – sound diplomacy and viable political strategies. He kept aloof from the politics of Hausaland for a very considerable period and maintained a cordial relationship with the Sulṭan of Gobir, Bawa, in order to enhance his standing among the people, and, as 'Abdullahi told us, that friendship gave weight to the Shehu's teachings. Those who did not listen to him out of conviction did so because of their fear of the Sulṭan. The Shehu did not see this as a compromise but as an integral part of his political strategy. It appears from the sources available to us, particularly *Tazyīn al-Waraqāt* and *Rawḍ al-Jinān,* that the Shehu used to advise the rulers on crucial matters and wielded, at least in one instance, a weighty voice in the politics of succession.

That "cordiality" in no way impinged on the basic fact that the Shehu was leading a movement dedicated to the overthrow of the corrupt order. Nor did it diminish the suspicion which the Shehu and his top advisers nursed against the intentions of the rulers. It seems that the Shehu was merely trying to avoid exposing his *Jama'a* to any unnecessary risks, such as the wrath of tyrants, before it was able to withstand direct confrontation.

The Shehu was also able to attract almost every segment of society and have in his *Jama'a*, as Abd al-Qadir indicated, not only the *'ulamā'* but also the business community, professional groups, elements of the army, and indeed, all the essential elements of society. The common people, of course, trooped to him in great numbers. These factors help explain how the *Jama'a* was able to conduct its lengthy wars and also how the *khilāfah* was able, within a very short time, to stand on its feet and thrive economically. This shows that the activity of the Shehu was not confined to preaching but, more importantly, involved the creation of a broad and sound base for the spread of true Islam. Through it he consolidated his hold on the business community, fraternized with artisans, itinerant traders, farmers and butchers, and spread his teaching network throughout the ranks of the army.

On a personal level, the Shehu possessed an iron will and extraordinary strength of character. Waziri Junaidu pointed out that it was this moral strength that enabled the Shehu to face the combined forces of the kings and sulṭans of central Sudan without being shaken in the least. "Indeed," Waziri Junaidu said, "in spite of their numerical strength and their enormous military prowess, the Shehu fought the combined forces of Hausa kings, striving against them with truth, and Allah opened for him all the lands of Kano, Daura, Katsina, Zazzau, the lands of Bauchi and of Borno as well as those of Kebbi, Burgo, Yauri, Nupe, Yoruba and others in the Sudan... He did not fear any of them until Allah gave him victory over them." It seems also that the Shehu was frequently afflicted by illness, in spite of which he remained active throughout his life.

Johnston sees in the Shehu the marks of a truly great leader. "Though a man of peace, he sustained a lengthy war and, though an unworldly mystic, he created a territorial empire." His "spiritual magnetism", Johnston says further, helped him to keep the loyalty of his followers for life. His moral courage enabled him, even in the most trying and desperate circumstances, to stand on his principles. His faith in his own destiny was so intense that "it fired all those who came in contact with him," inspiring them to turn defeat into victory in several instances.

The Shehu, moreover, remained totally unworldly, "unspoiled in triumph as he had been unshaken by disaster." "To the very end," Johnston says concluding his assessment, "the Shehu led a simple, pious and abstemious life, renouncing the world precisely at the time he had gained it... On these achievements alone, he deserves to be ranked among the greatest men whom Africa has produced. If his character and achievements are taken together, however, his place is unique."

Waziri Gidado interpreted the *tajdīd* in a parable, in *Rawḍ al-Jinān*:

> "Allah facilitated for him the building of a house for his community with four pillars and a roof. Anyone who adheres to it is saved and anyone who neglects it is doomed... The first of the pillars is judgment according to the Book of Allah and, if someone judges according to it, Allah will manage his affairs for him. The second pillar is the upholding of the Sunnah of Muhammad ﷺ and, if someone upholds it, the Prophet ﷺ will concern himself with his cause. The third pillar is kindness towards the common people, relying on the saying of the Prophet ﷺ, 'O Allah, treat with kindness all those who were appointed over the affairs of the people of my community and treated them kindly.' And Allah the Most High says: '*Make allowances for people...*' (7:199) And He also says: '*You will never cease to come upon some act of treachery on their part, except for a few of them. Yet pardon them, and overlook.*' (5:13) The fourth pillar is tact with those with whom we should be tactful, in accordance with the saying of the Prophet ﷺ, 'I have

been sent armed with tact.' As to the roof, this is taking refuge with Allah by means of prayer and good actions. The Shaykh had three qualities by means of which this house was built. They were knowledge, piety and firm resolution."

Bibliography

Texts written by 'Abdullahi dan Fodio

Ḍiyā' al-Ḥukkām
Ḍiyā' as-Sulṭān
Ḍiyā' at-Ta'wīl
Ḍiyā' 'Uli-l Amr wa-l-Mujāhidīn
Iḍā' an-Nusūkh
Minan al-Minan
Risālat an-Naṣā'iḥ
Sabīl an-Najāt
Tazyīn al-Waraqāt
Tibyān li-Ḥuqūq al-Ikhwān

Texts written by Shehu Usman dan Fodio

al-Amr bi-l-Ma'rūf wa-n-Nahy ani-l-Munkar
Asānīd al-Faqīr
Bayān Wujūb al-Hijrah ala l-'Ibād
Hidāyat aṭ-Ṭullāb
Ḥisn al-Afhām
I'dād ad-Dā'i ilā Dīni-Llāh
Iḥyā' as-Sunnah wa Ikhmād al-Bid'ah
Irshād Ahlu-t-Tafrīṭ wa-l-Ifrāṭ
Irshād al-Ikhwān ilā Ahkām Khurūj an-Niswān
al-Khabar al-Hādī ilā Umūr al-Imam al-Mahdi
Kitāb al-Adab
Kitāb al-Farq
Miṣbāḥ Ahlu-z-Zamān

Masā'il al-Muhimmah
Najm al-Ikhwān
Naṣā'iḥ al-Ummah al-Muḥammadiyyah
Naṣīḥat Ahlu-z-Zamān
Nūr al-Albāb
Qawā'id Ṭalabi-l-Uṣūl ila-Llāh
Taḥdhīr al-Ikhwān
Ta'līm al-Ikhwān
Ṭarīq al-Jannah
Tanbīh al-Ikhwān
Tanbīh aṭ-Ṭalaba alā anna Allah Ta'āla
Marūf bil-Fiṭrah
'Umdat al-'Ubbād
'Umdat al-'Ulamā'
Uṣūl al-'Adl
Uṣūl al-Wilāyah
Wathīqat Ahl as-Sudān
Wathīqat al-Ikhwān

Texts written by Muhammad Bello

Fawā'id Mujmilah fi-Mā Jā' fi-l-Birr wa-l Silah
Infāq al-Maysūr
Jalā' aṣ-Ṣudūr
Kaff al-Ikhwān
Shifā' al-Asqām
Ṭā'āt al-Khallāq bi-Makārīm al-Akhlāq
Tamḥīd al-'Umdat al-'Ubbād

Other Arabic sources

Iḥyā' 'Ulūma-d-dīn by Al-Ghazali
Anīs al-Mufīd by Abdalqadir the son of Waziri Gidado
Ḍabt al-Multaqaṭāt by Waziri Junaidu
Rawḍ al-Jinān by Wazir Gidado
Rawḍat al-Afkār by Abdalqadir ibn al-Mustafa (Dan Tafa)
Shurb az-Zulāl by al-Barnawi
Taj ad-Deen Fī Mā Yajibu 'Ala-l-Mulūk by al-Maghili
Tārīkh al-Fattāsh by Muhammad al-Kati at-Timbukti

Non-Arabic sources

Ajayi, J.F.A *and* Crowder, M. *(eds.), 'The Western Sudan from the Moroccan Invasion (1591) to the Death of al-Mukhtar al-Kunti (1811)'*, in *History of West Africa,* Vol. 1 (2nd ed.), 1976.

Arnett, E.J., *'The Rise of the Sokoto Fulani'*.

Bagley, F.R.C., *Ghazali's Book of Counsel for Kings,* OUP, 1977.

Balogun, Ismail, critical edition of *Iḥyā' as-Sunnah* as a doctoral thesis submitted to the University of London, 1967.

Balogun, Ismail, *The Life and Works of 'Uthman dan Fodio,* Islamic Publications Bureau, Lagos, 1975.

Batran, Abdal-Aziz Abdallah, *'A Contribution to the biography of Abd al-Karim ibn Muhammad al-Maghili al-Tilmasani'* in the Journal of African History, Vol. 14, 1973.

Batran, Abd al-Aziz Abdallah, *'Sidi al-Mukhtar al-Kunti and the Recrudescence of Islam in the Western Sahara and the Middle Niger'*. Ph.D. thesis submitted to the University of Birmingham, 1971.

Batran, Abd al-Aziz Abdallah, *'Sidi al-Mukhtar al-Kunti and the Office of Shaykh al-Tariqa al-Qadiriyyah'* in Studies in West African History, Volume 1.

Batran, Abd al-Aziz Abdallah, *'An Introductory Note on the Impact of Sidi al-Mukhtar al-Kunti (1729-1811) on West African Islam in the 18th and 19th Centuries'*, Journal of the Historical Society of Nigeria 6, No. 4, 1973.

Bivar, A.D. *and* Hiskett, M., *'The Arabic Literature of Nigeria to 1804: A provisional account'*, Bulletin of the School of Oriental and African Studies 25, 1962, pp. 118-35.

Bivar, A. D., *'The Wathīqah Ahl al-Sudan'*, Journal of African History, I, (2),

Boyd, Jean, *'The Contribution of Nana Asmau Fodio to the Jihadist Movement of Shehu dan Fodio from 1820-1865'*. M. Phil thesis submitted to the Polytechnic of North London, 1982.

El-Masri, Fathi, *'Bayan Wujub al-Hijra ala l-Ibad'*, Khartoum University Press, 1979.

El-Masri, Fathi, *'The Life of Shehu Usman dan Fodio before the Jihad'*, Journal of the Historical Society of Nigeria 2, 1962.

Gwarzo, Hassan Ibrahim, *'The Life and Teachings of al-Maghili'*, thesis submitted to University of London, 1972. [It is to date the most comprehensive study of the North African scholar.]

El-Hajj, M.A., *'The Mahdist Tradition in Nigeria'*. Ph.D. thesis submitted to Aḥmadu Bello University, Zaria, 1972, pp. 229-31 and 262-9.

Hiskett, Mervyn, *'Material Related to the State of Learning among the Fulani before their Jihad'* translation of *Ida an-Nuskh man akhadhtu anhu min al-shuyukh,* edited and translated, Bulletin of the School of Oriental and African Studies 1957.

Hiskett, Mervyn, translation of *Tazyīn al-Waraqat,* Ibadan University Press, 1963.

Hodgkin, Thomas, *'Usman dan Fodio'*, in Nigerian Magazine, 1960, p. 75.

Hubbare, Alhaji Sayyidi Maude, publisher of *'Tanbīh at-Ṭalaba 'alā anna Allah ta'āla Ma'rūf bil-Fitrah'* by Shehu Usman.

Hunwick, John, *'Aḥmad Baba and the Moroccan Invasion of the Sudan (1591)'*, in Journal of the Historical Society of Nigeria 2, 1962.

Johnston, Hugh, *'The Fulani Empire of Sokoto'*, OUP, 1967.

Journal of Historical Society of Nigeria, *'A neglected theme of West African History: the Islamic Revolutions of the 19th Century'*, 1961, pp. 175, 178-9.

Kani, Aḥmad, critical edition of *'Diya as-Siyāsat'* of 'Abdullahi ibn Fodio (1981) also contains a copy of the *Wasiya.*

Kani, Aḥmad, *'Between Theory and Practice: Changing Patterns in the Political Thought of the 19th Century Jihad Leaders in Hausaland'*, Seminar Paper, Muslim Institute, 1983.

Malumfashi, U.F., *'The Life and Ideas of Shaykh 'Uthman dan Fodio'*, edited translation and analysis of *Rawd al-Jinan and al-Kashf wal Bayan,* Kano: Bayero University, M.A. Thesis, 1973.

Last, Murray, *'The Sokoto Caliphate, Ibadan History Series',* 1977, pp. 33-4.

Martin, B.G. *'Unbelief in the Western Sudan: 'Uthman dan Fodio's Ta'līm al-Ikhwān'.* Middle Eastern Studies 4, 1967-8, p. 92.

Minna, M.T.M. *'Sulṭan Muhammad Bello and His Intellectual Contribution to the Sokoto Caliphate',* Ph.D., London, 1982.

Palmer, H. *'An Early Fulani Conception of Islam'* in which is a translation of Shehu Usman's *Tanbīh al-Ikhwān.*

Usman, Yusuf B. *(ed.), 'The Meaning of the Sokoto Jihad', Studies in the History of the Sokoto Caliphate,* pp. 10-13.

Usman, Yusuf B. *(ed.), 'A Contribution to the Biography of the Shaykh Usman', in 'Studies of the History of the Sokoto Caliphate',* p. 469.

Usman, Yusuf B. *'The Transformation of Katsina',* pp. 104-2.

Said, Halil, *'Revolution and Reaction: The Fulani Jihad in Kano'.*

Tukur, M. *'Values and Public Affairs: The Relevance of the Sokoto Caliphal Experience to the Transformation of the Nigerian Polity'.* Ph.D. thesis submitted to Aḥmadu Bello University, Zaria, 1977.

Smaldone, Joseph P. *'Historical and Sociological Aspects of Warfare in the Sokoto Caliphate'.* Ph.D. thesis submitted to Northwestern University, 1970, pp. 223-4.

Willis, J.R. *(ed.) 'The Cultivators of Islam',* Frank Cass, 1979.

Zahradeen, M.S. *'Abd Allah ibn Fodio's Contributions to the Fulani Jihad in Nineteenth Century Hausaland',* Ph.D. thesis submitted to McGill University, 1976, p. 175.

Glossary

IN THIS GLOSSARY, as throughout this book, two methods of transliteration are used. The first method is the literal transliteration of the word, that is to say the word has been transliterated as it is actually pronounced in Arabic. The second method is to transliterate the word according to the way it has been previously introduced into the English language by orientalist writers and western academics. These words are now commonly written in English according to the orientalist spelling method and have become so entrenched that it is now difficult to change their spelling to a more accurate form of transliteration – for example: Allah, Islam, Imam, Amir, *jihad*, Sudan etc. and similar words like these. These words are not transliterated according to the way they should actually be pronounced in Arabic. In this case, the transliteration of their proper pronunciation will be placed in parenthesis next to them in the glossary entries below. Also the names of people and places that have a preferred spelling, or where a particular spelling has been adopted locally, have not been transliterated according to the way they are pronounced in Arabic.

Doubled Vowels: The doubling of the vowels: a, i, u denotes the elongation of the sound each of these letters represent by two measures – for example: 'ā', 'ī', 'ū'. The principle of doubling a short 'a' to make a long "ā" is well established – for example the word '*salām*'. However, in some cases like in the word '*Seerah*' 'ee' is used in preference to 'ī'.

Sun Letters: The proper 'Sun letter' is used in the place of the letter *lām*: 'l' of the definite article 'al' – for example, the word will read: *as-Sudan* instead of *al-Sudan, ash-shaytān* instead of *al-shaytān, ad-dunyā* instead of *al-dunyā* etc.

Doubled Consonants: are written double and in the case of digraphs like dh, kh, etc., a hyphen is placed between the doubled consonant and what follows it like in the word: *madh-hab*. To avoid ambiguity however, two-letter combinations which are not digraphs but resemble them have been separated by a hyphen. Example: *aḍ-hā*.

Lower Case: The usage of the lower case in the words 'bin' and 'bint' in Arabic names follows the same rules for 'von' (German) and 'du' (French). The Hausa word 'dan' also follows this rule.

Tā Marbūtah: is used in its pause form with the letter 'h' rather than the letter 't' so we read the name: A'ishah and not A'ishat. The exception to this are the words: *ṣalāt* and *zakāt* which are read with 't' at the end rather than with 'h'.

abnā' ad-dunyā – worldly men who constitute the core of the oppressive class

adab – refinement, good manners, social etiquette, courtesy, discipline, self-control

'afw – forgiveness, pardon

ahlu-l-baṣīr – those people who possess broad insight, foresight and sound intuition

ahlu-d-dunyā – those people who are preoccupied with the acquisition of wealth and power and the *matā-l-ghurūr* (the alluring deceptive merchandise) of the life of this world; those who say, "Our Lord give us the life of this world" without any consideration of the Hereafter

ahlu-dh-dhulm – tyrants, oppressors; those who practise injustice; unjust rulers and leaders

ahlu-l-ijtihād – those scholars who are capable of formulating law and rendering independent legal judgment based on the legal rulings of all of the schools (*madhāhib*) of Islamic jurisprudence, as opposed to the scholars who have the need to adhere to one *madh-hab* (school) in order to formulate law or derive legal rulings; see also '*ijtihād*' and *mujtahid*

ahlu-s-Sunnah – the people who uphold the Sunnah of Prophet Muhammad ﷺ; his Sunnah consists of what he said, what he did and what was done by someone else in front of him and he remained silent about and did not forbid; see also *Sunnah*

ajamī – any non-Arabic language written with Arabic script; in the case of Shehu Usman, it was the Hausa or Fula language written in the Arabic script

'alā sabīl al-lutf – in a kind and gentle way

Allah (*Allāh*) – He Who is the Creator of all that exists; He besides Whom there is no other god; the Self-Sustainer without beginning nor end; the only Entity that the Muslim is allowed to worship

amān – an assurance of protection; protection offered to an enemy or disbeliever – which may include protection of his family and property when he has ceased to be belligerent; such protection may be offered by an ordinary Muslim but becomes binding on everyone including the Amir as long as it is not harmful to Muslim interests

amānah – something held on trust; a person or duty for which one has responsibility; the agreement to take responsibility for someone or something left in one's charge

amir (*amīr*) – one who is in charge; one whose leadership is to be followed; one whose commands are to be obeyed

Amir al-Muminīn – the Commander of the Believers; the one placed at the head of the Muslim community and placed in charge of their affairs while receiving their pledge of allegiance to follow him in every lawful command that is in accord with Islam

amr wa nahy – command and prohibition; that is to say, commanding the right (*al-ma'rūf*) and prohibiting the wrong (*al-munkar*)

anṣār – the helpers of the cause; the title given to those inhabitants of Madinah who gave sanctuary and support to the Prophet Muhammad ﷺ in his cause of establishing and spreading Islam

ʻaql – consciousness, comprehension and intellect; the ability to distinguish right from wrong

Badr – the Battle of Badr: one of the battles fought by the Muslims during the time of Prophet ﷺ in which the Muslims were granted a great victory

barakah – spiritual charisma; a gift from Allah given to certain individuals to attract people and guide them towards good and success

Bararoji – Fulani cattle raisers

baṣīrah – foresight; insight; sound intuition

bayʻah – the pledge of allegiance given to an amir by the members of the Muslim community that they will hear and obey his lawful commands

bidʻah – something that is newly introduced into Islam which was not part of it during the time of time Prophet ﷺ and the first three generations of Islam; Shaykh ʻUthman placed *bidʻah* in three categories: those things newly introduced that nullify Islam; those things that have been introduced that are consistent with the *Sharīʻah*; those things which are permissible to do or use to advance the cause of Islam or create ease and comfort in everyday life without going against Islam

bilād al-kufr – the lands ruled by disbelievers; the lands where their *dīn* (see below) is disbelief

Bilād as-Sudan (Sudān) – literally: 'the Lands of the Blacks'; the vast region of savanna grassland sandwiched by the Sahara and the dense forest stretching from the Atlantic Ocean to the Red Sea

caliphate – see *khilāfah*

dāʻi – literally: a 'caller' or 'one who invites'; one who explains Islam to non-Muslims and invites them to become Muslim; see also *daʻwah*

dajjal – literally: 'deceiver' or 'impostor'; the false messiah; the Antichrist who will come to deceive the Muslims and the rest of the world before the coming of Imam Mahdi at the end of time

dar al-bidʻah – the land where newly invented practices are undermining the true practice of the Prophetic Sunnah

dar al-kufr – the land where disbelief is the way of life and where its ruler is a disbeliever

Dar al-Islam (*Islām*) – the land of Islam whose ruler is a Muslim, whose people are mostly Muslim and whose law is the *Sharī'ah*

Dar as-Sunnah – the land where the Sunnah of Muhammad ﷺ is upheld and innovation is rejected

dasā'is dunyawiyyah – scheming and plotting attributed to worldly ambitions or desires; secret planning of something illicit or detrimental that is tied to worldly ambition

da'wah – the explanation of the tenets of Islam to non-Muslims followed by an invitation to them to become Muslim; see also *dā'i*

dhikr – remembrance; reminding one's self about the One who should never be forgotten: that is say, to remind oneself about Allah, the One Who should always be remembered; to remember Allah much so that you bear Him in mind at all times and in all conditions, remember to seek His assistance in every situation, and remember to turn to Him in *tawbah* (repentance) and seek His forgiveness of one's sins

dhimmi – a non-Muslim living under the legal protection granted to non-Muslim inhabitants of *Dar al-Islam*

dīn – way of life; life-transaction; literally the debt of exchange between two parties, in this case between the Creator and the human creature; Allah says in the Qur'an: "*The* dīn *with Allah is Islam.*" (3:19)

du'ā' – supplication; a prayer of request to Allah in which one asks for Allah's blessing, mercy, support, protection, forgiveness or intervention in one's personal affairs

al-Fātiḥah – the first chapter of the Qur'an

farḍ al-kifāyah – the collective duty of the Muslims as opposed to *farḍ ayn* (the obligations that have been placed on the individual Muslim); those Islamic obligations and responsibilities for which an entire community will be held accountable on the Day of Rising if that community did not have at least one member who was capable of performing them, such as: the duty of the imam, the duty of the amir, performing funeral rites, teaching Islamic knowledge, leading the *jihād*, giving legal judgments etc.

faqīh – literally: 'one who understands'; one who has an in-depth knowledge of *fiqh* (Islamic law) and is capable of rendering a legal opinion or judgment

fasād – wickedness; corruption; immorality, social decay

fatwā – a legal judgment/ruling rendered by a *faqīh*; also see *faqīh*

fiqh – literally: understanding, comprehension; the knowledge of Islamic law

fisq – deviation; sinfulness, immorality

fiṭrah – the natural disposition of human beings; the natural patterning which all human beings are born with

Fulanin Gida – the settled Fulani

furū' – branches or derivative aspects of Islamic law as opposed to *uṣūl*, which are the fundamental principles of the law; also see *uṣūl*

ghurūr – deception; delusion; beguilement; infatuation

Gobirawa – the residents of the town of Gobir

ḥadīth – transmitted and narrated reports about Prophet Muhammad ﷺ and his Companions ﷺ; what they did and what they said

haibah – social standing; prestige; awe inspiring appearance; dignified bearing

Ḥajj – annual pilgrimage to Makkah (Mecca)

ḥarām – a matter that is unlawful or prohibited in Islam

ḥaqīqah – the true realization of *tawḥīd*; an understanding of the true nature of the relationship between Allah and the human being, that is to say, Allah is the Creator and the human beings are creation; Allah is the Master and the human beings are His slaves; Allah is *al-Ghanī* (the One Who is not in need of anything) while the human beings are *al-fuqarā'* (the ones in need of everything from their Lord)

ḥijāb – any screen; a cover or veil that is used to protect a woman entirely or partially from the direct view of men or direct contact with them; a veil which covers the head and drawn across the bosom of a woman

ḥilm – forbearance; a gentle and pleasing disposition; mild-temperedness, reasonableness and approachability

hijrah – emigration from one place to another usually under duress; emigration from an impossible situation to a possible one; emigration from the land of unbelief, innovation or rebellion against Allah; emigration from *dar al-kufr* to *Dar al-Islam*

ḥikmah – wisdom; advice or argument put forth using rational judgment

himah – the department of government which, among other things, reserves grazing fields for animals given as *zakāt* and for the animals of the poor

ḥisbah – the department of government charged with maintaining and overseeing Islamic public policy and social morality

ḥubb ar-ri'asah – a love of leadership coupled with an ambition for power

ḥukm – command; authority; power; governance

hurūb – flight to escape danger

hurūb al-maṣāliḥ – the department of government established to combat apostasy, highway robbery and rebellion, protect the welfare of the people and to maintain unity, social cohesion and peace within the *ummah*

ḥusn as-siyāsah – sound diplomacy and viable political strategies

'Id – a day of feasting; the two most important days on the Muslim calendar: *'Idu-l-Fitr* which occurs at the end of Ramadān or *'Id al-Ad-hā* which occurs during the Ḥajj

ijmā' – the consensus of the *'ulamā'*

ijtihād – the ability to formulate independent decisions by those who are juristically qualified to do so, with regard to interpreting and applying laws that are based on the four schools (*madhāhib*) of Islamic jurisprudence, as opposed to the exclusive adherence to one *madh-hab* (school of Islamic law) to derive the law; also see *ahlu-l-ijtihād* and *mujtahid*

Iḥsān – *taṣawwuf*; the ability to conquer distraction and absent-mindedness in worship, and to perfect worship by keeping in mind that one is, in reality, always in the presence of Allah; "To worship Allah," in the words of the Prophet ﷺ, "as if you see him, for even though you do not see Him, He sees you."; see also *taṣawwuf*

'ilm – knowledge

'ilm al-kalām – knowledge of *tawḥīd*; a branch of knowledge developed as a means to protect the *dīn* from unbelieving or heretical philosophers

Imān – belief; to believe in Allah, His messengers, His Book, His angels, the Day of Judgment, and the Divine Decree (*Qadr*)

Imam (*Imām*) – The word Imam has broad usage: it may refer exclusively to the *Amir al Muminīn* – the supreme leader of the Muslims; it may be used to refer to one of the four Imams of Islamic jurisprudence: Imam Abū Ḥanīfah, Imam Mālik, Imam Shāfī' and Imam Aḥmad ibn Ḥanbal; it may be used to refer to the *imāmu-l-khams* (leader of the five prayers) in the mosque or *imāmu-l-Jumū'ah* (the imam who leads the Friday prayer); it may also be used to refer to the scholars of *ḥadīth* or any Muslim scholar in general; it may also be used to refer to any male Muslim who leads the prayer in any place where prayers are performed

Imam al-Mahdi (*Imām al-Mahdī*) – "The Rightly Guided Imam" who will appear just before the end of the world and who will fight the *Dajjal* (see above)

intidhār – waiting, patience, delay, respite; making allowance for a person in adverse economic circumstances until his situation has improved or writing off his debt completely

inā – proceed without hurry; taking one's time; proceeding cautiously; acting with patience

Islam (*Islām*) – complete submission and obedience to the will of Allah

isnād – the uninterrupted chain of authorities from whom a *ḥadīth* (see above) has been narrated

jāh – rank; social standing; dignity

Jama'a (Arabic: *Jamā'ah*) – a community of Muslims large or small; the community of Muslims who mutually assist each other and who live, work, pray, learn and fight in unison under the leadership of an amir

jangali – (a word derived from Fula) – the arbitrary cattle-tax collected by the Hausa rulers from the Fulani cattle herders

Jaysh al-Futūh – the victorious/triumphant army

jihad (*jihād*) – literally: exertion, striving, going through pain for the sake of something; fighting in the Name of Allah to defend *Dar al-Islam* against the enemies of Islam, unbelief, innovation or rebellion against Allah; fighting in the name of Allah to eliminate *kufr* (disbelief) and to establish Islam in its place

jihad an-nafs struggling with the weakness of one's lower self in order to overcome the base inclination of the self towards evil and immoral thoughts and behavior

jizyah – the tax paid by non-Muslims living under Muslim rule

jinn – created beings that exist in *al-ghayb* (the unseen world)

Ka'bah – the Sacred House located in Makkah built by the prophet Ibrahim 🕮 and his son Isma'il 🕮 for the worship of Allah; also see *tawāf*

khalīfah – literally: the one who follows in succession; that is to say, the one who comes after Prophet Muhammad 🕮 and becomes the supreme leader of the *ummah* (all the Muslims) wherever they are to be found. The first four were Abū Bakr, 'Umar, 'Uthmān and 'Alī 🕮 who are known as *al-Khulafā' ar-Rashīdūn al-Arba'* (the Four Rightly-Guided Caliphs)

khilāfah – the office of the supreme leader who governs the Ummah (the world body of Muslims); the original structure of governance for the Muslims established immediately after the death of the Prophet Muhammad 🕮; in the time of Shehu Usman, it was the structure of government which was established by him to rule the Muslims of Hausaland

khulafā' – plural of *khalīfah*

khawārij – literally: those who withdraw or separate; one of the earliest sects in Islam who separated themselves from the main body of Muslims and declared war on all of those who disagreed with them, saying that a Muslim becomes a disbeliever on account of his sins

kibr – pride; haughtiness; arrogance

lā khilābah – its meaning in Arabic: 'no fraudulent practices or deceitful behavior'

malik – king

Māliki School – one of the four schools of Islamic law recognized by Sunni Muslims

madh-hab – literally: way; opinion; principle; rule; the way so and so went; any school of Islamic law which evolved out of the collection, compilation and codification of the legal opinions and rulings of the early Imams and *fuqahā*

al-Maghrib – North-West Africa

mu'adh-dhin – the one who calls the Muslims at the designated times to the five daily prayers in the mosque

mudārāh – gentle courtesy; sociability; tactfulness; affability; legal rulings to meet new situations

muhājirūn – those who emigrated from Makkah to Madinah in the cause of Allah before the conquest of Makkah; anyone who emigrates for the sake of Allah from *dar al-kufr* to *Dar al-Islam* or an area where it is safe for Muslims to practice Islam and continue to do *da'wah* peacefully.

muḥtasib – the one charged with regulation of the market, promotion of justice in society and preservation of public morality

mujaddid – one who revives, resuscitates, restores; it has been related that at the beginning of every century Allah sends a *mujaddid* to the Muslims to regenerate and restore Islam back to its pristine pure practice; see also *tajdīd*

mujtahid – a *faqīh* (legal scholar) who is capable of formulating new legal judgments based on his own knowledge of the sources

mukhalliṭūn (syncretists) – those who mix the practice of Islam with paganism; see also *takhlīṭ*

munkir – denier; rejector; the one who denies the truth of Islam; the one who rejects the *dīn*

murīd – follower, student, disciple of a shaykh of *taṣawwuf*; see also *taṣawwuf*

muṣlihūn – the people who love right action and abhor evil and injustice; those who strive to reform society by commanding the good and calling for justice

mustad'afūn – those people in society who are looked upon as being weak and inferior; those who are the victims of tyrants, oppressors, or an arrogant upper class

Mu'tazilī – literally: seceder; a speculator or rationalist; a follower of the school of thought that rose up to introduce rationalist and speculative dogma into Islam; one of the views held by the *Mu'tazilī* was that the Qur'an was created

mutrafūn – those who live in decadent and undeserved ease and luxury and who thrive off of unbridled corruption

mulk – power; authority; sovereignty

Muwaṭṭa – literally 'the well-trodden path'; The *Muwaṭṭa* of Imam Mālik is the text written by Imam Mālik as a source book detailing the Sunnah of the Messenger of Allah ﷺ as expressed by the *'amal* (social and behavioral pattern) of the people of Madinah in the first three generations of Islam

nāfilah – literally, that which is extra or more than is required; the category of prayer that is neither *farḍ* (obligatory) nor Sunnah, rather a *nāfilah* prayer is performed for extra blessings and reward from Allah

naphta – a type of musket used in Hausaland during the time of Shehu Usman

naṣīḥah – sound advice; good counsel

naṣīr – helper of the cause; plural; *anṣār*; see also *anṣār*

nawāfil – plural of *nāfilah*; see *nāfilah*

nazghat ash-shaytān – satanic inspiration; incitement by satan to do evil; the suggestion of satan

qāḍī – a Muslim judge who is an expert in Islamic jurisprudence and therefore qualified to settle legal disputes, pass or pronounce judgment in favor of or against someone, pass sentence on someone and impose the *hadd* punishments according to what has been prescribed by the Qur'an and Sunnah

Qādirī ṭarīqah – see *Qādiriyyah*

Qādiriyyah – the *ṣufi* brotherhood that was founded by Shaykh 'Abdul Qādir al-Jilāni who lived in Baghdad, Iraq 1077-1166. The brotherhood spread from Iraq to Syria and other parts of the Muslim world and then reached the Western Sahara in the second half of the fifteenth century. It seems to have reached West Africa at the time of Sidi Aḥmad al-Bakkā'ī (d. 1515).

qiyām al-layl – standing for prayer in the middle of the night; also see *tahajjud*

raka'at – a unit of the prayer consisting of a number of standing, bowing, prostration and sitting positions

radd al-mazalim – the department of the ombudsman or public complaints, which deals with cases of oppression and usurpation that are beyond the powers of the *qāḍī* to adjudicate; the custodian of this office must be more powerful than the *qāḍī* since he deals with complaints against people of power, wealth and influence who must be restrained from resorting to coercion and intimidation against a weaker complainant with whom they are having a legal dispute

riyāḍah – rehabilitation of the *nafs* (lower-self), which entails self-purification, personal intellectual development and social restraint; spiritual training and fortification supervised by a shaykh

rubūbiyyah – Allah's absolute Lordship, Sovereignty, Ownership and control over the entire creation

rukū' – the bowing position in the prayer

rūḥ – spirit; life-breath; the essence of the human being that contains all his cognitive faculties

sāhah – battlefield

ṣabr – patience in the time of trials; enduring injury and mistreatment from others without retaliating; enduring hardship that is suffered while striving in the cause of Allah and the establishment of Islam

sadāqi – the dowry which is paid to a bride

ṣadaqah – voluntary charitable gift or act which may take many forms, ranging from a sincere smile, to removing an obstacle from someone's path, to assisting someone in times of ill health or financial difficulty

ṣalāt – the formal Muslim prayer

Ṣalāt aḍ-Ḍuḥā – a prayer performed any time after the sun has fully risen until the time just before noon

Ṣalātu-l-'Aṣr – the afternoon prayer

Ṣalātu-dh-Dhuhr – the midday prayer

Ṣalātu-l-Maghrib – the sunset prayer

Ṣalātu-ṣ-Ṣubḥ – the morning prayer that is performed after dawn and before sunrise

salaf – the first generations of Islam referred to as "the worthy predecessors"; the first three generations of Muslims about whom the Prophet Muhammad ﷺ said, "The best of the generations is the one to whom I came, then the one that comes after them and then the one that comes after them."

ṣawm – fasting; especially during the month of Ramadān

Seerah (*Sīrah*) – the recorded account of the life of the Prophet ﷺ

Sharī'ah – the body of laws revealed to Prophet Muhammad ﷺ by Allah; the universal, unalterable law that is absolutely binding on all Muslims wherever they may be

shahādah – literally, a witnessing, a testimony, a declaration; the first pillar of Islam; an open declaration of one's belief that there is no god except Allah Alone, Who is without partners, and that Muhammad is His slave and final Messenger

Shaykh – an honorific title meaning scholar; learned man; also used to give honor to men of esteem and senior rank in the community; the title of the teacher and guide for people on the path of *taṣawwuf*; also see *taṣawwuf*

Shaytān – the devil; accursed enemy of man

Shehu – the word used to mean 'Shaykh' in the Hausa and Fula language

shirk – associating partners with Allah

shūrā – counsel; consultation

silsilah – the uninterrupted chain of transmission and

authority passed from shaykh to shaykh or shaykh to *murīd* that reaches back to a scholastic authority or the original master of a *ṣufi tariqah*; also see *taṣawwuf* and *ṣufi*

ṣufi – the one who undergoes a systematized form of spiritual training under the guidance of a qualified *ṣufi* shaykh in order to receive guidance toward intellectual and moral elevation, so that he will be able to overcome the diseases of the soul (*nafs*) that prevent spiritual and moral development; also see *taṣawwuf*

Sulṭān – literally, rule; authority; ruler over a dominion;

Sunnah – the normative practice of the Prophet ﷺ; it is divided into three matters: *sunnat al-fi'l* – what the Prophet ﷺ did; *sunnat al-qawl* – what he said; and *sunnat at-taqrīr* – what was done or said in his presence and did not incur his disapproval

tabaṣṣur – reflection; thoughtful consideration of matters

tarbiyah – education; instruction; the spiritual training given by a shaykh of *taṣawwuf* to his *murīd*

tahajjud – prayers performed in the middle of the night based on a strong practice of the Prophet ﷺ; it is reported that the Prophet ﷺ said, "Allah descends to the lowest heaven in the latter part of the night purposely to listen to the complaints of people, to respond to their needs and to forgive the sins of those who seek His forgiveness."

tajdīd – the revival, regeneration, restoration of Islam and the Sunnah of the Prophet ﷺ; the work done by a *mujaddid* who is said to come at the beginning of every century to regenerate and restore Islam back to its pristine pure practice; also see *mujaddid*

tafsīr – explanation and commentary on the Qur'an

takhlīṭ – syncretic behavior, that is to say, mixing Islam and paganism; also see *mukhalliṭūn*

ṭalaba – students; seekers of knowledge

taqiyyah – denying one's religious affiliation when under the threat of serious harm or death

taqlīd – strict adherence to a particular *madh-hab* (see above) and the opinions and rulings of its jurists *taqwā* – guarding one's duty to Allah while fearing to offend Him

ṭarīqah – literally, path, way; the path or way the *ṣufi* travels in order to arrive at the destination of intellectual and moral elevation which brings him to nearness to Allah; a group of people under the guidance of a *ṣufi* shaykh whose *silsilah* (spiritual authority) and *idhn* (authorization) to use the method of spiritual training practised by the group goes back to the original master of the *ṭarīqah*

taṣawwuf – a systematized form of spiritual training (*tarbiyah*) which is used to guide individuals towards the proper Islamic attitudes to life and to guide them to intellectual and moral elevation in order to overcome the diseases of the lower self (*nafs*) that prevent spiritual development.

ṭawāf – to walk completely around the Ka'bah; the circumambulation of the Ka'bah by the pilgrims to Makkah (Mecca) also see Ka'bah

tawbah – turning away from sin to Allah in regret; repentance for past sins with the intention of not returning to those sins

tawḥīd – the knowledge of the Oneness of Allah

'ulamā' – scholars; plural of *'ālim* (scholar)

'ulamā' ad-Dīn – scholars of the religion

'ulamā' as-sū' – the corrupt scholars; the scholars who justify immoral behavior and practices and legitimize corrupt practices in Islam

'ulūm – sciences; subjects of study; branches of knowledge

'ulūmu-l-ḥaqīqah – knowledge of the true nature of reality; also see *ḥaqīqah*

ummah – the entire world community of Muslims

uṣūl – the fundamental principles of Islamic law as opposed to the branches of the law (*furū'*); also see *furū'*

uṣūl ad-Dīn – the fundamental principles of Islam

walīmah – a Muslim wedding feast

wara' – caution; carefulness; a pause to reflect before acting

wa'z – advice; counsel; instruction; inspiration

wazir (*wazīr*) – the deputy of the Amir; the right-hand

assistant of the Amir who has the responsibility, among other things, "of awakening the Amir when he falls asleep, giving him insight if he cannot see, and reminding him when he forgets"

wuḍū' – minor ritual ablution

zāhid – the one who strives to remove the love of this world (*dunyā*) from his heart; also see *zuhd*

zakāt – the two types of tax collected annually from Muslims; *zakātu-l-māl* (the tax on wealth) which is levied on money, crops, livestock, minerals when they exceed a certain amount; and *zakātu-l-fitr* which is a small tax paid with food stuffs by every Muslim on the occasion of *'Idu-l-Fitr* which occurs at the end of Ramadān

zuhd – the practice of simple living combined with social restraint, modesty and testing physical endurance with the aim of removing love for this world (*dunyā*) from the heart; *zuhd* is to give up the world willingly when one possesses it and to be at rest in one's heart if one loses it

www.ingramcontent.com/pod-product-compliance
Lightning Source LLC
Chambersburg PA
CBHW020349100426
42812CB00001B/5
9781842001127